HELL
ON CHURCH STREET

An abused child grows up
addicted to crime and violence

To my friends John + Marilyn

Bill Sizemore

By Bill Sizemore

PRESS

ISBN 9781498499477

www.xulonpress.com

Table of Contents

Dedication

I dedicate this book to our oldest daughter, Rebekah. Our Becky is a beautiful, intelligent young woman, who has always been full of life. From the moment of her birth, and even before, her mother and I have loved her dearly. Unlike Chuckie, the boy who is the focus of this book, our Becky grew up in a home where she was always safe and was smothered with affection. But her love of adventure and penchant for trying new things got her into deep trouble when, one fateful night, she tried meth and heroine "just for fun."

From that night on, Becky's life spiraled out of control. Before long she was living on the streets and robbing and stealing to support her habit. The authorities caught up with her and prosecuted her. Becky was on her way to prison, when, by the grace of God, she got into Teen Challenge, which is, in my opinion, the best drug rehab program in the country.

Thanks to the help of the dedicated staff there, our daughter found her way back from the precipice and today is free from addiction and substance abuse. Rebekah is a courageous young woman and her story of deliverance has been an inspiration to many. I happily and proudly dedicate this book to her. Cindy and I thank God every day that He faithfully answered our prayers and drew our daughter back to Him.

Acknowledgements

I acknowledge to all the world that I could not have written this book without the patience and faithful dedication of my wife Cindy. Cindy went to work every day for seven months, helping to pay the bills, while I plugged away at the kitchen table, putting all of the pieces of this remarkable story together. I must have told her a dozen times, "I'll be done tomorrow," only to start back at the beginning of the book the next day and go through the entire manuscript "one last time." Thank you, Cindy Sizemore. This book belongs to you as much as me.

I also want to acknowledge those who helped me edit the manuscript. Thanks to Adrianna, Kathy, and Joni for doing the tedious work of (hopefully) finding all of my typos and awkwardly worded sentences. Thanks to Chuck Dudrey and his wife Diana for reading the book over and over to ensure accuracy. I know that wasn't always easy, because a lot of old and often painful memories had to be dredged forth and relived. I hope you agree that the finished product is worth all of the effort.

Chapter One

Life or Death at the
Top of the Stairs

Somewhere in the middle of the night, I was awakened by someone yelling and screaming. The sound was coming from down the hall. Instinctively I covered my head with a blanket and closed my eyes in fear. All I could do was hope that I was not the cause of all the commotion, 'cause if I was...

Mingled with the screaming, I heard my name being shouted. "Chuckie! Chuckie!" It was Barbara! Still fearing what was likely ahead, I jumped up from where I slept on the closet floor and ran as fast as I could toward the voice. Whatever this was about, not coming when I was called would only make things worse.

"What did I do?" I whispered under my breath. "Am I going to be beat for something? Please, not again."

The past seven years had taught all five of us kids that when Barbara called for one of us, day or night, it was not a good thing. It never was. There *was* no good in our lives. We lived every waking moment in fear.

The house was ice cold that night. The power had been off for several days and there wasn't any coal in the bin for the furnace. Was this why she was screaming for me, because the house was cold? It wouldn't be the first time I had been ordered to get up and fill the coal bin in the middle of the night, even if we didn't have any coal.

When he was home, Dad would yell at me to get my lazy butt out of bed and go to the basement and fill the furnace. But Dad wasn't home that night and hadn't been for several days. He had a new girlfriend, a nineteen-year-old, and of late he had been spending a lot of time at her house.

I wiped the tears away and kept groping my way through the darkness, making my way toward the source of the yelling. Then, still half asleep and shivering from the cold, I saw Barbara; she was standing near the top of the stairs. I hated the top of the stairs. More than once, Barbara had thrown me down those stairs, sometimes beating me with her fists and pulling my hair all the way down, screaming at the top of her lungs how much she hated me.

I tried to make out what she had in her hands. What was she going to use to beat me? The buckle end of a belt? An extension cord? The mop wringer? Or would she just scream at me, spit in my face, and pound me with her fists?

I couldn't even guess what I'd done. I'd just been in bed, sleeping.

As I got closer I could tell that Barbara was in agony. Tears were running down her face. Apparently, something was seriously wrong with her. She was pregnant and close to her due date. I knew that. Maybe there was something wrong with her or the baby.

Suddenly, she doubled over in pain and began begging me to help her. There she stood, a woman who had starved me and my little brothers and sisters, beat us unmercifully, and kicked and slugged us more times than I could remember, a woman who had screamed or hissed how much she hated us, all of us – and now she was begging me to help her.

That's when it occurred to me. This was the moment I had dreamed of. This was it. This was my chance. I could end it all, here and now. No more beatings. No more being kicked in the ribs, punched in the face, or whipped with a hose or an extension cord or a two-by-two.

I wouldn't have to look at the pain in my brothers' and sisters' faces, as Barbara abused them. No more living hell. I could jump her, smash her face into the wall, put her in a head-lock, and ride her down those hard wooden steps, all seventeen of them, pounding her face into each one, all the way to the bottom. Yes! I could kill her. I could do it right now. This witch who had caused me so much pain, and had even tried to kill me. This cruel monster who'd choked me, and even thrown urine in my face. Yes, I could end it now. And who would ever know that I did it?

I bet this all sounds nuts to you. Even crazy. A kid dreaming of killing his babysitter or stepmother, whatever this woman was. But if you knew the circumstances and the kind of living hell Barbara had turned our lives into, doing what I was contemplating at that moment might actually seem rational. Well, at least to a kid who knew no other way out.

I hate you! I wish you were dead! I have to do it! I have to! Dark, homicidal thoughts raced through my head.

As I stood there looking at her, full blown murder in my young mind, something came over me, something I had never experienced before. For no reason that I could think of, I started feeling sorry for Barbara. I felt compassion, and somehow that emotion overpowered the intense hatred, anger, and bitterness that had defined my very existence.

Out of nowhere, Barbara had become a helpless, suffering human being who was in pain. She needed help, and she was begging me to help her. The thoughts of murder began to fade from my mind to be replaced by emotions that honestly made no rational sense to me.

Almost before I realized what I was doing, I put my arm around her and gently helped her down the stairs toward safety. I got her to a chair in the living room and told her I was going for help. Out the front door I ran, as fast as I could. We lived on the last street in town, so I had a ways to go. I ran toward the square in the center of town, looking for the police.

My side ached and I was out of breath, yet somehow I felt new inside. My mind was clear. I was focused on savings someone's life, and the life of an unborn child. I had never felt anything like that before.

I felt stronger and I ran even faster. Human lives were in the balance and it was up to me to save them. I found a policeman and waved him down. Between gasps, I told him what was happening and where we lived on Church Street. Then I turned and started back toward home, running as fast as I could. All the way home, I could hear sirens and see flashing lights.

The police and the ambulance arrived before I did. By the time I made it to the house the ambulance people had already picked up Barbara and were on their way to the hospital.

I watched and listened as the police and others huddled together outside. They were talking about the appearance of our house. And the smell. Suddenly, I was embarrassed at the condition of our home. There was no electricity so it was completely dark, as if the house was deserted. I remember my eyes following the beam from someone's flashlight, as it revealed the conditions we lived in.

What they were seeing was not pretty. And the smell? There's no describing that. You see, our house sat on a low spot on the outer edge of a small town. For some reason, the city sewer would, with some regularity, back up and flood our basement. The raw sewage would sometimes rise to a depth of two feet or more. Everything on the floor would float to the top. There were weeks' worth of laundry and garbage floating in the standing sewer water in our basement.

Also, with the power off, all of the meat in the freezer, mostly beef Dad had stolen, had rotted. The putrid smell of rotten meat filled the house, mixing with the smell of raw sewage drifting up from the basement. If you were not used to filling your lungs with rancid air, you would probably throw up the first time you breathed it in. I can still recall the expressions on the policemen's faces when they walked inside and shined their flashlights down the basement stairs. They were barely able to breathe. The stench was so great they tried to cover their mouths. Some visibly gagged.

But this was our home. This was where Dad and Barbara and her two kids, and me and my younger brothers and sisters all lived, and slept, and ate our meals. Outsiders could barely breathe for a minute the air we breathed in every day.

I wondered what they would think if they came back and saw our home in the daylight. The linoleum floors were dirty and littered with cigarette butts. The couch and chairs were stained with spilled Pepsi and cigarette burns. Most of the windows were covered with old sheets that served as curtains. In the backyard, 500 chickens were milling around in the bare dirt. That many chickens in one back yard made for a lot of added stink.

At the time, I didn't quite understand why the police and other officials hung around for so long. I thought they would just leave as soon as the ambulance left with Barbara, but they didn't. They stood around outside, whispering and talking.

Eventually though, everyone left and the house was quiet. It had been hours since I'd run for help and I was completely exhausted. I collapsed on the couch and fell asleep just as the sun began peeking through the window. I woke up an hour or so later to the sound of my two brothers, John and Kenny, and my youngest sister, little Frances, talking and moving about. Susanne, the oldest except for me, wasn't there. Everyone was wondering what was going on. I filled them in on what had happened.

What I am going to tell you now might sound a bit strange, but to us it was just a way of life. We were all starved. We weren't just hungry, we were starved. We hadn't eaten anything for days. Yes, there was some food in the house, but it was locked up in a cabinet. The groceries were always kept under lock and key so we wouldn't get into them. We were considered "wasteful, ungrateful little brats," who could not be trusted with access to food of any kind, because "we would just waste it."

Most kids you know would probably be upset if their breakfast or lunch was late, but not us. For the Dudrey kids, eating was not always a daily activity. When we did eat, it was only under adult supervision. We would sit at the kitchen table and eat Barbara's disgusting goulash, while Dad and Barbara enjoyed their baked chicken in the living room.

There was also some food in the freezer, or what used to be food anyway. It was all spoiled. Everything in the refrigerator was spoiled, too. There was a chain around the fridge and a padlock, so it wouldn't have mattered what was in it anyway.

We were raised to believe that adults ate good stuff and the kids ate whatever the adults put on the table. For us, that was almost always some unrecognizable goulash comprised of leftovers that should never have been mixed together in the same pot.

Most of the food we ate was USDA commodities. If you've never had warm, lumpy powdered milk, you might not know what it's like. It can gag you. No matter how warm and lumpy the stuff was, or how disgusting it tasted, if we didn't willingly drink ours, Dad or Barbara would hold our heads back and pour it down our throats. We would choke and gag, and sometimes we would throw up.

But on that particular morning, there wasn't even lumpy powdered milk to drink. There was nothing. I was so hungry my stomach hurt, and I'm sure the other kids felt the same way.

Later that morning, several complete strangers showed up at the house unannounced. They identified themselves as being from the State. They told us that they were there to take care of us until they could locate our father. They said we had to leave with them right away. I noticed that the lady doing all the talking held a handkerchief over her mouth when she spoke.

In a matter of minutes, all four of us kids were loaded into cars and off we went. There was no packing or gathering of things. In fact, we were told not to take anything with us. They explained that they would get us everything we would need to take with us to our first foster homes.

I recall telling them that I wanted to wait for my dad to come home, but they would have none of it. "No, you have to leave with us now," the lady in charge explained. There was no compromise in her voice, so that was that.

Us kids were split up and we left in different cars. It would be quite some time before I would see my brothers and sisters again, except for Susanne. Being the oldest, Susanne and I were assigned to the same foster home. As we drove away that morning, I turned and looked back. I wanted to forget the hell we'd gone through on Church Street. But, I doubted that I ever could.

I would find out later that the circumstances of our escaping Church Street came together in a perfect storm, of sorts. You see, there was a reason Susanne wasn't at home that morning. A few days earlier, she had somehow made her way to a preacher's house in our town. She showed up on their doorstep starved and exhausted. The kindly couple tried to feed her some bacon and eggs to revive her strength, but she couldn't even gather the strength to eat. They rushed Susanne to the hospital where she sunk into a coma and lay unconscious for three days, diagnosed with starvation and extreme exhaustion.

When my sister finally came to, there was a police detective and a state attorney sitting at the end of her bed, waiting to talk to her. She told them everything she knew, things you are going to learn for yourself, as my story unfolds. What you are going to read here is all true, though the author has changed some of the names for legal reasons. But I should also tell you this: Some of the things that happened to us are simply too gross to put in a book for decent people to read. However, if you read between the lines a bit, I think you will get the gist of most of what happened.

Also, when I tell you about my life on the wrong side of the law, some of the things I did were omitted, because wisdom dictates that, for various reasons, they should not be published in a book. I hope you understand that.

I was in the seventh grade when the folks from the state came and took us all away. I was of course much too young to have spent so much time fantasizing about ways I might kill Barbara, a woman you have just met. But as we continue with this story, you just might understand why I did.

Barbara was eighteen when Dad brought her home. That was some seven years before the night I ran for help. She moved in ostensibly to be our "babysitter." That would prove to be a fateful day for the five Dudrey kids. I was seven at the time. The youngest, Frances, was about a year old, and the other three were in between. But for all of us, the next seven years would change us. They would mark us, and challenge even our will to survive. And for me personally, they would set me on a path that could only lead to death or prison, or both. But I get ahead of myself.

When she first moved in, Barbara bathed occasionally, and she kept her false teeth in her mouth most of the time. (Yes, she had false teeth when she was a teenager.) But eventually the woman abandoned all pretense at hygiene, at which time standing within three feet of her would literally nauseate you. If you've never experienced close proximity to someone with extreme body odor, you might not be able to comprehend just how overpowering the smell can be. But that was Barbara.

None of us knew back then that there was a plan for Barbara to take our mom's place, or why. None of us had any idea what was about to happen or just how evil this eighteen-year old girl would soon become. And, of course, there was no way for us to know what was going to happen to our mother after Barbara suddenly appeared in our lives.

This all happened at our house on Church Street in Georgetown, Illinois. But my story actually began in Minnesota. Before we go back there, though, let me tell you how the Dudrey family came to be.

Chapter 2

Mother Grew Up Rough

My mother was raised in a home where work, hard work from sunup to sunset, was just a way of life. Young Audrey was slender of frame, weighing about a hundred pounds, and had golden blonde hair. Her slight build notwithstanding, she was required from a very young age to work harder than most adults do today.

As a young teenager, mom had to clean the house and cook and bake. In the spring and summer months, she helped plant and do most of the work of maintaining a large family garden. Besides planting and weeding, she kept the garden alive and growing by carrying endless buckets of water that she drew by hand from the well. All summer long, Momma spent much of her time on her knees in that garden, digging and pulling out weeds.

Mother grew up in the time period that included the great depression and the Second World War. The family survived the entire year largely on what was grown in that garden, so after the weeding and watering, there was, of course, the harvesting and preparation of the vegetables for canning. Canning back then required chopping wood, building a fire and keeping it burning hot enough to boil water for the pressure cooker.

Mother had no choice but to become accomplished in the kitchen. She was expected to have a full supper ready for the men every evening when they returned from the fields. (By the way, I know all of this stuff about Momma's early life because later on, after my mother was killed, Grandma Mausolf shared with me the kind of life her only daughter lived growing up.)

Momma's days as a young teenager were always long. She had to get up early every morning because, in addition to the cooking and gardening and regular housework, she was responsible for doing the entire family's laundry. Back then, there were no washing machines or electric dryers. Doing the laundry meant building a fire to heat water and then carrying the buckets of hot water to the washtub to do the clothes. Everything had to be washed by hand. Mom used a scrub board, a stiff brush, and a large bar of lye soap to clean the clothes. Then she would have to rinse them, wring them out, and hang them on the clothesline to dry.

Life on a family farm was hard enough in those days, but being the only girl in the family made it even more so. Momma killed, plucked, and dressed chickens. She milked the cow. When she needed to take a break of some kind, she sat in front of the sewing machine, making her own clothes and doing any other mending that needed to be done.

This was the life my mother lived as a fourteen-year old girl. It was a tough life, but for her it was about to get a whole lot tougher.

In the summer of 1946, my mother, through no fault of her own, suddenly found herself pregnant. In the 1940s and 50s, being pregnant outside of wedlock was considered a grave offense, something that brought great shame to the family name.

I can only imagine what this poor girl must have gone through. The raw emotions, the confusion, the shame, and the daunting task of having to share the embarrassing news with her mother.

As a frail teenager, she was stuck with having to answer the tough questions that were on everyone's lips. "How did this happen? Why did you let this happen? How long have you known? Why didn't you tell me?" All the while feeling guilty for her situation.

Still, there was no hiding what was going on inside her body. When she finally found the courage to tell her mother, the response was harsh. The condemning words cut deep into Mother's already crushed heart. She was still almost a child herself, a victim of sexual abuse, and yet she would have to bear the shame alone. No one could know the identity of the father. That had to be kept secret at all cost. Why? Because the father of her baby was a member of her own family. Momma not only bore the public shame of her pregnancy, but she had to sit across the dinner table from her assailant every night.

Still, life went on. Being pregnant didn't mean her chores didn't have to be completed. There was still the gardening and the canning and the cooking and the baking. There was still a house to clean, wood to chop, and laundry to do every day. Young Audrey Mausolf could brush and scrub the clothes and make them clean, but nothing she did could keep her from feeling dirty and cheap because of her "condition".

Momma was still young, so I can't help but believe that deep down inside she still would have at least hoped for the things that other girls her age experienced. Things like hanging out with girls her own age, or perhaps going to a movie or a dance.

I'm sure other things occupied her thoughts, crowding out things like hope and fun. She had to wonder what life would be like when her baby was born Would it be a boy or a girl? Would the baby be okay, given the fact that the father was an immediate family member?

And I'm sure that sometimes she would think about the Dudrey boy down the road. Maybe she shouldn't have. According to the rest of her family, he was a "no account, good for nothing," who was always stealing from their little farm.

Well, it turned out things were not okay with the baby. It was born with profound mental problems and died at the age of four. The boy down the road was two years older than Momma and eventually would be my dad.

Mom's folks, the Mausolfs, did their best to keep the two of them apart. They even sent young Audrey away for a while to keep him away from her. But their efforts were in vain. At age eighteen my mom married my dad and went on to bear him five children of which I was the oldest. I was named Charles, after my dad. But everyone called me Chuckie.

When our story picks up again we were all living in Minnesota. Mom was still alive and Barbara was not yet living with us. But even with no Barbara around, our dad was pretty scary in his own right.

Chapter 3

Who Wet the bed?

"Gunsmoke, starring James Arness." Those were the words coming out of the black and white television set in our living room.

As a young boy of seven, I loved that show. As soon as I heard the announcer say it was coming on, my heart would always beat faster in anticipation. You knew it was going to be good, because every show started with some bad guy outdrawing Marshall Dillon, but still going down, due to the Marshall's calm but deadly aim.

But there would be no Gunsmoke that night. My excitement was interrupted by, "All of you kids, get your _____ down to bed."

There was no warning, no hugs, no one saying "good night." It was just, "Get your _____ in bed. Now!" There was always yelling and cussing in our home. And threats. That was the way Dad communicated.

I remember with some timidity appealing to him that night to let me stay up and watch Marshall Dillon and Chester. My plea, however, was met with a slap upside the head and the words, "Get your ___ in bed now, if you know what's good for you."

So, with tears rolling down my face, down the steps to my basement bedroom I went. I choked back my disappointment. My stomach and chest heaved, but I caught my breath, holding it in so Dad wouldn't hear me crying. The last thing I wanted to do was make Dad mad. He was not a man who responded favorably to crying, warranted or not. And crying over something so small as not being allowed to stay up and watch Gunsmoke would not go over well.

"What the _____ are you crying for? Knock it off before I give you something to bawl about." Those were not just idle words when Dad said them. Bad things could follow immediately thereafter. So I kept my disappointment to myself.

I climbed the ladder to the top bunk and crawled under the covers. Years later, when we moved to the house on Church Street, I would sleep on the closet floor, but at this time Mother was still alive and I slept on an actual bed.

For some time, I lay there awake, staring out the window and choking back the sound of my crying, wiping the tears from my eyes and blowing my nose on my sleeve. Eventually, I fell asleep.

As soon as I awoke the next morning, I knew it would not be a good day. Lying there under the covers, a mind-numbing sense of dread began to creep over me. I could hear the coffee pot percolating on the stove upstairs. I could make out the sound of cups being set out on the counter. The coffee was boiling faster and faster. The aroma, mixed with the smell of cigarette smoke, gradually made its way down to the room where we kids slept.

I knew it wouldn't be long before I would hear Dad yell, "Let's go! Get your ____ out of bed." The command was going to come any moment now. And when it did...

Why the fear and dread? Why the ominous sense that this was not going to be a good morning? Well, as soon as my eyes had opened, my nose had caught the unmistakable smell of urine hanging heavy in the room. Someone had wet the bed! Someone was in for it.

I know it was selfish of me, but I was so glad that the smell of pee wasn't coming from me. I felt all warm and comfortable there under the covers. I was relieved that at least I would be able to proclaim with confidence that I hadn't wet the bed.

However, as I moved to climb out of my bunk, I felt a sudden coldness and wetness that I hadn't felt before. I knew instantly what that meant. I had indeed wet the bed, and had only felt warm and safe because I hadn't moved yet. And for that crime against humanity, there was going to be a serious reckoning. There was no getting around that.

Again I heard the shout from the kitchen upstairs, "Get your _____ out of bed, now!" The fear in my head was building now. My whole body felt like it was going numb.

I saw the look on my brothers' and sisters' faces as we all glanced at one another. We were all pretty little. Like I said, I was seven. Suzanne was six. John was four. Kenneth was two or three, and baby Frances was thirteen or fourteen months old. I didn't realize it then, but that was a look we would all share many, many times as we grew up together. We would all come to recognize, all too well, the face of fear.

Frances might have been too young to understand what was about to happen, but four of us weren't. We all stood there trying not to look like the guilty one. Smoothing out our pajamas, so as not to look wet, we stood huddled together, afraid to move, afraid of being singled out, all of us feeling hopeless and afraid.

You had to live with my dad to understand the danger we felt. Dad stood six foot three and at the time weighed 220 pounds. He was a strong man, and when he was angry there was no telling what he would do, except it would be bad.

Ironically, Dad put some effort into looking good in the eyes of the community. He was a Scout leader. He taught young boys canoeing, and how to shoot. He taught them how to bicycle and camp. At Christmas time, he even played Santa Claus for the local Jaycees. But behind that public persona was an angry and sometimes very dangerous man. A few months earlier, in one of his fits of anger, he had held me out over Minnehaha Falls, a drop of a hundred feet or so, and threatened to drop me to my death, just because I had cried about something. A hundred feet is a long drop, so as you can see, it was hard for us kids to not be terrified of the man.

Dad was different in other ways. Our dog, when we lived in Minnesota, was three-fourths wolf. And leaning against the back of our house were several large cages for the critters he liked to collect. There was a cage for the chicken hawks, one for the horned owls, and one for Dad's pet crows. There was another cage for the three red foxes for which Dad had some strange affinity.

When Dad would do a job for the company he worked for, he would invariably buy more parts than he needed, and then bring the surplus home. He almost never did a job straight up. He was a thief and a swindler and stole any time there was an opportunity. You wouldn't have believed the things you would've found, if you'd looked in our garage. Copper could be sold anytime for cash, so Dad was always buying more copper pipe than the job required and bringing the extra home to sell – after he'd stuffed some dirt up inside it to make it weigh more.

Even at our very young ages, we'd talked several times about running away, but we could never think of a place where we could go. We didn't know that it was possible that strangers might be concerned about the life we were living. The best we knew, there was no one out there to rescue us. We were on our own. Our life was our life, and all we could do was try to survive it. But I digress.

Huddled there at the bottom of the stairs, we were afraid. I noticed that I was trembling, at least on the inside. That was bad. Somehow, I had to get control of that or risk getting punched in the face for "acting like a baby."

But be that as it may, the time had come to go upstairs and face what lay ahead. There would be no more stalling.

I heard Dad's voice again. It sounded more ominous. So, like condemned men, forced to walk the gangplank, the five of us headed up the stairs. From that point on it was every kid for himself. We shoved and elbowed one another, each of us trying to make someone else go up first.

I was pushing my way up and holding back at the same time. Dad heard the ruckus, the "Stop pushing! Quit it. Chuckie hit me! No I didn't! Ouch, you hurt me."

"Get up here. Now!" Dad was getting angrier.

Apparently the smell of urine was strong, because the next words out of Dad's mouth were, "Which one of you pissed the bed?"

"I don't know," came out of several little mouths at the same time. Frances was too young to talk, so she just looked scared.

"What do you mean you don't know, stupid? Get over here. Kenneth, get in line. Stand here. Stop that _____ bawling."

There we stood, all in line and all scared half to death. I was still trembling inside, pleading with myself, hoping my lip would not quiver when he asked me the critical question, face to face.

Don't whimper. Don't let him see you tremble. Look innocent.

After you've been held over a hundred foot drop-off for crying, you have a pretty strong sense that you cannot whimper with impunity.

But try as I might to hope otherwise, I knew what was to come. There would be no avoiding it. But still, I had to at least try to control myself. I was going to be found out and I was going to get a beating, but it would be better if I wasn't a wimp about it.

Don't look at him. Don't let the tears come. It will be worse if you cry. Stop trembling.

It wasn't just me. We were all scared out of our minds. Other than Frances, we had all been at the receiving end of several of Dad's whippings and knew that our fear was justified.

He demanded again, "Who wet the bed?" My eyes stayed glued to the floor.

"Who wet the _____ bed? We are going to stand here all day, if that is what it takes. I want to know right now which one of you little _____ wet the bed? Chuckie, did you wet the bed?"

I knew that I had, but I knew what would become of me if I said yes, so I assured Dad that it wasn't me. Down the line he walked, asking the same question. As he paced, he held his belt with one hand, hitting the other hand over and over with the loose end. Each hit made a sharp snapping noise.

Why does he hate us so much? I didn't do it on purpose. It just happened.

Back and forth he went. Finally, he stopped in front of me and asked again if I had wet the bed. I meekly assured him that I hadn't. At that point, he leaned down and felt my pajama bottoms. "Then how did your pants get wet?" The anger in his eyes was hotter now, and it was all focused on me.

I answered that I didn't know. Then all of a sudden he turned around and started whacking me with the belt.

"This is for lying!" he said, as he continued swinging. "Don't you ever lie to me, you _____. Stop that bawling, ___ you!"

I tried to cover my backside with my hands to protect myself, then cried out "My hands, oh, my hands!"

But he kept hitting me over and over, yelling over my crying, "Get them out of the way then."

This probably sounds a bit repetitive, but when Dad gave you a beating it wasn't just a few slaps with a belt. When he got started, he just kept swinging. He would swing, cuss, then swing some more.

"Shut up and stand still. Stop your bawling, _____ you."

I fell to the floor in pain. He hit me several more times after that. The blows landed on my arms and across my back. Then, finally, he stopped.

He told me to get up and go to my room until I was done bawling.

I glanced up and saw Mom. She was standing off to the side, a helpless look in her eyes. I was only seven, but I could see the pain in my mother's eyes. I knew even then that she was a hurting, abused woman.

Our mom had tried to defend us. She'd spoken to Dad about the way he treated us. Through the closed bedroom door, I'd heard her pleading with him. Her appeals were not without risk. Sometimes, Dad would slap her or push her. Sometimes he would get mad and throw her across the kitchen. It was not unusual for Mother to have swollen, black and blue eyes for weeks on end.

27

But like lots of abused women, Mom did her best to hide it. Sometimes, I would hear her talking to her mother on the telephone. She would beg her mom *not* to come to our house. She never wanted her mom and dad to know how things really were in our home. Maybe she was embarrassed. Maybe she didn't want them to know how much she regretted not listening to them when they told her that that Dudrey boy was nothing but trouble.

Even as a kid I wished that there was something that I could have done to help my mother. But I was so numb with fear, and lived in such a continual state of terror, that I never dared say anything that might make myself the target of my father's rage.

As bad as things were at the time for me and my younger brothers and sisters, they were going to get a lot worse, as in, "put you in the hospital" worse. And try as she might, Momma couldn't save us. She couldn't even save herself.

Chapter 4

Head Injury

I was watching television in the living room one evening when I heard the familiar refrain, "Bedtime. Everyone, get your _____ downstairs to bed."

With the memory of the whipping I had received for wetting the bed still fresh in my mind, I ran to the bathroom before going downstairs. I tried to hurry and get to bed quickly so I wouldn't be slapped for taking too long.

Besides, the bed was my "safe place." Climbing up the ladder to the top bunk at day's end meant two things for me. I was less likely to get a beating if I was in bed being quiet; plus I could pull the covers over my head and, at least in my mind, escape the world around me. I could wrap myself tight and feel less vulnerable.

So I hurried. As I was finishing up in the bathroom, I heard Dad yell, "You better wash your hands when you're through!" So I did.

As I left the bathroom and crossed the living room floor headed for the stairway, Dad asked me if I had washed my hands. Before he could answer he added, "You better not be lying to me, if you know what's good for you."

Without thinking, I had paused in front of the television set on my way to the stairs. Dad motioned angrily, then growled, "Now move. Get out of my way. You make a better door than a window."

I moved quickly.

There were six steps that led down to the next level of our bi-level basement. Just as I reached the bottom step I felt a hand grab hold of the back of my neck and slam my face into the wall. The force of the thrust crashed my head through the wallboard. Just as my head snapped back from the first blow, another followed.

I was dizzy and my head was spinning, but still another blow came. Someone was beating my head into the wall. On the next blow, my head hit something solid, a stud in the wall, I assume. My body went numb and everything went black. I heard a loud ringing in my ears, as I sunk into unconsciousness. I barely remember crashing to the floor. Then motionless. Then nothing.

When I woke later in the night, I was in my bed. My body was thrashing uncontrollably, back and forth and up and down. My skin was cold, but wet. My head was throbbing with pain. I was dizzy and my chest was heaving. I could barely breathe. I lay there, flopping wildly on the bunk bed.

My throat was swollen and my tongue had slipped to the back of my mouth, choking me. I couldn't speak or call for help. My mind was running in circles, faster and faster. There were flashes of light in my head and I was making strange noises, sounds I'd never heard before.

My whole body felt stiff and rigid, like every muscle had contracted at once. I had no control over anything. I was thrashing helplessly in the dark, afraid and alone, trying in vain to call out. It is difficult to explain the panic I felt.

Then, someone was shaking me, talking to me, yelling at me, asking me questions. "What's wrong, Chuckie?" I could detect worry in the voice. I vaguely remember the voice coming from my Uncle Ron. He was staying with us at the time and slept in the basement where we kids slept. I didn't answer him. I couldn't.

Then I was alone again. Fear gripped me. The next thing I knew, a hand was forcing my mouth open. Fingers were digging into my cheeks. I felt the cold metal of a spoon at the roof of my mouth. The top side of the spoon was facing down in the back of my throat. Someone was using it to press down and pull forward on my tongue.

In spite of their efforts, I still couldn't breathe. Instinctively I knew I was choking to death. Then I felt someone lying on top of me, holding me down. In the background, I heard concerned sounding voices. In panic and desperation, I clamped my jaw tighter and tighter, but fingers kept prying my mouth open. The spoon scraped across my teeth as someone continued trying to pull my tongue forward.

I heard new voices, more people in the room. I could hear my mother sobbing as I was picked up and placed on a stretcher. They strapped me down and hurried me up the stairs and across the living room floor. I was thrashing harder and harder. I hazily recall being carried out the front door. The thrashing continued; it was completely overpowering.

I saw the flashing red lights of the ambulance as my stretcher was loaded into the back. Immediately, someone placed a strap over my head. Additional straps were fastened over my body and my arms. Then the doors closed.

As the vehicle began moving forward, I felt a needle pierce my arm. The siren was loud at first, then faded to nothing as I slipped from consciousness.

I don't know how long I was out, but when I awoke I could hear the sounds of people in the room. My eyes were heavy. I attempted to open them, but drifted back to sleep again. I wasn't feeling any pain, but I could feel and hear the heavy drumbeat my heart was making inside my head. I felt a heavy pressure behind my eyes, as though they were somehow too large to stay in their sockets. Then I mercifully drifted off to sleep again.

I don't know how long I was out, but as I slowly regained consciousness I sensed that my mother was there in the room with me. Through a haze, I could smell her perfume and hear her voice asking someone, "Will he be okay?" I drifted off again before I heard the answer.

When I awakened the next time, it was immediately apparent that whatever they had given me was beginning to wear off. My entire body ached. I wasn't sure what had happened to me or where I was. I slowly took in my surroundings. So many strange and unfamiliar sounds. Noises were coming from somewhere outside my room. The sound of rolling carts hitting a wall, the squeaking of wheels turning. And distant voices.

The smells were all strange and new. Some were pleasant. Others made me nervous and uncomfortable. Then, just like that, I was asleep again, dreaming.

All of a sudden I saw bright flashing lights. Things started moving rapidly. I didn't realize it, but I was seizing again. I was thrashing about involuntarily, my teeth tightly clinched. My neck was so stiff it hurt. I noticed that I was shivering from the cold.

Later that day, at least I think it was that day, I found myself wide awake. My mother was standing beside me while a nurse took my blood pressure and checked the bag of fluids that were dripping into me.

At the time I had no idea what the term meant, but the nurses said I had been having *grand mal* seizures, dozens of them. They had lasted for more than eight hours.

I kept wondering why I felt so very, very cold. When I complained, Mother explained that I was lying in a bed of ice. My fever was 104 and the doctors were concerned that I had a suffered a brain injury. A doctor walked in and I could hear him talking to my mother. Then he turned and spoke to me.

"How are you doing? Are you okay?" he asked. "You took some fall down those stairs. You will need to stay here for a few weeks, because we need to run some more tests before we can send you home."

My body felt numb. My emotions were either numb or too confused to grasp what was happening to me, and what had happened before. But, at least I could feel my heart pounding inside my head. That told me that I was indeed alive.

I didn't realize it then, but I was a very sick little boy. I was only seven, but at the time, the outlook for any kind of future for me looked pretty grim.

Some things were hazy, but one thing wasn't. I knew I hadn't fallen down the stairs. Someone had repeatedly bashed my head into the wall. But if falling down the stairs was the story the doctors had been told, well, I dared not contradict it. If I got my dad in trouble, I would be the one who was really in trouble. Of that I was certain.

Chapter 5

Off to the Mayo Clinic

E ventually, the doctors sent me home. They'd decided that my case required special help, the kind the local hospital was not able to provide. A couple of days later, the doctor had me come to his office for a follow up.

I sat on the table in one of the rooms while he slowly ran his fingers through my hair. He paused now and then, and gently pressed on my head, all the while making small talk with my mother. The small office we were in was located on the third floor of a large building in downtown St. Paul, Minnesota.

Mother and I had caught the bus that morning at the same stop where she always caught it when she went to work. Today was a good day. Today I was with her. I was alone with my mom. I loved that. That's when I felt the safest.

The door opened and a nurse came in with a large folder, which she handed to the doctor. He opened the folder and took out several x-rays. One at a time, he clipped the large pieces of film onto a light-box, so we could see them. While the doctor worked, Mother and I sat on large wooden chairs, the kind with a square piece of padded leather on the seat, and round brass tacks holding the pad in place.

I still remember the sadness on my mother's face. After sorting through several x-rays, the doctor asked her to take a look at one of them. He had a measuring device and was making notes on the film as he talked. Then he came and stood next to me and carefully measured my head. He scribbled some notes in a folder, then turned and talked to my mom.

In a calm voice, the doctor explained that he thought it would be best if I were taken to some place in Rochester, a special place he called the Mayo Clinic. Then he turned off the light box, placed the film back into the folder, and handed it to Mother. I remember him saying something about the importance of my sleep and giving my mom a prescription for some medication to help with that. As we left his office he wished me good luck and said he would see me in a few weeks.

It's funny the things that matter to a child. I remember that I loved being with my mother as we walked together down the hall and stopped in front of the elevator. Everything was better when it was just the two of us. And I remember the elevator. It was one of the old style contraptions that had a large lever for opening the door. After the door was opened there was another door that folded to the side. This was fun for me because Mom let me close the elevator doors by myself. Of course, like mothers do, she had to warn me not to let my figures get pinched. Once inside, with the outer door closed, Mother let me push the big button with the number one on it, and I got to turn the crank that closed the inside door. It was a wonderful and amazing thing to do. I would have stayed there and done that all day.

All too soon, however, we were downstairs, walking through the large revolving doors and exiting the building. With Mom holding onto my hand, we quickly blended with the multitudes of people out on the sidewalk.

It was a busy afternoon in the city. Cars were constantly stopping for the traffic lights, then speeding off again. There was a steady din of horns honking and the smell of diesel trucks and buses. It was all very exciting to a seven-year old boy from a small town.

We walked a few blocks to our destination, Stein's Pharmacy. That's where my mom worked; I'd been there with her several times. As was common back then, the pharmacy had a soda fountain. I liked to sit on the stools at the counter and spin around. But alas, even before we walked in the front door Momma made it clear that there would be no spinning for me today.

Everyone greeted us when we walked in. After Mother ordered lunch for me, she walked to the back of the store to talk to her boss. The two of them talked for quite a while. Occasionally her boss looked my way, and once he even smiled at me. When they finally finished their conversation, Mother walked back to the counter and waited patiently while I finished my grilled cheese sandwich and fries.

There were a lot of bus stops between Mom's work and the stop by our house. For me, the more stops the better. Thanks to all of the nice people on the bus, I got to pull the cord and sound the buzzer for every stop. My mother made this ride everyday at this same time, so she was acquainted with the other passengers. She seemed pleased to introduce me to people and would always smile when she did.

Today, however, I could tell that she was hurting inside. I knew she was concerned about me. But I sensed that it was more than that, that there were other things haunting her too. She seemed distant and withdrawn. Looking back, I realize that she was caught up in an intense drama that was spinning out of her control. My heart ached for her. I had seen how Dad treated her. I had seen him knock her across the room many times. I had seen the helplessness on her face when she saw us kids being abused.

At the time I was too young to comprehend the emotions that must have been tearing her apart. All I knew that day, was my mom was hurting and it seemed worse than usual. I wondered if it was partly my fault; if my going to the hospital had made her hurt more than before.

When we could see our stop coming up, Mother said, "Go ahead and pull the buzzer." She had anticipated my request before the words came out of my mouth. Moms are like that.

When the bus came to a stop, Mother held my hand tightly. "No jumping off the bus today," she whispered. It was fun jumping from step to step and then to the ground, but I wouldn't be doing that today. With Mother still holding my hand, we stepped off the bus. She turned and waved as the bus pulled away. Mother was always friendly and polite, even when her whole world was coming apart.

As we walked up the street, I saw my friends riding their bikes and playing. They rode up to us and asked where we had been and if my mom had bought me anything. They asked me to stay with them and play. As Mother gently squeezed my hand, I replied, "No. I have to go home now."

I wanted to stay, but I didn't appeal. I knew by my mother's mood that I would not be able to change her mind. As we walked toward home, my friends rode their bikes in circles around us. Some rode with no hands, showing off.

I didn't know it then, but I would not be playing with those kids ever again.

Chapter 6

Rochester Trip

T he sun wasn't even up, but the lights were all on and people were talking. I could hear Mother, Dad and the new babysitter, Barbara, talking upstairs around the kitchen table. Mother was giving instructions about the house and the kids and what to do about this and that. Eighteen-year-old Barbara would be living with us and babysitting the other kids until I was well again. We needed help because Dad had to work, and Mother and I were going on a trip and would be gone for a few days.

Barbara was supposedly a friend of Mother's. She had been around the house on and off for a year or so, but I never got the sense that she and Mom were close.

While I prepared to hop in the bathtub, my mother showed me the new clothes I would be wearing on the long bus trip ahead of us. Then, right after breakfast, we caught the city bus that would take us downtown to the main Greyhound Bus Station.

As we rode along, Mother made sure I didn't go to sleep. I was tired and my head hurt, but the doctor had given strict instructions that I was not to sleep before we got to the clinic and some tests were run. I was sure Mother needed sleep too, possibly more than I did. But she stayed on guard and made sure neither of us dozed off.

I had never been to a bus depot before; it was really something. Buses and trains were the main means of travel for long trips back then, so the bus depot was a busy place. There were several buses lined up under the large overhang that ran the total length of the depot, and people hurrying here and there, everywhere you looked. The place was bustling with activity. There were people carrying suitcases. Some had shopping bags with handles on them. Others carried cardboard boxes that had been closed up with tape and tied up with heavy string.

Depot employees with matching uniforms were busy loading suitcases into cargo compartments. I would have liked to have stayed and watched. There was so much going on, so many people and so many new sounds. But my mom gently directed my attention to the café counter and before long I was sitting there sipping hot chocolate.

From where we sat I could hear someone talking over the loud speaker. In vain I looked around, trying to see who was doing the talking. Whoever this mysterious person was, he was directing passengers toward the buses that would take them to their destinations. Each time a new announcement was made I glanced up at Mother and she would shake her head. Finally, just as we finished our drinks, the man over the loud speaker announced, "Rochester, Winona, Des Moines – Gate Two." Mother nodded her head and began gathering our things so we could get to our bus on time.

I was in no hurry. There was so much going on and I didn't want to miss a thing. But the buses all had schedules to keep, so there was no time for a seven-year old boy to stand around gawking. The voice came back on the loudspeaker, "Des Moines and points south, final call, Gate Two." Holding my hand, Momma picked up our pace.

The Greyhound we boarded was a lot bigger than the city buses I was used to. We sat up really high, and even though I had not slept for almost two days I was wide awake now. I watched out the window as other passengers climbed aboard their buses. As our bus lurched forward, I saw a man across from me lean his seat back, so I found the button on the side of my seat and tilted mine back, too. That was fun.

Around us, people were settling in. Some were preparing to sleep, while others puffed on cigarettes or sipped cups of coffee. But for me, this was my first long bus trip and I was enjoying myself. I sat up on the front edge of my seat. Outside the window I could see people on the street. If they looked up, I waved to them; it was fun when someone waved back.

We were going to stay with my mother's aunt in Rochester. I didn't know who she was, but Mother explained that she was her mother's sister, and that this made her my great aunt. I had never seen a great aunt.

As the scene outside my window changed from city to countryside, I suddenly realized that I was really tired and desperately wanted to sleep. I started wishing that this trip was over already. But Mother faithfully stood guard and made sure the doctor's orders were followed and I didn't sleep. Not being able to sleep felt like torture.

After a long, long ride we finally pulled into the bus station at Rochester. Looking out the window, Mother whispered, "Look, there's Aunty now!" I pressed my face to the window and saw a pleasant looking woman smiling and waving at us.

After a short car ride, we arrived at Aunty's home. When we walked in the front door, it felt like we were at Grandmother Mausolf's house. Everything was clean and fresh and smelled really good. The air was heavy with the wonderful smell of something baking in the oven. I noticed a fresh apple pie sitting on the kitchen counter. I liked this place. I wouldn't have minded staying a long time.

Chapter 7

The Mayo Clinic

I was too young to realize it at the time, but the Mayo Clinic was and is one of the world's premiere medical facilities. The fact that I was sent there is pretty good evidence that I was a really sick little boy.

When Mom and I arrived in radiology, we were met by a nice lady in a white nurse's uniform. She was holding a clipboard. The lady asked me my name, looked at my new armband, and then told me to please sit in one of the wheelchairs. This was exciting. My very own wheelchair! I was already thinking about wheeling myself down the long hallway as fast as this baby would go. Alas, the nurse and my mother had other plans. The nurse got behind me and rolled my chair slowly down the corridor to another waiting room.

Too much waiting. Waiting was the one thing I disliked about this trip, because when we waited, my body and my mind tried desperately to drift off to sleep. If no one was paying attention, even for half a minute, my head would fall forward and I would start to doze off. Sometimes, I would snap out of it from the motion of my head suddenly lurching forward; other times my mom would catch me and shake me gently until I was awake. She would then engage me in conversation or squeeze my arm with her hand. That's what she was doing when my name was finally called.

I was wheeled to a room with a large window. Moments later, a lady walked in and said that she was there to give me a haircut. There was no explanation. She simply fastened an apron around my neck and started shaving off all my hair. As soon as she was finished, another woman came in and washed my head with soap and water. While this second lady was drying me off, a third lady came in pushing a cart with all kinds of stuff on it. I tried to turn around and see what was on the cart, but I was instructed to remain still. The third lady took some ointment from a small silver tube and rubbed it on my head. Whatever it was, it was cold. She apologized for that.

I was tired and cold, but again I was instructed to not fall asleep. I sat as still as I could while they started attaching wires to my bald head. Whatever they were doing, the testing went on for a long time. At least it seemed like a long time to me because I was constantly being reminded to not fall asleep. Finally, another nurse came and said that I would probably like the next test.

After she closed the door, someone over a speaker asked me if I could hear them. I answered, yes. Then they began conducting some kind of light test to measure my brainwave pattern. The lights in the room were turned off and I was instructed to close my eyes for a moment.

"Now, Charles, open your eyes," they said. They repeated this several times. But every time the lights went off, I wanted to fall asleep. My body desperately wanted to sleep.

Someone came in and checked the connections for all of the wires; then they started another test. This time using strobe lights. The light flashed really fast and I could see the people behind the glass taking notes.

Finally, one of the nurses came in and said that they were done testing for the day and I could sleep now. Sleep! Finally, I could sleep. As you might imagine, it didn't take long for me to drift off.

When I awoke, there were people taking wires off of my head. With warm soap and water they washed my head. They told us it was okay for Mother and me to leave for lunch. I remember being pretty embarrassed about my shaved head. Momma must have realized that, because the first thing she did was stop at the clinic's gift shop and get me a brand new baseball cap.

As soon as lunch was over, we headed to our next appointment. The clinic had tunnels that led to different buildings. I liked the tunnels and I was having fun, but I could tell my mother was tired and worried. Looking back, I'm sure her anxiousness was not just about me, but also about the other children back home with the new babysitter. Barbara was only eighteen and there was no way for Mother to know in advance whether she was up to the task of babysitting four young kids, especially in a house where none of us had ever felt safe.

Our home was far from a peaceful place. Sure, there were times when the atmosphere was more pleasant than others, like when we had people over for a birthday party for one of us kids, or when our grandparents would pick us up for church. My mother's parents, the Mausolfs, went to a Methodist church that was close-by. Sometimes we would go with them on Sunday mornings, and afterward they would take us out to lunch.

Whether at church or at a restaurant, our grandmother always introduced us to people. Most of the time they would ask if we were Audrey's children. I remember the sadness on our grandmother's face when she would talk about our mother. Grandma thought she knew what life was like at our house and it made her sad, but in truth she had no idea.

Our mother's parents were rarely at our house. Even as a young kid I knew they didn't like our dad. They never said anything negative about him to me, not back then, but I could sense it. I think if they really knew what we were all going through, they would have tried to do something about it. Grandmother Mausolf was that kind of person. She could be a real mother hen when the situation called for it. At times she was downright fearless.

Getting back to my story. As we sat in the clinic waiting for our last appointment of the day, I was glad my mother was there with me, even though today she seemed more withdrawn than usual. Maybe it had something to do with the fact that my own father had bashed my head into the wall and she'd been forced to say that I had fallen down the stairs. The big holes and dents in the stairwell wall, however, told a different story. Those didn't happen from someone falling down the stairs, and Momma knew it.

Every once in a while, Mother would pull out a hanky and wipe the tears from her eyes. When I asked her if she was all right, she only replied, "Now don't you worry about me, Honey."

Finally, a doctor walked into the room where we had been waiting. He had a folder in his hand. Step by step, he explained the results of all the tests they had run. He told Mother that I had suffered a brain injury from blunt force trauma to the head. He said that I had some scar tissue on my brain, and that they would like to remove it. He explained that this would require surgery and could possibly have lasting effects on me, including the rather ominous fact that I might not survive the surgery.

Momma had lots of tears in her eyes when we left the doctor's office that day. She seemed so sad and alone in her thoughts. But what was there for me to do? I was only seven and it seemed the more I showed concern for her the more she showed concern for me. We took a taxi to Aunty's house to spend one more night with her before the bus trip home. That night, Mother talked to Aunty about what the doctor had said. After talking everything through, Mother decided not to go ahead with the surgery, not if there was a chance I might die from it.

When we arrived back at our house the next day, I noticed that things were oddly different. At first I wasn't quite sure why or how, but things were not the same as when we left for Rochester. Dad wasn't any kinder to mother. It wasn't that. He continued to get angry and yell at us kids and give us whippings over the smallest things. That part hadn't changed. Then I realized what it was. It was the babysitter. For some reason, she was now living with us. She had moved in. She was suddenly part of our family, whether Momma liked it or not.

I remember there being a loud argument between my parents over the matter. One night, after being especially mean to Mom, Dad walked out the door and slammed it behind him. He didn't come home until the next morning. That kind of thing went on for some time after that.

I would find out later that Dad had gotten Barbara pregnant while we were away at the Mayo Clinic, but that was never talked about in front of us kids. In fact, that was Dad and Barbara's secret. I don't even think Mother knew.

Things started getting weird after Barbara moved in. A lot of strange people started coming around. Late one night, I woke up to the sound of loud yelling and someone crying. I sneaked quietly up the stairs to see what was going on and saw a man I'd never seen before sitting at our kitchen table. His face was covered with blood and he looked really beat up. Dad was giving him wet towels so he could wipe the blood off his face. When Dad looked over and saw me, he told me in less than polite terms to get my rear end back to bed. I obeyed quickly enough, but as I lay there in my bed that night, wide awake, I remember being scared. And I remember worrying about my mom. There never used to be so many people coming and going at our house. Now there were lots of strangers and they weren't always nice people. Mostly, they were friends of Barbara.

In some ways, I welcomed all the coming and going, because for the moment we were not being treated quite as badly. But I could tell that my mother didn't approve of all the people Barbara was bringing to our home. They came all hours of the night. They smelled strongly of hard liquor, and were so loud they routinely woke everyone in the house.

I'm not quite sure how Barbara pulled it off, but before long her brother Walter also started living with us. It was becoming increasingly clear that the babysitter, Barbara, had taken over our house – in more ways than one. And that marked the beginning of the end for our mom.

Chapter 8

Mother Is Shot

It was a little before five a.m. and still dark outside when Barbara and her brother Walter got to the house. They had been out all night long with their friends, drinking and partying.

A few minutes after those two arrived there was a loud knock at the door and three of Barbara's friends showed up. I could hear them talking and laughing, and the strong smell of alcohol and cigarettes drifted down the stairway to my bedroom. The two who came in last were carnies, and had that rough look about them. They had been out partying all night, but apparently had not yet had enough. So, rather than go to bed, they brought their fun to our house. At least that was what it was supposed to look like.

Be that as it may, their loud voices and laughter woke me up. I lay there in bed and listened to the noise and tried to make out the different voices. Then I heard my mother speak. It was clear that she too had been awakened by all the ruckus. But being the kind of woman she was, rather than kick them all out, she got busy making the revelers coffee and breakfast. I heard Momma ask them to please keep the noise down, so as not to wake the children. They seemed to pay her no mind.

I hadn't heard Dad's voice yet. He was supposedly leaving for an early morning hunting trip, so I was surprised that I hadn't heard him up, getting ready to go.

Dad's hunting gear was sitting on the countertop. He had set everything out the night before so he could just get up and take off. Along with his other gear were his hunting rifle and his pistol. His pistol was always hanging from a hook on the kitchen wall by the refrigerator. We were used to seeing it, but all of us kids knew better than to ever touch it.

While the coffee was brewing on the stove, Vernon, one of Barbara's carnie friends, picked up Dad's rifle and started messing with it. He held it up and looked down the barrel, as if he was preparing to shoot. No one said anything to him about messing with Dad's guns, which was odd, because Barbara and Walter both knew the rule about touching Dad's guns and would not have broken it themselves.

After messing around with the rifle, Vernon laid it down and picked up the pistol and examined it. He didn't do what everyone knows to do when picking up a firearm, make sure it's not loaded. Instead, for no "apparent" reason, he pointed the pistol directly at my mother, in what he later would call "reckless fun."

Mother placed her hand over her heart in disbelief, shocked that someone would point a real gun at her chest, a gun she knew was loaded because Dad's guns were always loaded.

Then Vernon quipped, "I gotcha." As the words left his lips, he pulled the trigger. There was a loud crack as the gun went off, and a bullet passed through my mother's hand and into her heart, mortally wounding her.

I heard the shot, but had no idea what it meant. When my sister Susanne heard the gun go off, she ran into the kitchen where she saw Mother lying limp on the floor with blood all over her.

The police were called. When they arrived a few minutes later, they picked up Mother's all but lifeless body and rushed her in their squad car to Ancker Hospital in downtown St. Paul. Surgeons worked for five hours in an attempt to save my mother's life, but in spite of their best efforts they were unable to repair the damage the bullet had done to her heart. My dear, sweet mother died at eleven-thirty that morning. She was 27 years old. The date was Saturday, November 11, 1961.

Five little kids lost their mom that day. I was eight at the time. We lost the only person who had loved us and tried to protect us from the hell that was slowly gathering around us, like some kind of dark, brooding cloud. There is no way to explain the hurt and the loss.

One moment there were sounds of loud laughing and partying going on upstairs in the kitchen; then without warning. the loud crack of a gunshot reverberated through our house. That gunshot was going to change all of our lives forever.

Little Frances had no idea what was going on, and neither did Kenny. Susanne, John, and I had at least some sense of it. As you might imagine, the three of us cried a lot of tears that day. Little Kenny and Frances eventually joined in the crying, even if they had no idea why everyone was so upset.

On the Monday afternoon following the shooting, all of us kids were seated on a pew in the second row at the Methodist church where my mother's parents attended. My sisters and brothers and I were dressed in new clothes just for the occasion. As I looked around the church, I could see people I knew and some I couldn't recall ever seeing before.

My mother's parents, the Mausolfs, were sitting across the aisle from where we were. On our side were my father's mom and dad, the Dudreys, and the rest of Dad's family. Occasionally, Grandma Mausolf would bring someone over to see us kids and they would give us sad looks and hug us or give us kisses. Everyone looked so hurt and sad that my mother was gone. Up in the front of the church, people were walking past the casket, stopping for a moment to gaze down at Momma's body.

Some of the people cried and sobbed. Others shook their heads in sad disbelief. I needed to know what was going on and what those people were seeing. Before my dad could grab my arm to stop me, I jumped up and ran over to the side of the casket and looked inside. There was my mother. She looked so peaceful and pretty. She was wearing her glasses and her lips were red with the lipstick she always wore.

Of course I couldn't grasp the full magnitude of what this all meant, but I understood well enough to know that this would be the last time I would ever see my mom. I started crying. My mind went numb with pain. What would become of me now, with Mother gone? What would happen to my brothers and sisters? Looking back, it was probably best that I didn't know.

Grandmother Mausolf came over and stood beside me. She took me by the hand and assured me that someday I would see my mother again in a place called heaven. I had heard of this heaven place the few times we had been to church with our grandparents, but at that moment I don't recall finding much comfort in that thought. There was nothing real about it.

While I was standing there, Susanne came running up. She looked at Momma, peacefully lying there like she was asleep, and started begging her to wake up. "Wake up, Momma. Wake up!"

When Mother didn't respond, Susanne began sobbing uncontrollably and making a big enough fuss that eventually one of the relatives came forward and took all of us kids out of the room. There was a restaurant close by, and we went there and had lunch while the adults proceeded with the funeral service.

That afternoon, our dear sweet mother was laid to rest. The emptiness and the pain I suffered that day would not pass quickly. Years later, seemingly out of nowhere, I would find myself desperately missing my mother and wishing I could see her just one more time.

There was something else about that time that would not pass quickly, the questions. On the morning our mother was shot, the police took the shooter into custody on suspicion of felonious assault. On Tuesday afternoon, however, the day after mother's funeral, my father stood in a courtroom beside the man who had killed his wife and testified on his behalf. Standing before the judge, Dad had a Bible in his hand, which was somewhat of a surprise, given the fact that we had never seen him with one before. He passionately pleaded with the judge not to charge Vernon with any crime, calling the entire affair just a terrible accident.

Vernon Drake was set free that day. He was not charged with anything, not even negligent homicide. He had pointed a loaded gun at my mother's heart, said "I gotcha," and pulled the trigger, and yet he got off scot-free, thanks largely, I'm sure, to my dad's testimony.

I was probably too young to grasp everything that was going on around me. But looking back, I'm certain that my dad had our mom killed. There were several reasons why he might have done that. Had Mother threatened to go to the authorities about the fact that Dad had been abusing us, including sexually? Was he afraid Mom would find out that Barbara, our "babysitter," was pregnant by him?

There were reasons to believe that that was the case. Shortly after Mother's death, Barbara left for an extended visit with her sister in Wisconsin. When she returned, her sister in Wisconsin had a new baby named "Chucky," the same name as my dad and me.

One thing, however, was for sure. After Mom died, Barbara was no longer our babysitter. She was Dad's "woman." She took Mom's place in our house and in his bedroom.

After that, day by day, week by week, all of the anger and guilt our babysitter had been hiding in her dark heart began to come to the surface. The darkness would be unleashed on five little kids who had no idea just how bad their sad little lives were about to become.

At that time, we were still in Minnesota. We had not yet made it to Church Street. That's where the real hell would begin.

Also, at that time I had no knowledge of the ties my dad had to people in the mob. In those days, the mob was quite active in the Minneapolis/St. Paul area. Back then, I didn't know that Dad had connections with people who killed people for other people. I would find that out years later when Dad showed me the fully automatic machine gun he kept in the closet, and told me where he got it. We will get to that in due time.

I confess that I'm hesitant to say things like this about my own father, but I am not a kid now and I'm neither naïve nor afraid. As I grew up, things that were only suspected back then would become increasingly clear.

A lot of time has passed since these things went down, and there are things that still today I don't want to talk about. The sex abuse. The unspeakable perversions. Or the time when Dad was angry because I wouldn't stop crying about something, and looked me in the face and with a snarl told me, "I should have sold you when I had the chance."

Someone had offered to buy me and my dad had turned him down. And now he regretted it? I was pretty sure I knew the guy he was talking about, and trust me when I say if you were a little boy you would not want to belong to that kind of person.

Chapter 9

The Road to Church Street

W e spent the entire day loading our humble belongings into the big U-Haul truck parked outside our Maplewood home, the only home we kids had ever known. Once the truck was finally full, the steel ramp tucked back into place, and the back door closed, we were ready to hit the road.

Dad and Barbara and all of us kids somehow packed ourselves into the cab of the U-Haul and headed south. Our new house was a little more than 500 miles south of Maplewood in a place called Georgetown, Illinois.

It would be an understatement to say that the cab of that truck was a bit crowded. There were four of us kids, two dogs and a cat, plus Dad and Barbara. Unbeknownst to us kids, the load was going to get lighter as we traveled south.

I should mention that the reason there were only four kids in the cab was because my younger brother John had been hit by a car crossing the street a few weeks earlier. He would be staying with our mother's parents until his cast was off and then joining the rest of us at our new home later. Too bad for him that he wasn't able to stay with the Mausolfs and never join us. The real hell was about to begin and he could have missed it.

The cab of the truck was hot and stunk with the smell of the cats mixed with Barbara's body order. Barbara's hygiene was not so bad when she first started living with us, but she had gradually let herself go. By this time, I'm pretty sure she had stopped taking baths altogether, because she always smelled awful. Sitting next to her in the cab of a hot, stuffy truck was nearly unbearable. Often I would take a breath and hold it as long as I could, then after exhaling, put my mouth to my sleeve to take in the next breath to keep from gagging. Try doing that for 500 miles.

It was on the trip to Georgetown that the darkness of Barbara's soul began to show. Whether it was hatred or pure evil, that's when it first began to manifest. Riding along in the truck she would, for no reason, pull Susanne's hair or dig her fingernails into Kenny's arm. She seemed to get some kind of fiendish pleasure out of causing us pain.

From time to time, she would grind her elbow into my ribs, just for fun. Down by Barbara's feet, poor baby Frances was trying to get comfortable in her designated spot on the cab floor. Every so often, and for no apparent reason, Barbara would give Frances a sharp kick in her side or her back. When Frances would cry out, Barbara would say, "Oh I'm sorry, Hon," and pretend that she had done nothing intentional. But the fiendish look on her face said otherwise.

For some reason the woman hated us kids. It was plastered all over her face. And her behavior got increasingly worse the further south we went. None of us knew it then, but this woman who had taken our mother's place was going to become increasingly more aggressive and venomous as the years dragged on. She was just getting started.

It is hard to describe Barbara's countenance. Her eyes were dark and set deep in her face. When she looked at us, her brooding eyes seemed to pierce right through us. It was as if she was trying to cut us to pieces with her stare. By this time, I was really missing my mother.

About halfway to Illinois, the cat urinated on the floor of the U-Haul. It smelled awful. Without stopping the truck, Dad grabbed the cat by the hair on the back of its neck and tossed it out the window. I doubt it survived the impact with the pavement, but then you never know about cats.

Because of all the cat pee, my little sister wanted to get up off the floor, but with an expletive thrown in for emphasis, Dad told her to stay where she was until we stopped somewhere to get something to eat. The poor child was only about two years old at the time. She was at an age when any normal person would have gone out of their way to make her comfortable. But Dad and Barbara seemed to lack any compassion whatsoever.

When we finally stopped for gas, Barbara went into the station to get us something to eat. When she came back to the truck, she made us all peanut butter sandwiches, shoving them at us one at a time, as if she resented us eating. It was as if we were being punished for existing. As she shoved the sandwiches at us, she made it clear that we would not be getting anything else to eat until we got to our destination.

As soon as the truck started moving again, I got a really hard elbow in my ribs. Then for no reason other than proximity, Barbara took a hold of my face and twisted it in her hand. When Dad heard me moan in pain, he slammed on the brakes and pulled the truck to the side of the road. As soon as the U-Haul had lurched to a full stop, he turned to me and told me, in an expletive laced threat, that I was to stop my complaining or he would give me something to complain about. I won't repeat his words exactly, but it was pretty nasty and pretty scary. I was used to Dad's bad moods, but things were darker and uglier than I had seen before.

Before we took off again, Dad decided it was time to lighten the load a bit more. He opened the driver's door and unceremoniously threw our two dogs out. With a heartless, "Good luck, boys," we started off toward Illinois.

By this time, I had learned to internalize a lot of my feelings. After Mother was killed, I started suppressing my emotions, holding back for fear of getting a beating. And with good cause. Even on this trip, if I asked a question or said anything, Dad would reach across the cab and bust me upside the head and tell me to shut up. I would wipe my tears on my shirtsleeve and hold my arm against my mouth, so Dad wouldn't hear me cry. As a defensive measure, I tried to not speak at all. Sometimes this would go on for hours until eventually Dad would yell at me for not paying attention, or yell at me for being stupid. As you might imagine, it is pretty hard for a kid to hide or stay out of harm's way in the cab of a U-Haul truck.

Around noon the next day we pulled up to our new home on South Church Street in Georgetown, Illinois. Back in Minnesota we had been renting, but Dad actually bought the house on Church Street. He used Mother's social security money to do it.

This two story house was where we were going to spend the next several years of our lives. I remember wondering at that moment if Mother could see us from up in heaven. I sure missed her and the comfort I'd only felt when she'd put her arms around me. Later on, after we got settled in, I thought I saw Mother walking past our house on Church Street. Sometimes I woke up in the middle of the night and thought she was there beside me.

Of course, all of that was just my imagination. In the real world, dark clouds were beginning to settle over us.

Chapter 10

My Report Card

Lying in my bed in the early morning I listened closely to the sounds of the house. I didn't hear Barbara yet. It was a report card day at school and I planned to get out of the house before she knew I was gone. I really didn't want to go to school. Not today. I didn't want to be handed a report card that I knew I had to show Dad and Barbara when I got home. But staying home would mean getting a beating for something else. That was a certainty.

With our move to Georgetown, Barbara just kind of assumed her place as our stepmother. When Dad wasn't around, she was free to mete out whatever punishment her dark heart imagined. With little or no provocation or reason, one of us would get whipped with a belt, a mop handle, or an extension cord, or Barbara might just haul off and slug us in the face.

Eating Barbara's cooking was almost as bad as getting one of her beatings. Last night's supper had been more of Barbara's disgusting goulash. I am sure she had urinated in it. It wouldn't have been the first time she had done that. She loved to torture us in any way she could, and urinating in our food was just one of her fiendish means of making our lives miserable.

Now you might think I'm just making that up, but Barbara literally kept a pitcher of urine in the fridge, supposedly for her doctor to test. Susanne and I saw her pour some of that in the food she was cooking for us kids.

Before I left the table the night before report card day, I was told that what I didn't finish at dinner would be my breakfast the next morning. As you might imagine, I chose to not eat at all, which required leaving the house the next morning before Barbara got up. It may sound strange, but all of us kids learned to not eat for what would sometimes be days at a time. We got used to eating when Barbara decided to feed us – and that was not always daily.

I should add that sometimes Susanne and I ate at school or shoplifted food from the grocery store. But the little kids who were still at home never had those opportunities.

When I slipped out of bed that morning, I noticed that my brothers and sisters were already awake. Like me, none of them were anxious to get up and face the day. So as to not make noise or draw attention to ourselves, we had learned to communicate with our eyes. The unspoken question in everyone's eyes that morning, as with most mornings was, "Is Barbara out of bed yet?"

By now, we were all living in constant fear of this woman. Barbara's hatred was no longer veiled. You could see it on her face any time she looked at you. You could feel it in the room, if you were in her presence. If she was awake and you were where she was, there was trouble. There was screaming. There were threats. There were hits. It was not occasional; it was constant.

Maybe she had taken a lot of her pills the night before and would sleep all day. Those were good days. There would be no meals, because the food was kept under lock and key, so us thieving little ungrateful vermin wouldn't get our hands on it. But at least while she slept we weren't being beat on. Maybe she had overdosed on her pills and was lying in her bedroom dead. I always hoped in vain for that day.

I was careful not to make any noise. The others followed suit. My pants were damp but dry enough to put on. I had washed them with Ivory Hand Soap in the kitchen sink the night before, rinsed them, and wrung them out the best I could. Then I laid them over the radiator to dry. I did this often, always hoping that the next morning my pants wouldn't be too damp or too wrinkled to wear.

I had gotten dressed and was just starting out the front door when I heard the cussing and swearing begin. It was Barbara telling Susanne that she was going to be late for school. I heard her ask where I was. I heard her slap my sister in the face, screaming that she had to eat breakfast before she left.

"I wouldn't want you telling anyone at school that you didn't eat at home," she yelled. As if going without meals never happened.

Making my sister eat breakfast was not what it seemed. Barbara didn't care if Susanne ate. She was just trying to cause my sister to be tardy, so when she got home from school that afternoon there would be an excuse to beat her for being late. I had heard enough. I got away from the house as quickly as I could. The sounds of Barbara's swearing faded behind me as I made my way down the sidewalk.

That morning I sat at my desk, totally oblivious to what was going on around me. I was lost in my own thoughts, hoping that I didn't get an F in any of my classes. If I did, I would be in big trouble when I got home. We always got in trouble if we did anything that made people think we might be stupid. Dad was big on people not thinking his kids were stupid.

The last time I got an F on my report card, it was in Spelling. Dad made me sit at the kitchen table for hours until I could spell every word correctly. He would come into the kitchen and say, "Okay, spell this word." If I got it wrong he would hit me in the back of the head and call me by my nickname, stupid little _____. I would try to memorize the words, but frankly was never any good at it. The more I misspelled, the dumber I was, and consequently the more I got hit in the back of the head. Finally, Dad told tell me to get my stupid _____ to bed before he really got mad. "And stop that _____ bawling before I give you some-thing to cry about, you _____ baby."

I could never understand what was going on in the classroom. It wasn't that I didn't try. I did, but I just didn't get it. I couldn't stay focused because my mind was busy worrying about what was going to happen when I got home. I'm not trying to make excuses for my bad grades. I truly and honestly did spend most of my time at school dreading going home when classes were over.

Imagine that you had never been in a fight before. You were little and couldn't defend yourself, but the bully of the school had just told you that when school got out at three o'clock he was going to be waiting for you outside the school door and was going to beat you up. How would you feel? Would you be able to focus on what the teacher was saying in the classroom that day? Or would you spend all day thinking about what was going to happen to you after school? Well, that's what it was like for us kids every single day of our lives. And it showed on my report cards.

If Barbara had seen me that morning before I left the house I would have been forced to eat last night's supper, or I would have gotten a beating. Or if I had actually eaten my dinner the night before, she

54

would have given me corn flakes with powdered milk for breakfast. That stuff made me sick. It was never mixed well, always warm and the lumps floated to the top of the glass. If you've never had warm, lumpy USDA powdered milk, you might not get what I am saying. But if you have, you know.

When Barbara did get around to making us something to eat, not eating her ghastly fare was not an option. If any of us resisted and didn't eat whatever she'd made, and eat it in her time frame, that kid was deemed an ungrateful little _____. She would then grab whomever it was by the face, dig her fingers into their cheeks to force their mouth open, then pour whatever it was down their throat. She seemed to take fiendish delight in watching little kids gag.

But for the moment, I was at school and for a few hours I was safe. That's what school was for me, and probably for all of us kids. It was a place where Barbara wasn't, and any place Barbara wasn't, was a good place.

As lunchtime approached I had a decision to make; go home for lunch and get a beating for something or stay at school and clean tables for a free lunch. I chose to stay.

Sometimes between classes I would see Susanne in the hallway. When that happened, we'd always ask each other the same question, "What kind of mood is Barbara in?" Barbara's mood affected our lives more than anything else in life, so this was valuable information.

Of course, no matter what the answer to that question was, we knew the mood could change in an instant and we could be subject to a beating at the drop of a hat. That's just the way it was. She had threatened to kill us all more than once and her eyes told us she meant it. Whether she meant it literally, I don't know. But kids tend to take death threats seriously.

As I sat at my desk that afternoon, dreading going home, I thought about what had happened to little Frances a few days earlier. Barbara had beat her with a belt. Then she picked her up by her hair and threw her across the floor. The welts on Frances's little four year-old body swelled up and turned red and blue, especially her hands and arms where she'd tried to protect herself. To hide the abuse, Barbara filled the bath tub with water and ice cubes and put my little sister in it to soak and force the swelling to go down. The entire time Frances sat shivering in ice cold water, Barbara stood over her and yelled at her for not keeping her hands and arms out of the way while she was being beaten. When Frances cried, Barbara screeched at her to shut up before she got her face smashed.

Another time, Barbara knocked Frances into a radiator. My little sister hit the radiator so hard that you could literally see her skull bone through the cut. As bad as she was hurt, Barbara would not let anyone take Frances to the doctor, saying, "I'm not going to jail for anyone, especially one of Audrey's kids."

I felt so hopeless that day, not being able to help Frances. But what could I do, really? Well, I could fantasize about killing this woman. I could do that, and I did it a lot. I sat at my desk and dreamed about killing Barbara for what she had done to Frances and to me. I would imagine how I would pull it off, how I would make her suffer.

The hatred I had for this woman was a growing thing, something festering deep inside me. I wanted her dead more than anything in life. I would think about it until the rage would build up inside of me to the point where my head would hurt. All the while, my poor teacher had no idea why I wasn't grasping the things she was trying to teach me.

Walking home that cold afternoon, the cold wind and snow blew hard against my face. I turned around and walked backward to protect my face from being frost bitten. I wondered if maybe my dad would be home when I got there, if maybe he would deal with Barbara as he had on a few occasions, taking her upstairs and bending her over his knee and whipping her with the belt.

When that happened, we could hear him hitting her. We could hear her yelp with pain. We would just stand and look at one other without saying a word. On the inside we were all celebrating, but at the same time we knew that she would, for sure, take it out on one of us kids the first chance she got.

There was only one reason why I hoped that Dad would be home when I got there. If he was home, I would only get one beating, instead of two.

As I approached the house, I saw that Dad's truck wasn't there. So rather than going in, I stood outside, shivering next to the fireplace chimney. I held my fourth grade report card in my hand, fearing what would happen to me if Barbara saw it before Dad did.

It was a strange relationship between Dad and Barbara. For some reason, Barbara thought that if she gave us a good beating for getting a bad report card, Dad would approve of her parenting skills. Even then, Dad would beat us, just to make sure we were fully aware of his disapproval. That made it a pretty straightforward choice for us, stay outside and freeze until Dad got home, or go inside now and get two beatings.

I had only been at my hiding place for a couple of minutes before I was joined by Susanne and John. They too had received their report cards. Together the three of us huddled outside by the chimney, afraid to go inside.

Finally, we heard the loud sound of the cracked muffler on Dad's work van coming up Church Street. The time had come. As soon as Dad walked in the door we marched in behind him, prepared to take the beatings we'd been dreading since the moment we woke up that morning.

Chapter 11

Helping Dad Steal

In the summertime, I always enjoyed sitting in the front seat of Dad's company truck with the window rolled down. I would stick my head out the window and feel the wind blowing in my face and through my hair. The wind made my head itch, but still, I loved it. I was eleven now and school was out, so most days I got to go to work with my dad. I was out of the house and that's what mattered.

Truth be told, those days were the only good times I ever recall spending with my father. I pretended he liked being with me and conveniently ignored the fact that he probably brought me along merely as an accomplice for his work related thefts. In fact, it was while I was working with Dad that I first learned to steal.

With my head out the window, I liked to count the telephone poles as they whipped by. Dad was somewhat of a self-professed speedster, so I had to count fast. To Dad, all of the other drivers were slow pokes, clogging up the road. He was always yelling and swearing at them and calling them names. If someone yelled back or otherwise ticked him off, he would swerve toward them as he passed and try to scare the daylight out of them. Sometimes he thoroughly succeeded.

My father's current job was as a water system installation man. Company salesmen went to customers' homes and sold them a water softener and Dad's job was to install the system and hook it up. I had my role in the process as well. I came along to help install the new water softeners. Dad would introduce me to customers as his oldest son and his assistant.

When we arrived, the homeowners would show Dad where they wanted the unit installed. Dad would look over the situation, then send me to the truck to get the tools he needed. There were certain things he always needed. I would start with the torch, the striker, pipe wrenches, fittings, and several other miscellaneous things. When my errands were done, I would stand by and watch my dad work. Like a dental assistant, I got so I could anticipate what he would need and have it in my hand ready to hand it to him the moment he asked.

When it was almost time to install the actual water tank, I would go out to the truck and carry it into the house all by myself, while Dad finished doing the plumbing. Once the tank was delivered, I would go back to the truck and start bringing in the salt bags. Salt was used for the regeneration process in the water softener. The bags weighted fifty pounds each and I felt really strong carrying them in all by myself.

This was when Dad would use me to help him steal stuff. As he was finishing up, I would gather up all of the tools and other equipment and take them out to the truck. The last thing I would do is gather up all the empty salt sacks and throw them into the back of the truck. Sometimes when I carried out the empty sacks, I noticed that they were not actually empty. Dad was using his son as his bag man to help him steal personal belongings from the customers.

I felt uneasy about what he was doing and I'm sure Dad could tell that I knew something wasn't quite right. Still, we never talked about it. Eventually I learned how to read my dad's face like a book. It was easy to tell when he was up to no good or had gotten away with something, because invariably it would be written all over his face.

In spite of all the illegal stuff, going to work with Dad and riding in the truck with him on those warm summer days were some of my favorite times growing up. Those were the only times I felt something toward my dad other than fear mixed with hatred and resentment.

We drove the back roads of southern Illinois all summer long, installing water softeners and iron filters, and stealing from customers. The thing is, when Dad and I were out installing jobs, I was able to block out thoughts of home and Barbara and abuse. In fact, I usually didn't think about home and Barbara clear up to the time we stopped to fill the truck up with gas at the end of the day. But like clockwork, as the truck would get close to home, I would begin to go numb. I would look out over the fields of corn and grain and once again face the fact that with each passing mile we were getting closer to the darkness of my everyday life.

There was something else that bothered me and made me feel guilty. While I was away from the house and away from Barbara, the other four kids were still there. They were still in hell. I know it was selfish of me, but I was just glad I wasn't with them.

I hated my life, but there was nothing I could do about it. I didn't dare bring up the subject with Dad, not even on one of his best days. No way. I tried once, and he turned and looked at me with a guilty stare and said nothing. Nine times out of ten, if one of us said something about her, Dad would take Barbara's side and we would be rebuked or beaten for complaining or for whining like babies.

By the time we pulled into the driveway at home it was usually dark. My job was to take all of the salt sacks out of the truck and put them in the shed. When I was finished with that, if Dad had filled the company truck with gas that day, I had to siphon out two five-gallon gas cans of the fresh gas for his personal use. That was something I did for dad every Friday night. I liked the smell of gas and had learned to siphon it without getting any in my mouth. Dad told me once that I was getting pretty good at it and to keep doing a good job. It was a rare thing indeed for my dad to commend me for doing something, so I was eager and willing to steal his gas for him.

Yep, at the age of eleven I had learned to be pretty good at being a bag man for my dad and stealing gas out of the company truck. Dad was teaching his son how to be a criminal and I was soaking it all in. It would take a while, but robbing and stealing would eventually become a way of life for me.

Chapter 12

Camping and Pop Bottle Trickery

I t was a spring day and a Friday. I had plans to go to the river after school and do some fishing and hunting for crayfish. Crawdads, as some call them, are especially tasty cooked in butter over an open fire.

I don't know why, but my dad had a new job. He was working the late shift for the City Waterworks Department at the dam. So, all summer long I spent my weekends camping by the river with one of my cousins and my brother, John. By this time, John had rejoined the family after healing up from being hit by that car. My cousin and I let him come camping with us, as long as he pushed our wheelbarrow full of camping stuff.

We would set up camp on the riverbank about a quarter mile upriver from the dam. If Dad wanted us for something he would just walk out on the catwalk and call us. We would hear him and head back. Those were some exciting and peaceful times for me. I was away from Barbara and free to be a boy of twelve. All I could think about all day, while I was at school, was the upcoming weekend camping trip.

I knew that as long as I didn't let Barbara see me, there would be no beatings. Out of sight, out of mind. But if she was around, there was no telling what she would do. One day I would kill her and bury the body where no one would ever find her and let her rot. I know that is a terrible thing for a twelve-year old boy to be thinking, and often I would shake my head to try and get rid of the thoughts, but some days that was all I thought about. They say people need goals. Well, I had one. Killing Barbara and ending the misery me and my younger brothers and sisters suffered every day was my goal in life.

The moment we got home from school on Fridays, John and I would start getting ready to go. I would collect my cane pole and other fishing stuff, along with the fancy new reel I had recently ripped off from the local hardware store. I was turning into quite the little thief. From my perspective, I liked the reel, so I took it. Eventually I would show it to my father and tell him that I found it at the river. I knew him well enough to know that he wouldn't inquire further.

We would need fishing bait for our weekend at the river, so I headed to the basement to fetch some night crawlers. Dad raised worms in large tubs for the purpose of selling them, so we had all the fish bait we needed. Mind you, if Dad had ever found out that I was stealing his worms I would have gotten my head knocked off, but if I could steal a pricey fishing reel from the hardware store, I could pull off stealing a few worms from my dad.

We planned for these camping trips all week long. We were always gathering up neat, useful stuff and hiding it away for the river – things like rope, matches, blankets, and old canvas tarps. In the imagination of a twelve-year old boy, almost anything could be useful at a campsite.

John and I had been secretly collecting food for our trip all week long and hiding it so Barbara wouldn't find it. But it was never enough, so we needed to buy a few things. We had no money, but we knew how to get some. We gathered up a bunch of Barbara's pop bottles and headed for the store.

We'd figured out early on how to go shopping with pop bottles and buy an impressive amount of stuff. At the local store, regular pop bottles could be redeemed for three cents each and quart-size bottles brought a nickel. So, with a few twelve packs of empties under our arms, we headed out to do some shopping.

When it came to redeeming bottles for cash, we had quite the little racket going. There were times when the money from our little "bottle redeeming enterprise" provided all the food we ate. So we had to make the best with what we had.

When you walked into the local grocery store, there was a large wooden bin for empty bottles. You would show them to the checker, put them in the bin and then go up to the cash register and get your cash. I had been doing this "profitably" for years. You see, Barbara and Dad were both big Pepsi drinkers. They would go through three or four twelve packs in a weekend. The pop bottles would pile up until Barbara needed cigarettes, at which time she would tell me to take the bottles to the store and get her some smokes.

Like I said, I had been doing this for years and it didn't take me long to realize that the hand is quicker than the eye. I would walk into the store with bottles in each hand and under one arm. I would put them in the bin, being sure to make enough noise that the cashier would hear me. When she turned to look I would say, "Six twelve packs." In reality, I had only deposited three. I saw that little fabrication as a one hundred percent business profit.

Back then, $2.16 would buy enough food for a full weekend at the river. Just to give you a frame of reference for the times, gas was $0.31 a gallon back then, a first class postage stamp was four cents. You could buy a candy bar for a nickel, a loaf of bread for 20 cents, and a gallon of milk for less than half-a-dollar. So, $2.16 went a long way.

Besides, we mainly sat around the campfire and ate our freshly caught fried fish with bread and butter. I assure you, that was a lot better eatin' than anything we got at home.

So, with everything loaded in Dad's truck, and with my faithful dog Trooper lying on the floor by my feet, we were off. I loved Trooper. Aunty gave him to me when he was a pup, and he pretty much went with me everywhere I went. Lots of days he would be waiting for me after school and would walk home with me. When we were camping, Trooper would warn me if someone or something was close by in the woods. He would growl if anyone walked past our campsite or drifted by on the river. Trooper was the best friend I ever had.

As soon as Dad dropped us off, we got to work setting up camp. I got the fire going and then threw my line into the water. It wouldn't be long before I would be catching sunfish. With the bread and butter we had "purchased" at the store, we were set for a great weekend of fine dining on fish sandwiches.

Our camping adventures were an escape for me. I would do my best not to think about home and what was going on there while I was at the river. But it was hard to erase the thoughts from my mind, knowing what Kenneth and my sisters were probably going through and what Barbara was almost for sure doing to them. Many times I had seen her grab a handful of hair in her fist and slam one of them into the wall in a fit of hate-filled rage. So while I was fishing, I couldn't help but wonder if they were being beaten or choked, or maybe being forced to stand in a corner all night long – or worse yet, being forced to eat Barbara's meals.

You are probably getting tired of me describing such things, but I would not want to leave you with the sense that these things were occasional. They really were an every-day, all day long kind of thing.

By that time, Barbara had borne two children by my dad. Biologically, she was a mother, but in real life she was too lazy to raise her own kids. To accomplish that task she stole Susanne's childhood, or what there was left of it. Susanne fed Barbara's kids, babysat them all day, and changed their diapers. If one of them cried for more than a minute, Susanne would get a beating. Barbara should never have had kids and I am pretty sure she didn't want to, but Dad made sure she did. My dad wanted more kids, though to this day I have no idea why.

One day Susanne left for school earlier than usual and didn't change Barbara's kids' diapers before she left. I don't know if disposable diapers had been invented yet, but in any event the ones we had were the old cloth kind. Barbara was furious that morning. She had to change her own kids' diapers, and there was no way she was going to let my sister get away with that.

Before I tell you what happened to my sister that day, I should explain that one of Susanne's jobs was to wash the soiled diapers and make sure there were fresh ones on hand. Barbara, on the other hand, was not so conscientious. When she removed a soiled diaper, she merely tossed it out on the back porch. That was less of a problem in the wintertime because the diapers would freeze and not stink up the place. But in the summer, that was a different story.

On that particular day, when Susanne got home from school, Barbara met her at the front door. She dragged Susanne to the back porch, picked up one of the messy, stinky diapers and rubbed it in my sister's face and hair. Then she tossed the diaper down and picked up a baseball bat and proceeded to beat Susanne with it. All that was to teach her not to leave for school without first changing Barbara's kids' diapers, even if she had to wake them up to do it.

If I could have, I would have lived there by the riverbank for the rest of my life and been happy. I could lie awake at night, looking up at the stars, and just enjoy the peace and safety. And I could dream about how things would be when I was far away from Georgetown. Sometimes I dreamed of a happy home where there was peace, and no threats or beatings.

Thinking about such things sometimes brought tears to my eyes. Eventually, I would wipe them away with my shirtsleeve and crawl into the tent with Trooper and drift off to sleep. I was young and there was not much I could do about my life. But I did my best to hope.

On a later trip, Trooper was hit by a car and killed while we were on our way to our campsite. I buried him behind the garage, crying my eyes out with every shovel full of dirt I dug. But I get ahead of myself.

A change was coming our way. The Dudrey kids were about to get a reprieve, a break from the nonstop abuse.

Chapter 13

Grandma and Grandpa

I t was an unusual day. No one was being beaten or slapped around. There was too much going on for that. Barbara was running around with literally nothing on except her tee shirt. She hadn't even bothered to put her teeth in her mouth. When she was scurrying around like that, stirring up the air around her, her body odor was especially disgusting.

Thankfully, all the windows in the house were open that day. I remember the radio blaring out "One, Two, Three, Red Light" by the 1910 Fruit Gum Company. I liked that song. All of us kids were busy doing something rarely if ever done at our place, cleaning the house. Why? Well, school was out for the summer and my dad's parents, the Dudreys, were coming to live with us.

Cleaning our house was quite an undertaking. You would have had to see it to believe it. Everything was pushed in one direction toward the back of the house and the basement door. Then everything was swept down the stairs. The basement was a pit full of everything you could imagine, including all the dirty laundry.

Our washing machine was the old wringer type, which meant you had to empty out all of the water when a load was finished and then run the clothes through a wringer. When they were all wrung out, you had to rinse them and start the process all over again. The clothes washing continued all through the night, because we had company coming.

We had a pile for whites, reds, dark colors, and one for rugs. Then there were the "throw away" items. The throw away items were the clothes and bed linen that had rotted from being left unwashed for weeks or months.

Everything went to the basement – bags of trash, empty cans and bottles, anything we wanted to get rid of went down the stairs. Out of sight, out of mind. It was a day for making things look good, and for leaving the impression that they were always good. In other words, we were putting on the shine!

If you've seen the play or the movie, "Annie," you might remember the famous scene where all the little orphan kids are down on the floor scrubbing with brushes. Well, that was us. Only we weren't singing while we worked. The chlorine bleach we were using didn't exactly put us in a singing mood.

We used rags and buckets full of hot soapy water to wash the walls. If the water was too hot for our hands and we said anything about it, we were lazy little _____ and were threatened with having our faces smashed. So we scrubbed and kept our mouths shut.

We literally worked all day and all through the night without sleep. When the walls were clean, we got down on our hands and knees and scrubbed and rinsed the floors. The entire time our eyes burned from the bleach fumes.

Cleaning the kitchen cabinets was especially tough. That project alone took almost two days. Dad made us remove everything from the cupboards and stack the dishes in one area and the pots and pans in another. He sat and watched as we cleaned the cabinets. If he found one streak, we got slapped upside the head. I always wondered how my dad, who was a big man, could move so quickly across a room to land a blow on one of us kids.

While we were still cleaning, Dad took his baked chicken out of the oven and disappeared into the living room to eat. He ate while we worked. We hadn't eaten all day and the smell of the baked chicken made us all the more starved. I've never quite understood how he could eat good food like that while his own kids went hungry, or were forced to eat disgusting goulash.

Once the cabinets were clean and had passed inspection, it was time to wash the dishes. Every dish in the house had to be washed, rinsed, dried and placed on the countertop for inspection. When we said we were finished, Dad would pick up the dishes, one at a time, and look for some slight imperfection. If he found one single thing he didn't like on one dish, we were slapped and forced to start over and do them all again.

So, there we were, lined up at the kitchen counter, tired, hungry, and scared, but still washing dishes all night long.

The next morning, we had to finish anything that hadn't gotten done the night before, plus keep watch for the arrival of our grandparents. I kept thinking of how life was going to change once they arrived. There would be no more yelling and beatings or getting punched in the face. I would be happy. For once in my life, I wouldn't have to be afraid anymore.

I wished they would hurry up. There was still time to get pounded or whipped with a belt. It seemed like forever, but finally they arrived. We were five happy kids when our grandparents' car finally pulled into the driveway. All of our fear just melted away. We had never been hit, slapped, or beaten when we had company, and now people were coming to live with us and be there every day!

The next morning, we woke up to the smell of pancakes. Pancakes! Our grandpa was up early working in the kitchen. The house smelled amazing! I couldn't recall the last time someone had made a real breakfast for us kids. Grandpa was whistling and singing a tune. The smile on his face was warm, and I could tell that he was genuinely happy to be at our house. Soon, the other kids joined us in the kitchen for what we considered a dream morning.

There were so many pancakes! And lots of stuff to put on them. We had honey, maple syrup, and homemade jam. Grandma had brought all of that with her, just for us. We had chocolate milk and orange juice and the house was filled with joy. It had been too long to remember the last time that I had felt like this. We even had real milk to drink, not the warm powered stuff with dry lumps in it. It was like heaven.

Then, all of a sudden Barbara walked into the dining room where we were eating. That woman had a way of sucking all of the joy out of a room, just by walking into it. Grandpa was still in the kitchen when she gave us all her look of hate – eyes that said she would rather beat us than look at us. Without saying a word, she stole our happiness. The first words out of her mouth were, "Stop eating like pigs!"

Then she told us that our grandpa had better things to do than spend his day cooking for us ungrateful little _____. Then without missing a beat, she turned and spoke to Grandpa in a sweet voice, as if the previous thirty seconds hadn't just happened.

My grandpa was an interesting man. He had raised his family during the Great Depression. The man could make toys out of just about anything. With an empty oatmeal box and some rubber bands he made us a car. When you rolled it on the floor, it would stop and roll back to you.

With a piece of wood and his pocketknife he could whittle out a whistle that made real noises when you blew it. We all wanted one.

One day, Grandpa took an old tire, and with his knife, fashioned it into a swing. We took some rope, climbed that big oak tree out back, and hung the tire from the largest limb. Just like that, we had a swing. We swung on that old tire for years.

My dad's mother was a real champ, too. She and I got along really well. I liked the way she said my name. No one could ever say it like she could, kind of the way my mother used to.

Grandma Dudrey was special to me and I know she felt the same way. Most afternoons, I sat alone with her in the living room, watching her favorite television programs together.

Grandma liked routines. Every day at the same time she did the same thing. After fixing lunch for us kids and being nice to all of us, she would send the others to take a nap and the two of us would spend the afternoon together. I would sit on the arm of Grandma's big chair while she watched her shows and ate her lunch of grapefruit and cottage cheese. How she never got tired of eating the same thing every day was beyond me. Now and then she would have some fresh cheese with rye crackers; I even learned to enjoy them myself, but it took a while.

I never knew why, but Grandma always acted like I was special. That wasn't just my imagination. The tenderness with which she treated me was real. The two of us talked about everything. She always wanted to know what I thought about things. I was definitely not used to that. I would sit on the arm of her chair and share all of my thoughts and dreams with her, except the part about killing Barbara, of course. That was my secret, and I was pretty sure she wouldn't understand.

We talked about the wife I would have someday and of how special she would be. Grandma was a good listener and she would ask me questions about the things I shared with her. She had a way of resting her elbow on the arm of her chair, raising her forearm, and then letting it fall down again, if she heard something she liked. That was one of those mannerisms a person has that is unique to only them, kind of like the way she said my name.

I still hold those times close to my heart. I will always remember the peace I experienced with Grandma on those warm summer afternoons.

But in the end, Grandma and Grandpa were still Dudreys. They were still my dad's parents, and there was a real downside to that.

Chapter 14

Right before My Eyes

As I walked up the sidewalk, just arriving home from school, I heard yelling and fighting coming from inside the house. It sounded like Grandpa and Grandma were going at it. I didn't know what to think. I ran around the house to see what was going on. Just as I bolted through the back door I heard Grandma Dudrey yelling, "Who are you? Who are you?"

Then I saw dishes flying toward Grandpa. He ducked one, but the next one hit him in the back of the head. "Please stop," he said. He was pleading with Grandma not to throw her good dishes at him.

Totally shocked, I turned around and darted back outside. I went around the side of the house and took my place by the fireplace chimney. That was still my hiding place when bad things were going on inside the house.

I was lost in a sea of conflicting emotions. My mind felt numb. I couldn't understand how this could happen right when things were going so well for us kids.

"I hate you, you _____," Grandma screamed.

"Please stop this!" Grandpa pleaded with her.

I didn't know what to do. I clenched my teeth and closed my eyes as tightly as I could. I wanted to somehow escape the drama unfolding in our kitchen. I heard the china cabinet crash loudly to the floor. Then I saw Grandpa run out the back door and race for the safety of the shed. Two cups flew after him, both barely missing his head.

I peeked around the side of the house, where I had a good view of Grandpa cowering in the shed. He was weeping. His hands were up in the air, and he was pacing around in a circle. I felt so bad for him, but I didn't want him to know that I was watching. I was seeing something that I wished I had never seen, and it broke my heart.

Things were never quite the same after that day. For a few months, we had lived without yelling, and screaming, but right in from of my eyes that peace and tranquility was being shattered.

I eventually discovered that outbursts like I had just witnessed were nothing new for my grandparents. They had carried on like this for many years. Even when their own children were still living at home the fighting got so bad that neighbors half a mile down the road could hear the yelling and screaming.

I didn't know it at the time, but Grandpa Dudrey was a sex abuser. He abused his own daughters, and abused my dad, too. The sexual abuse Grandpa afflicted on his own kids eventually found its way into our home with my dad doing the same kind of things to his kids. My dad's behavior was a continuation of what he had seen and experienced growing up.

The day I witnessed my grandparents fighting was a terrible day. The shattered dishes in the kitchen were nothing compared to the pain and brokenness the unexpected outrage inflicted on my young emotions. My dream of peace and happiness had come crashing down around me.

After things calmed down and Grandpa went back into the house, I ran to the shed and climbed up the ladder to my secret hiding place in the loft and lay there with my head pounding. I cried and cried. I cried for myself and I cried for my grandpa too. I had never seen my grandparents fight and I'd never heard some of the words I'd heard them use. Mean, cutting words meant to inflict pain. Of course, at the time I knew nothing of Grandpa's sexual abuse. I would learn about that later.

The next morning, I got up early and headed to the woods with my dog, Trooper. I didn't want to see anyone. I was too embarrassed to even look at my grandparents. I couldn't understand why Grandpa let Grandma treat him that way, and I had no idea why this woman, who had been so sweet to me, was so mean to her husband. My opinion of both of them had changed dramatically in just one day. They had disappointed me and destroyed the image I had of them. I doubt if either of them had any idea how much faith I had placed in them.

But, alone in the woods with my dog, I found a place of peace, a place of safety from my family. I had a secret spot that no one else knew about. When I got there, I lay down on the ground and began to cry again. I eventually fell asleep wondering what would ever become of me and my brothers and sisters.

I had lived so long without hope, in constant fear and despair. Then, when I finally found someone to give me hope and peace, they'd ripped it away.

Would it have been better if our grandparents had just mended fences that day, like they probably had a hundred times before, and stayed with us? I don't know. As things turned out, their visit ended up being just a temporary reprieve.

Years later I learned that the reason for that big fight was Grandma had caught Grandpa in the act of trying to abuse Susanne. Eventually, Grandma decided that she had taken all that she was going to take, and divorced him.

Chapter 15

The Two-by-Two Beating

T he final bell rang and school was out for the day. For most fifth graders, the end of school is usually the best time of day.

My walk home always took me past my old stomping grounds in the woods. We lived on the corner of Church Street and Division. Division was the last street in town and marked the city limits, and across the street from our house lay woods and farmland.

Our neighbors had a farm and we kids played in their woods as much as we could. Sometimes we would spend the day picking up black walnuts with Grandpa, back when he lived with us. A river ran through the woods. If we followed it one direction it took us back toward the school. The other direction took us to our summer camping spot upriver from the dam. We walked this way home from school every day. Sometimes, if we could catch one, we would jump on the back of one of the neighbor's horses and ride bareback and take the long way home. We were, after all, never in any hurry to get there.

On this particular day, I came up the hill toward our house with a freshly picked pear in each hand. I was about to cross the street when my sister Susanne ran past me yelling and screaming, racing toward the house. I could hear her carrying on for blocks and I was sure everyone in the neighborhood could, too. It seemed a little odd that she was running home screaming, but I was more or less accustomed to hearing yelling and screaming, so I just shrugged it off.

As I approached the front yard I could hear a second voice, Barbara's. She sounded as angry as I'd ever heard her. As I walked up the steps to the porch I could see that she was in a total rage, the kind where you can see the hate literally radiating from her eyes. Anger and hatred were written all over her face and for some reason it appeared to be directed at me. I had no idea why.

Barbara barked an order at me, telling me to get into the house. The second I passed through the door, I got a fist to the face, followed by a barrage of kicks and punches. She was screaming at the top of her lungs, yelling, "Why did you hit Susanne?"

A she yelled, she continued pounding me with her fist. She had completely lost it, spit was flying from her mouth with every word.

Without stopping the pummeling, she ordered Susanne to go get a stick. While Suzanne was away looking for a stick to beat me with, Barbara kept hitting me and screaming, "You're going to get it, you little _____."

I was going to get it? I was already being punched in the face and kicked. I kept pleading with her, asking what I'd done. "I didn't do anything," I insisted, while she continued hitting me.

"I'm going to kill you, you son of a _____," she shouted as she hit me in the face again and again. Her voice went lower and raspier. It was a deep, hate-filled voice.

She hit me with one especially heavy blow that knocked me to the floor. Just then, my sister arrived with a heavy two-by-two picket that had come loose from the railing on the front porch. I tried to get up from the floor, but was met with a vicious blow to the ribs, then another. A two-by-two is a piece of lumber. It is a lot heavier than a "stick." It is more like a weapon or a club.

I fell back trying to defend myself with my arms over my head, but Barbara kept landing blow after blow, pounding and bruising my hands and arms. I had no choice but to raise them up to protect my head and face.

I could hear the thump and feel the pain of the heavy picket hitting my body. In desperation, I rolled into a ball with my arms over my head trying to at least protect my face. Barbara kept swinging and kicking and calling me a liar.

"You lying little _____," she screamed as she landed blow after blow. The woman had completely lost it. She had gone crazy. I'm pretty sure she would not have stopped until I was dead.

Maybe I had slipped into shock. I don't know. But I wasn't feeling the pain anymore, even though the blows were continuing to rain down on me. I stopped thinking. My mind went numb.

Then suddenly, without conscious thought, I found myself up on my feet and running for the door. That was probably the only thing that saved my life.

I felt another blow as I rolled down the porch steps and still another when she threw the two-by-two at me, hitting me in the back. I ran as fast as I could, falling and getting up. Somehow I ended up across the street on the neighbors' front steps. I threw myself at their front door just as I went out cold.

When I regained consciousness, I was on the couch in the neighbors' living room cradled in the arms of the neighbor lady. Looking back, I'm certain that I would have been killed that day had I remained in our living room much longer. It is a mystery to me still today how I found the strength and will to get up and run.

I remember begging the neighbor lady, "Please don't send me home," while she gently placed ice on my face and washed my back with a cloth.

The welts on my back were beginning to swell and burn with pain. I was pretty sure I had broken ribs. It seemed like hours before I heard the unmistakable and familiar sound of my dad's 1959 Mercury coming up the street. For a long time, that had been the sound of help coming. Safety, of sorts, was on the way. When dad was home we didn't get beatings from Barbara. We still got them from him, but it wasn't all the time like it was with her.

I was sure that day that I was going to get the belt from Dad, even in my condition, because my sister, for some reason, had told Barbara that I'd hit her. But at least I knew he wouldn't try to kill me.

I recall my dad asking me once why Barbara would lie. I guess the question was supposed to be rhetorical, because if I was bold enough to speak up, she would vigorously deny whatever I'd said. If Barbara said I was lying, I would be the one in trouble, usually with a bar of soap in my mouth.

I would stand there with soap suds coming out of my mouth, while the one who was really lying looked on, gloating and smiling her sadistic grin. Of course, if I spat out the soap, I was forced to swallow it. Somehow, this was all supposed to be for our own good.

I was sure it wouldn't be too long before my dad would show up at the neighbors' house to take me home, where a second round of trouble would begin. The thing was, I still had no idea why I'd been beaten. I had no idea what had happened to my sister or why I had been blamed for it.

There was a knock at the door. When it opened, there stood my father, all 290 pounds of him. He was maybe forty by this time and had gained some weight. More than once, this six-foot three, barrel-chested man had, with one swing, knocked me clear across the room, then ordered me to walk back to where he was, so he could backhand me across the face for crying from being hit the first time.

When I saw my dad standing in the doorway, all I felt was fear. Dad crossed the room and sat down beside me on the couch and put his arm around me. I wondered if this was to comfort me or to impress the neighbors, or maybe it was just guilt for letting things go on for as long as he had. I had no idea, but his behavior was definitely not what I'd expected.

Dad must have felt uncomfortable sitting there with his arm around me knowing that everyone in the neighborhood and most of the relatives had known for years what had been going on at our house. I wondered what my dad was going to say to these people, or to me.

I was totally taken aback when he announced that Barbara felt sorry that she had punished me and that it wasn't me who'd hit my sister after all. It was a boy down the street, who was also named Chuckie.

The woman had beaten me half to death with a piece of lumber for something I hadn't done, and now it was supposed to be all better because Dad said it was.

"You can come home now. This will never happen again. Barbara loves you." His words made me less afraid to go home, yet at the same time nauseated me.

I'm not sure how she did it, but Barbara's demeanor was completely different when Dad and I walked in the front door of our house. Maybe her demon had gone back into hiding. Maybe she was afraid of what my dad might do to her.

There was definitely no denying what she had done to me. The evidence of her brutality was written all over my body. Dad and Barbara took me inside and put me in an ice bath to bring the swelling down, or as was more likely the case, to hide the damage Barbara had done to me. Nothing more was ever said about it. The woman had almost killed me and we never spoke of it again.

I hesitate to go beyond what I know to be fact, but looking back I suspect that Barbara and my dad were in some kind mutual protection league over the killing of my mother. They had to cover for one another, and that made it possible for her to get away with going way over the line with us kids. I know Dad could have stopped a lot of the hell we went through, but he rarely intervened. I can't believe he didn't know.

Then again, maybe he just hated us, but didn't personally want to take things so far that he would end up in jail. I don't know. It could have been that simple. My dad was pretty good at getting other people do his dirty work and avoiding being in a position where he might get caught and be held accountable. I'm getting ahead of myself here, but down the road I would be sentenced to the state penitentiary because I took the rap for some scheme my dad had cooked up. So, I know what I'm talking about when I say that my dad had a propensity for letting others do his dirty work.

Chapter 16

My First Foster Home

We lived with Dad and Barbara in the Church Street house for approximately seven years. It was a long, dark period for all of us kids. None of us had it easy. None of us were treated well. Even being the one-year-old baby of the family didn't make little Frances immune from Barbara's cruelty.

Harkening back to the opening chapter of my story, you may recall that Barbara was pregnant and in terrible pain at the top of the stairs. I was tempted to push her down and make sure she died that night. I overcame that temptation and did the right thing. I ran into town and found help, and Barbara and the baby pulled through.

Knowing the background for what happened that night, maybe you understand now why I thought so seriously about killing Barbara. It was part hatred. I admit that, but it was also partly pure survival instinct.

As it turned out, that night was a real turning point in all of our lives. When the authorities saw the filth and wretchedness in which we were living, when they had to hold their breath to not gag or retch, just going inside our house to bring us out, when they heard Suzanne's hospital bed account of the things that we were enduring, they recognized the inescapable truth that something had to be done about us.

In the end, maybe it wasn't the torture or the beatings or the sexual abuse that made them take us away from Dad and Barbara. Maybe it was just the stench. If you recall, the city sewer routinely backed up two feet or more in our basement and made the inside of our home smell worse than the bottom of an outhouse.

Add to that, the fact that the power had been turned off for several days and all of the meat in the freezer had spoiled – and you have yourself the makings for a pretty nasty stink. The five of us kids had been living and sleeping in squalor for years, and probably would have continued doing so had I not gone for help that night.

God only knows how things might have turned out had we been left with Barbara for much longer. One of us might have been killed, whether on purpose or because in one of her fits of rage she misjudged and went too far. Maybe I would have killed her. I was growing and getting stronger, and I was definitely of a mind to put an end to her. All it would have taken was one ill-timed event to trigger it.

It turned out to be fortuitous for us kids that Dad was away that night and Barbara was the only adult at home. There was really nothing else the authorities could rightfully do but get us away from there. Those events all happened back before there were cell phones or email, so Dad didn't find out for several days that his kids had been taken away from him.

The five of us were divided up that morning and sent in different directions. My sister Susanne and I were close to the same age and ended up in the same foster home.

When we arrived at our new foster parents' home, the lady from the State got out of the car first. While we waited, she walked over and shook the couple's hands. They looked very friendly. The three of them talked for a few moments, glancing over toward us once or twice, before finally coming over and opening the car door so my sister and I could get out.

I knew who these people were. I didn't recall ever talking to them or being in their home, but they were the pastor and his wife from the Adventist church our Dudrey grandparents went to on Saturdays. The man's name was Greg and his wife was Betty. They were a good-looking couple, full of joy, and they had a little girl named Emilee.

The house was the nicest I'd ever seen. The lawn was mowed and well kept and the shiny car out front was clean and polished. I thought to myself that theirs was the nicest place ever. The couple was warm and friendly and graciously invited us inside.

Standing in the entryway, I could hardly believe my eyes or my nose. The inside was painted white, and in their living room was the most beautiful furniture I had ever seen. The place smelled fresh and clean, almost too clean. What a different world this was from the ugliness we had been living in just a few hours earlier.

As our new foster parents showed us around their beautiful home, I began to feel uncomfortable and out of place. It was all so far from anything I had ever experienced. Yes, Grandmother's home was always fresh and clean, but that was so long ago and so far away that I could barely remember it. I wondered if our mom's folks even knew where we kids were. Had anyone contacted them? I was sure that Grandma Mausolf would be worried about us, if she knew we had been taken away from Dad.

And what about little Frances and my two younger brothers, John and Kenny? Where had they been taken? Were they together? Were they scared? I hoped they were all right.

And what about Dad? With so much going on, I had forgotten about him. I hadn't seen my dad for over a week and wondered if he had any idea what was going on with his kids. Did he know that Barbara was in the hospital or that we had been taken away from him?

So many questions were going through my mind. I finally decided that Dad was likely still with his nineteen-year-old girlfriend Elaine, and not thinking about us at all. I knew that if Dad wasn't coming for us, we were on our own and would just have to learn to adapt.

"This is where you will be sleeping, Charles," our hostess explained. Then she showed me the bathroom and pointed to where the towels and washcloths were kept. I noticed how everything was in its place. And wow, my own bed with clean sheets and pillow cases. How totally strange.

Our tour of the house ended in the kitchen. Lunch was already in the oven, and smelling good... really good. I looked around the room and saw a bowl of fruit on the counter. Obviously a kid could get a beating for touching the fruit. But Betty saw me looking and informed me that I could have some fruit anytime I wanted. Really? How odd.

I remembered the time my little sister had been forced to eat a jar of peanut butter. Barbara had accused Frances of getting into the cupboard and putting her fingers into the jar and licking her fingers. So, to punish her, Barbara poured a handful of salt into the jar and force-fed it to little Frances, who was maybe four or five at the time. Barbara took spoons full of the salt-laced concoction and forced it into Frances's mouth, holding her down until she choked. Then she beat her and threw her into the closet, warning her not to come out until she had finished the entire jar.

And now, here I stood, being offered all I wanted to eat in a peaceful home with no threats or beatings. It made me feel strangely uncomfortable and out of place.

There was a baby sitting in a high chair at the table when we entered the kitchen, and the table was set for the four of us. Betty served us lunch while she and Greg made plans for the afternoon. I couldn't get over the fact that this young couple was sharing their lunch with two strange children, ages twelve and fourteen, who had just shown up on their doorstep. I wondered how much they knew about us. I doubted that the State lady knew much about us herself, so there was no way she could have told this couple what they were getting themselves into.

Well, I hoped they didn't know too much. I hoped that no one had told them what our house looked like or that we didn't have a single clean thing to wear. I hope they hadn't heard that the sewer was backed up nearly three feet in our house. Did they know about Barbara and all the things she had done to us? That didn't seem likely.

I was sitting at their table eating lunch, feeling embarrassed about my entire life, when Greg spoke up.

"Charles," he asked, "how would you like to go with me this afternoon? I would like to take you shopping." I was not quite sure what to think, but I shyly nodded my approval.

I don't recall the name of the store he took me to, but when we got there Greg pushed a shopping cart up and down the aisles, tossing stuff in the cart as we went. There were bags of new underwear and socks and undershirts. Greg seemed to know what sizes I needed. We moved on to the pants section and Greg asked me to pick out what I would like to wear. I had an uneasy feeling about this. No one had ever asked me what I wanted to wear – not ever.

Weird thoughts flashed across my mind. None of this seemed real. I felt like I was in some kind of vacuum. I could almost hear my dad saying, "You will wear what I get you and that's that." It's hard to accept something that is entirely foreign to everything you have ever known.

At the beginning of each school year, Dad always took us kids shopping for school clothes. We got two pairs of pants, some shirts, and tennis shoes. The pants were always way too long and too big around the waist so we could "grow into them." I had to roll the pants legs up two or three times so I wouldn't trip on them. Grandpa would tie a cord around my waist to hold my pants up. The kids at school would laugh at me because I was holding up my pants with a cord, so to hide that

I would leave my shirt untucked. The down side of leaving my shirt untucked was that if Dad saw me, he would slap me for "looking sloppy."

I think that somehow Greg sensed how I was feeling. He walked over and quietly assured me that everything was all right. "You take your time and find exactly what you want to wear," he whispered. I had not been treated with such gentleness in a very long time, but I liked it. I picked out some things I liked and to my amazement they actually fit.

Susanne and I stayed with Greg and Betty for about a month. I'm sure that our being at their house put some strain on their relationship. It had to. Neither of them ever spoke in a negative tone or did anything to make me feel that I was a burden or not welcome. But my sister and I came with a lot of baggage. We never got along. I hated her and had no problem reminding her of the fact. And she felt the same way about me.

I was older than Susanne by almost two years. That probably affected the dynamics of our relationship. But whatever the problem was, we had always gone to some lengths to get back at one another. She would routinely tell Dad something to get me in trouble and then look at me with her stupid, 'I got you' look while I was being threatened or beaten for being mean to her. On more than one occasion, I had been forced to stand and look her in the face until I would say I was sorry for something she had accused me of doing. All the while she would stand there, quietly mouthing words in my face and taunting me.

In those moments, all I wanted in life was the chance to grab her by her long, red hair and throw her across the room. I had seen my dad do that and I was big enough now to do the same.

That was the kind of relationship Susanne and I brought into our first foster home. That nice couple, maybe in their mid to late twenties and probably not married for too long, had opened their home to two troubled teenagers who literally had no idea what a normal family was, and had almost no concept of right and wrong. What could go wrong? We were two almost wild kids, who could look you in the eye and lie without missing a beat, and who never missed an opportunity to get into a fight with one another. So, it couldn't have been easy.

I'm pretty sure Greg and Betty gave it their best shot before concluding that they were in way over their heads.

After about a month, the social worker showed up to "give us all an update on our situation." She thanked Greg and Betty for being so good to us and for opening their home. Then she told us we would be moving to another place. I was conflicted. On the one hand I was excited about trying something new, yet at the same time I knew that I would miss this sweet, kind couple.

At any rate, with bags packed full of new clothes, we loaded ourselves into the social worker's car and headed off to our new digs – The Vermillion County Children's Home.

Chapter 17

The County Home

When we pulled up in front of the Vermillion County Children's Home, the first thought that crossed my mind was, *I won't be here very long.*

The facility was a large brick building with a grove of mature oak trees in the front. On one side was a fire escape with stairs that led up to the top of the building. On the other side was a parking lot filled with cars, and out back was a playground with swings, slides and other playground equipment.

It was obvious when she marched us inside, that our social worker knew her way around. Inside the front door was a waiting area. There was a woman sitting behind a desk in the office to our left. She said hello and asked us to take a seat. Actually, it was more like an order with just a hint of niceness.

The social worker left us in the waiting area and went into an inner office. I could hear her talking to some man. I couldn't hear what they were saying, but I was sure they were talking about Susanne and me.

The place had that institutional smell, kind of like the Mayo Clinic buildings I'd visited with my mother when I was seven. This place looked kind of like those buildings too, and sounded like them. Everything sounded distant and hollow.

I didn't like this place. I wondered where my dad was and why he hadn't come to get me. It had already been more than a month since I'd seen him.

When the social worker and the man were done visiting, they came out and she introduced us. He was the Home's director.

"Welcome to the County Children's Home," he said. His voice was almost friendly, but not quite. He told us he was sure that we would enjoying living there and that if there was anything we needed, to please let him or one of the staff know.

I thought, *One of the staff? What does that mean?* I don't think I had ever heard that term before, but I was pretty sure I didn't like it. And I was already convinced that I didn't like this head guy either, friendly or not.

A few moments later, the supervisors over the boys' and girls' sections came in and greeted Susanne and me and then led us off in different directions. It was all so strange and foreign. As I walked down the hallway toward the boys' section, for the first time in my life I felt totally alone in the world.

To be honest, I was scared, but I wasn't about to let anyone know it. I had done some growing the last few months. I was bigger and stronger now. I had a new sense of physical strength, but I don't think my mind was quite in sync with my growing body. On the inside, I was still very much the same. I had a whole bunch of anger and bitterness, and a lot of hate. I was sure that I hated this boys' supervisor, too. He was telling me the rules, and I hated rules.

"Nine o'clock is bedtime and lights out," he explained without turning to look at me. "No talking after lights out. You can only get out of bed once per night to use the bathroom, if you need to." Yep, I for sure hated him.

My guide led me to my assigned room and introduced me to my roommate. The kid was about my age. He was sitting in front of the window looking out when I entered. We sized up one another quickly, as teenagers do. After we talked for a few minutes we concluded that we were in this place together and ought to make the best of it. My roommate obviously knew the lay of the land better than I did, so he filled me in on the high points, like the fact that there was a river right behind the facility. A river in our backyard, and we were free to go down there? That was all I needed to know for the moment. My roommate and I immediately headed for the river to go swimming.

To my surprise and delight, it was the same river where I had spent several summers camping and fishing, the Little Vermillion. At that moment, I was closer to home than I had been in weeks. I started thinking about my special spot upriver from the dam where Dad had worked. Those were good memories, so I decided that this place would do until Dad came to get me and take me far away.

I can't explain why I wanted my dad. He had never loved me or protected me. Quite the opposite. He hadn't even made sure I had enough to eat. He'd allowed Barbara to torture and my brothers and sisters. Worse yet, he had abused us himself, in ways that I don't feel comfortable talking about. But in my convoluted world, he was still my dad and the closest I had to someone to love. I don't know; maybe I just missed that with which I was familiar.

There were lots of kids at the river that day. Some of them lived close by, some at the County Home. My roommate made sure that everyone knew where I lived and that he and I were roomies. We were probably a bit of an odd looking couple. He was black and I was a white guy with blonde, curly hair. The race thing never mattered to me. To be perfectly honest, I never cared one bit about stuff like that.

After my new friend introduced me around, I nodded, then turned and jumped into the water and deftly swam to the other side. There were girls there and I wanted to show off my swimming abilities. I was a teenage boy. What can I say?

From the opposite bank I spotted a rope swing that someone had tied to a large branch that hung out over the deepest part of the river. I climbed up the cliff and took hold of the rope, swung out, and let go. When I popped to the surface, I didn't look to see, but I sensed that people were watching me and were impressed. With that, I was in. I was accepted.

Moments later, kids gathered around and started talking to me and asking all kinds of questions. They wanted to know all of the usual things: Why was I there? Where else had I been? Had I been in any foster homes? And, where did I live before the State got me?

I had fun that afternoon. Time passed quickly and before long, someone said it was time to go get ready for supper. With that, we all started walking back toward the home. I was surprised when I saw some of the kids kissing and holding hands. Some were even smoking cigarettes, passing them back and forth, drawing deep and then blowing the smoke out of their lungs. One guy was blowing smoke rings and walking at the same time. I was impressed. I had never seen that before.

When we got close to the Home, everyone with smokes hid them in their pants before entering the building. There were rules, but apparently they were not all that strictly enforced.

The dining room was nearly full when we walked in, and it was noisy. I spied my sister over in a corner with a bunch of girls. Her long red hair was easy to spot, even in a crowded room. I wondered how she was doing.

My roomie started filling me in on all of the dos and don'ts. His list was a bit different from what the staff guy had outlined for me. I liked this new viewpoint a lot better.

There was a sign on the wall, "NO THROWING FOOD AWAY! EAT WHAT YOU TAKE." I stood in line and got my food, then walked over to the table where my roommate was saving a place for me. Just then a big, ugly staffer walked up and announced, in no uncertain terms, "No saving chairs!"

Too bad for him; I was already there. The staffer swore and walked away, apparently disappointed that he was not able to come down on my friend.

The meal wasn't that bad. Of course it was a far cry from the home cooked meals Betty had been feeding us at the foster home. But, compared to home, it was heaven.

I understand not having good food to fix or having to make do with a little, but while we ate garbage, Dad and Barbara would retire to the living room to eat something good. Dad kept five hundred chickens in the back yard, so there was no reason his kids couldn't have had decent food. But no, those chickens were for them.

It bothered me that sitting in the dining hall, safely out of her grasp, I still couldn't help but think of her. The experiences were too recent and the memories too fresh. Little things, like a decent meal, would make me think of her and force me to relive some tortured memory. Seeing a two-by-two or some other piece of lumber, or even an extension cord lying on the floor would remind me of beatings.

I hated her, and over the past few weeks I had asked myself over and over why I hadn't shoved her down the stairs and killed her that night when I had the chance. No one would have ever known. Every day I vacillated back and forth between being glad I did the right thing and feeling stupid for not pushing her down the stairs.

At the County Home, the first weeks were rather uneventful, well, other than I started smoking and learned how to blow smoke rings. One day, as I was headed to the swimming hole, a girl came up and started walking beside me. She started telling me about a friend of hers who had a crush on me. I asked which girl she was talking about and she pointed her out. I turned to look and saw a pretty black girl looking at me and smiling sweetly.

Up to then, I'd only had romantic feelings for one girl, Sherry Thomas. I would occasionally dream of the time we kissed. I was always reminded of her when our song, "Angel of the Morning," by Merrilee Rush and the Turnabouts, came on the radio. That was a popular song back then and was aired a lot.

Sherry Thomas wasn't present that day, so I smiled back at this new girl. Then, playing my cards close to my chest, I turned away and proceeded to wade out into the water to cool off. A few moments later the pretty black girl was standing next to me and we started talking. She was cute and easy to talk to, so we spent the day together. Sherry's memory was fading fast.

The other guys in the dorm had girlfriends, and now I had one too. It was a good feeling. In fact, I felt more alive than I ever had. I had a girlfriend, three meals a day, and no beatings. Life was good. Of course this new girl and I didn't really know each other. That takes a while. But at our age we thought we did.

Out of nowhere, I started missing my dad again; and I convinced myself that he missed us too, and was trying to find us. I assumed that he had not come for my sister and me because the State had kept our whereabouts a secret from him. I asked the staff what they knew about my dad, but got nothing substantive out of them. Not that it would have mattered; I didn't believe a word they said anyway.

I decided that it was time to take matters into my own hands. I came up with a plan to sneak out at night and go find him. Wasting no time, I found someone who was willing to go with me. After supper I went to bed with my clothes on. The plan was to meet my friend in the boys' bathroom after lights out and then sneak down the hall and out the side door. We made it out without a hitch. When we closed the door behind us, I slid a matchbook between the latch and the catch, so when we returned, we could get back in the same way we got out. Hopefully no one would ever know that we'd left.

We made it to the street out front undetected, then ran as fast as we could toward Georgetown. I was scared, yet at the same time I felt free. The feeling that we were getting away with something was exhilarating. A guy can get hooked on that rush. It can be a real high. But craving that high can also get you into a lot more trouble than it's worth. Later on, I would definitely find that to be the case with me.

We had just made it to the bridge that crossed the river when some fellow stopped and gave us a ride the rest of the way to town, which turned out to be several miles. Before long, we were back in my hometown. Sherry probably had a new boyfriend by now, so I decided not to look her up. Besides, she was old news now. This trip was about my dad. So off we went to find him.

I knew all of the side streets in town, so I was pretty sure we could move around without the cops seeing us. Truth is, I hadn't really thought about the cops until we got to town. That's when it occurred to me that if they caught us out and about at night, it would be big trouble. We would be considered runaways.

I didn't know it, but that night would not be the last time I would be a fugitive, on the run from the law, not by a long shot. Compared to what lay ahead for me, that night's little drama was small potatoes.

The first place we looked for dad was at his girlfriend's house. Even if he wasn't at Elaine Dixon's, I was sure someone would know where to find him. When I knocked on the door, the people living there were surprised to see me. They asked where I was living. I lied and told them in a foster home. Then they explained that they hadn't seen my dad for a week or two; so we left.

The next place I checked was the tavern in Westville. Dad hung out there sometimes, but his car wasn't in the parking lot. I was stymied. I had no idea where else to look. Disappointed, we decided to head back to the County Home. We had to be back in our beds before daylight, if we were going to avoid getting caught and being punished.

We found the side door just as we'd left it. A minute later we were back in our beds with no one the wiser. I lay there for what seemed like hours before I fell asleep. I was thinking about my situation. The more I thought about where I was, the angrier I got. I didn't know if I despised where I lived or was just angry because my dad hadn't bothered to try to find me. As the days passed, my feelings for him began to turn more toward hatred. If ever there was a love/hate relationship, I had that with my dad. My feelings for him were an ever-changing, emotional roller coaster.

A week after my midnight trip to Georgetown, it came my turn to work in the kitchen. I didn't like that. The director of the home was constantly breathing down my neck. At least that's how it felt. I hadn't liked the guy from day one, and by this time I was sure that my initial instincts had been spot on. Word was, he swung the paddle fast and hard and I wanted no part of that, so I did my best to steer clear of the guy.

I had already outsmarted him once by sneaking out and going to Georgetown with my buddy. Now there was a new plan in the works.

My buddy and I were going to sneak out of our rooms and go see our girlfriends on the second floor. All we had to do was make our way outside the building, get to the fire escape, and then make it to room twelve undetected. That had to be easier than hitchhiking all the way to town and back. We would go out the same way we did before, sneak around the side of the building, climb the fire escape, and crawl into the window. It would be a snap.

In my mind, we were playing "The Man from U.N.C.L.E.," and I liked the feeling. I had been rehearsing the plan in my head all day; now it was time to put it into action.

Once we were outside and had made our way around back, I jumped up and caught hold of the ladder and pulled it down. The noise the iron ladder made was light enough that I was sure no one heard it. I climbed up and my partner came after me. As I crawled through the second floor window I noticed that my heart was beating fast, really fast. I shot my partner a nervous smile and he smiled back. I hoped I didn't look as nervous as he did.

Boys were not supposed to be on the second floor. That was No Man's Land. Literally. But there we were. Girls were waiting and we were not about to turn back after making it this far.

Down the hall we sneaked to room twelve. We opened the door and slowly made our way toward the beds. I was looking for bed number four. It was hard to see the numbers in the dark.

All of a sudden, someone screamed. Uh oh! That scream was followed by another. A second later, the whole second floor dorm was yelling and screaming.

We bolted. With my partner only a step behind, I ran past the dorm mother's door. The light in the hall was dim, but it was enough to make out our faces, if she opened the door at the right time. There would be hell to pay if she saw our faces.

Her stupid little dog was barking and jumping on the other side of the door. I knew the door could open any second, so I tossed aside all effort at stealth and ran like the dickens for the window. Down the fire escape we went. At the bottom we jumped off the ladder and raced for the door to the boys' dorm. We had just made it to our beds and pulled the covers over us when the light in our room came on. A quick inspection revealed that all of us were in our beds, so the light went back off and footsteps receded down the hall. I breathed a sigh of relief. Another stealth mission accomplished, well, sort of accomplished. And we hadn't been caught.

I lay there in bed that night thinking that maybe I really was as good as the Man from Uncle! *No one catches me!*

At breakfast the next morning, the atmosphere in the dining room was heavy. The director was there, and he didn't look happy. In fact, you might say he looked downright mad. He walked from table to table, eyeing everyone, scanning every face, searching for any hint that might lead him to the guilty culprit or culprits.

Good luck, Buddy. You can't pin a thing on me. I made a clean break. I was in my bed when the lights came on. It will be a cold day in July before you catch me. So don't look my way, Chump!

Of course there are cold days in July, and I was about to find out just how cold. Before breakfast was dismissed an announcement came over the loudspeaker, "All boys from dorm two to the director's office." I wondered what that was about.

Getting up from the table and looking ever so innocent, I made my way toward the office with the other guys from my dorm. I noticed that there was a lump in my throat and for some reason my head hurt, but I wasn't aware of being scared. I stood in line with all of the others while the director walked back and forth in front of us, checking us out. He stopped in front of each boy, looking each of us in the eye for a long moment before moving on.

All of a sudden he said, "You can all leave now."

My head was spinning fast. I'd made it! I'd gotten away with it twice. *You're not so smart, Big Shot!*

But the director wasn't quite finished. He continued, "Except you," pointing to my friend, "and you." His finger was pointing right at me! I felt the fear well up in my face.

As the other boys filed out of the office, the director crossed the room and retrieved a large, rather ominous looking paddle. He told us to bend over and touch the floor. My friend did as he was told and got two hard swats across his rear end. He was a bit of a tough guy, but I noticed that the second swing brought tears to his eyes.

Then it was my turn. The words that came out of my mouth at that moment surprised me. I didn't think before saying them; I just spoke. "You're not hitting me," I stated defiantly.

The director was not in the least deterred. He stepped toward me, clearly angry and fully determined to mete out the justice he had determined was required. I warned him that he was not going to hit me, and that if he did, my dad would take care of him. Surely the "dad" card would put some fear into him.

It didn't. Well, it sort of worked. I got three really hard swats, instead of two. As much as that paddle stung my backside, the director saw no tears in my eyes. Not in this lifetime.

I left the room as defiant as when I'd arrived. I'm not saying that others were not deterred by the punishment my friend and I received. I'm sure they were. But I was not ready to learn anything I didn't want to learn. And I, for certain, wasn't ready to respect any kind of authority.

After the paddle incident, I began looking for a way to escape. It would be easy to just walk away. There were no bars or fences. But, eventually I would probably get caught, and when I did the social worker would send me to the boy's ranch. That's where they sent the tough cases. I definitely didn't want to go there. My roommate had spent two years at the ranch and he'd made it quite clear to me that I didn't want to take that trip.

The thing that really troubled me was that I had been here long enough that my dad should have found me by now, and yet he hadn't. So I hated him more.

I was sitting in the dayroom one morning, watching a game of ping-pong, when I heard my name called. The voice over the loudspeaker instructed me to come to the office. I had no idea why I would be summoned to the office. I hadn't done anything wrong in a week or two. But having no say in the matter, I made my way down the hall. I had just entered the waiting room when I heard the unmistakable sound of my father's voice coming from the inner office. To my surprise, my hating heart leaped for joy.

I was so happy to see him. I asked where he had been all this time and he answered me with a lie. I could always tell when my dad was not telling the truth. He was probably a terrible poker player because he had this dead giveaway, a tell, if you will. When he would answer untruthfully, his lips would inevitably tighten. And he would tilt his head forward just a bit, just enough to be noticeable. If you studied my dad's face, you could tell when he was lying. I know I could.

So, as happy as I was to see my dad, I was quickly reminded that I didn't trust him. I had worried about him. I had gone looking for him. And now he was lying to me about why he hadn't come looking for me.

We walked outside and climbed into the back seat of dad's car to talk. Susanne and one of the other boys from the Home were sitting in the front seat. I had no idea why this kid was in my dad's car. Dad reached over and put his arm around my shoulder and proceeded to tell me how bad he felt about everything. He asked me why I hadn't told him about the things Barbara had been doing to us kids all those years. He said that if he had only known he would have stopped it. He told me how much he loved Susanne and me and the other kids. He assured us that things would be different from that moment on.

All the time he was talking I kept thinking, *I'll never trust you or believe you again.*

Suddenly, out of nowhere, the boy in the front seat turned around and pointed a pistol in my face with the hammer cocked. I froze. I thought for sure I was dead. As my eyes focused on the gun, I recognized it. It was my dad's gun, the one he always kept under the front seat of his car. That gun was always loaded. "A gun is worthless if it's not loaded," he'd always said.

Time seemed to stop. Looking down the barrel of that pistol, I felt like I was being engulfed in a deep pool of hopelessness. My dad seemed shocked as well. At least I was under the impression that he was.

My eyes remained glued on the gun. The kid held it there for what seemed like an eternity with the business end never wavering from my face. Then I saw my dad's arm slowly reaching forward. He gently took hold of the gun and took it from the kid's hand and let the hammer down. The kid let go of the weapon without a struggle. Then he got out of the car and walked back toward the facility like nothing had happened.

All the three of us could do was sit there and look at one another. It was obvious that I had come very close to being killed. The strangest thing was, I knew of no reason why that kid would be out to get me. Whatever he was up to, though, he was obviously serious. He had not only aimed a loaded gun at my face, he'd pulled the hammer back. I know of no more certain warning sign that someone is serious about using a gun than that.

My sister and I were not exactly close. We rarely talked and never hung out together at the County Home. But years later she told me that she did not see the event with the gun the same way I did. She told me that she believed that Dad had arranged the whole thing and had intended for the kid to kill me that day, but for some reason had changed his mind. It's a little difficult for me to wrap my mind around that possibility. But now that I am older, and all but certain Dad had our mother killed with that same gun, it seems well within the realm of possibility that he had wanted me dead, too.

Before Dad drove away that day, he told me that he would get in big trouble if I ever told anyone what had happened with the gun. He made me swear that I wouldn't say anything. As he drove off, he stuck his head out the window and told me that he loved me. I didn't know it then, but that was the last time I would see my dad for a few years, other than one day at the courthouse.

Some weeks after the gun incident, I was sitting in the dayroom when a voice came over the loudspeaker ordering me to the office. I had no idea why, but I had become all too familiar with being in trouble, and expected more of the same. I got up from the chair that I had been grounded to for two days, for fighting, and headed for the office.

I didn't want to fight. But some kid had grabbed my watch and shoved me for no apparent reason. I told him to give it back. He laughed at me and taunted me, saying, "What are you going to do about it?"

"Nothing," I replied, as I pounced on him and started beating the cheese out of him.

Everyone started yelling, "Get him! Don't let him do that to you," while I was on top of the guy punching his face. It wasn't me they were cheering on, however. It was the other guy.

That happened two days earlier. Now I was on my way back to the office to see what else they had in store for me. I really hated this place. But on that day, I was in for a surprise.

Standing there, waiting for me, was Grandma Mausolf, my mother's mom. She looked at me and said in her sweet voice, "Oh Honey!" She crossed the room and landed a big kiss on my cheek.

"Why didn't you call Grandma?" she asked with genuine emotion in her voice. "I would have come for you a long time ago."

I knew she meant every word she said. She was that way. She put her arms around me and pulled me close and held me. I can't explain the emotions that coursed through my being right then. Up until that moment, I had felt completely alone. I had wanted to lash out and get even with somebody, anybody. I was a bitter young man, full to overflowing with anger and hatred. But as this sweet woman, mother of my mother, held me in her arms, I felt love and comfort and peace, feelings I hadn't known since my mother had died.

I didn't know it at the time, but since the day my mother was killed, Grandmother Mausolf had wanted to rescue us kids. She had always held my dad in contempt. She told me later that she had believed from day one that Dad had had our mother killed, and believed he would have had her killed, too, if he'd had the chance.

I remember the way she stood up to Dad, all five-foot five-inches of her standing toe to toe with him after the funeral. She begged him to let her raise us kids. She confided to me later, that over the years, since Mom's death, she had harbored strong suspicions that we kids were being sorely mistreated and abused by Barbara. But she'd had no proof and knew of nothing she could do.

Well, Dad had denied her request the day of the funeral, but today would be different. Today she would have her way. I had a feeling you could take that to the bank. With pleading eyes, she made her case to the director, but he didn't seem to be buying what she was selling. Maybe the Home got money for every kid they housed and his reluctance was budget related. I don't know, but he clearly wasn't budging.

He did, however, allow Grandpa and her to take Susanne and me out to lunch. After dinner we returned to the Home. The four of us sat in the car out front and talked for a while.

"I have been praying for years for you children to be out of his hands," she said. "God has heard me. How would you like to come with us to Florida to live?"

Was I ever happy to hear her ask that! From the County Children's Home to living with my grandparents in Florida! That sounded like heaven, but immediately I felt a wave of doubt come over me. "Will they let us go?" I asked. I was afraid of the answer.

Grandma shot a knowing glance at my grandfather and announced, "Let Grandma worry about that, Honey."

The next morning found my grandparents sitting out front of the Vermillion County Children's Home in their shiny clean Buick. Behind the car was the trailer home they'd told us about at lunch the day before. I don't know what that determined little lady said to get her way, but whatever it was, it worked. That very morning, everyone I knew from the Home was standing out front saying goodbye to Susanne and me.

I was overjoyed to be finally getting out of that place, though I felt a sense of sadness for those I was leaving behind. So many sad stories. So many lonely, hurting kids like me. Sure, I'd made some friends there, but none that I would ever see again. My new girlfriend and my roomie at the Home disappeared into my past that morning when we drove away.

Just as the car started moving, the director leaned in the window and looked at my sister and me in the backseat. He said to us, or to our grandparents, I couldn't tell which, "I'll see you back here in two weeks now, okay?"

Grandmother looked up at him, but none of us said a word.

Chapter 18

Grandma Tried

The trip from Danville, Illinois where the County Children's Home was located, to our grandparents' home in Florida was a fun experience for me. I was amazed by the meals Grandmother could prepare in that little travel trailer. The first night she made pot roast with all the fixings. Earlier in the day she baked a peach pie with fresh fruit that we picked up in Georgia on the way down. The smell of peach pie baking and pot roast cooking was enough to make a pair of young teenagers feel right at home, and we weren't even at their home yet.

I hadn't done much traveling before, so my eyes were constantly glued to the window, careful not to miss a thing on the way down. As we rode along, my sister and I shared with our grandparents the things we had gone through over the past seven years. More than once I saw my grandma wiping tears from her eyes. More than once she turned around and looked at Susanne and me and said, "I didn't know. I didn't know. Why didn't you call Grandma?"

I had assumed that our mother had told them, before she died, how life was for us, but apparently she'd kept most of her pain to herself. And, of course, there was no way for them to know what had happened to us under Barbara's reign of terror after Momma was killed. We would not have dared tell them. Telling could get a kid in big trouble.

I remember one time when Susanne told the principal at school about some beating Barbara had given her. That night, the principal called the house and spoke with Barbara, who calmly explained what a liar Susanne was and that nothing like that had ever happened and that she really loved us kids. You can only imagine what happened to Susanne after Barbara hung up the phone.

As we rode along in my grandparents' Buick, I would sometimes start a story about our lives with, "You won't believe this, but ..." More than once Grandma would interrupt me right then and there with, "There isn't a thing I would put past that man, Chuckie." It became increasingly obvious as we traveled south that this sweet little lady had a very strong dislike for our Dad. And that she had felt that way for a long time.

We told them about the beatings with extension cords, with mop wringers, or anything else Barbara could get her hands on at the time. I told them about my vicious beating with the two-by-two. We told them about the sexual things too. That was hard to share. Most of what happened was too disgusting and too deviant to put in print, but we told it all to our grandparents. I told them about my dad saying one time, in a fit of rage, that he should have sold me when he had the chance.

Susanne told them about the time Barbara had wrapped Susanne's long red hair up in curlers, those old wire curlers that were kind of like a hairbrush. A couple of hours later, Barbara came back and took out the curlers, but instead of unrolling them she yanked them out, ignoring Susanne's shrieks of pain and pulling out chunks of hair with every pull. Susanne tried to fix the mess that was left. She cut her hair in places and tried to make it look presentable. When Dad came home, he was furious with Susanne for cutting her beautiful red hair. He gave her a beating and then called someone to come trim her hair and make it look better.

The first thing the hair lady did was ask how Susanne's hair had come to be such a mess. Susanne explained what Barbara had done and how she'd tried to fix it herself. Barbara overheard the conversation and stomped in and told the hairdresser in no uncertain terms, "If you ever tell anyone what Susanne just said, I will kill you." That was not the first time Barbara had threatened to kill someone to keep them quiet.

Many times, the stories we told made our grandmother break down sobbing. But after she was done crying, she would get a determined look on her face, the same determined, protective look I had seen back at the County Children's Home when the director had hesitated to let us go with them.

Grandpa, on the other hand, never said much. He just drove and listened, and occasionally cast a sad look over at Grandma. It wasn't the man's nature to talk a lot. He had been a skilled finish carpenter by trade and liked it when things were perfect. He had suffered an untimely stroke and had consequently been forced to retire from working full-time. His mind was fine, but the stroke hampered his communication skills a bit. We could tell that the kind of chaos we were describing was hard for our grandfather to hear. The man may have let Grandmother do the talking, but we never doubted that he was sorry for us and was angry about what we had been forced to endure.

I was sitting in the back seat of the car with the window rolled down, the wind blowing in my face, when for some reason my thoughts turned to my little sister. It had been months since I had seen little Frances back at Church Street. To the best of my recollection, she was by that time about seven. I started tearing up, recalling the horrific treatment she had endured at Barbara's hand, like the night before her fourth birthday.

The night before her big day, Dad had told Barbara to bake Frances a cake. She did as she was told, but while everyone was in bed that night, Barbara went down to the kitchen and messed up the frosting. I'm sure she did it. The next morning, she called little Frances down to the kitchen.

"Why did you do this?" She glared at the little birthday girl with that same old hatred in her eyes. Little Frances meekly replied, "I don't know."

"Chuck!" Barbara yelled to my dad. "Come look at what Frances did to the birthday cake I made her."

Even on our birthdays we were not immune from that woman's anger and hatred. In fact, anytime there was a chance we might be happy, even for just a few minutes, she did her best to steal that away. I'm sure Frances never messed with the frosting of that cake. She was too terrified of getting in trouble to ever do something like that.

I don't want to leave you with the impression that we never saw our mother's parents. We did. But they were snowbirds. They would travel to Florida for the winter every year. On their way down south they would stop by our house on Church Street and take us out to eat, or maybe take us shopping for the afternoon. The times we saw them were short, but always special.

When Barbara and my dad would find out that our mom's folks were in town and might stop by, we would all be taken to the living room for a "talking to." We were always threatened big time with what would happen to us if we didn't keep our big mouths shut, or if we whined about the way we were treated.

Even though my dad's parents came over sometimes, and for a while even lived with us, as I mentioned earlier, Mother's parents were never allowed to enter our house. If we went anywhere with them, they would pick us up outside.

Part of me was kind of glad they never came inside. It was one thing to tell them, now, how things were, but if they had actually seen it with their own eyes, there might have been violence. I was embarrassed now just thinking about it. If the police and social workers couldn't walk into our house for two or three minutes without gagging, can you imagine how horrified Mother's parents would have been?

As we rode along, we were discovering that our grandparents were not at all like my dad had described them to us. Over the years, he'd never stopped trying to turn us against our mother's parents. He would say the most horrible things about them. But after getting to know them up close and personal, like we were, and seeing how wonderful they were, I hated my dad even more for slandering them so dishonestly.

My view of my dad was evolving. I was beginning to see him as a frightened, weak man. He had let an evil woman all but destroy the lives of his five little children. He had abused us himself. It was no wonder he hadn't come looking for us as soon as he'd discovered that the government had become involved and might be asking questions. When the police pull out the ole polygraph and start asking questions, guilty people usually start looking for the exit. Sorry, I'm getting ahead of myself. We'll get to the polygraph story soon enough.

Not long after we got settled in at our grandparents' home in Florida, we found ourselves sitting in the hallway of the county courthouse waiting to see a judge. That had been Grandmother's plan from the beginning. Grandma was in the judge's chambers talking to the judge one-on-one, while Susanne and I sat with Grandpa in the hall outside. Grandma had promised the director back in Illinois that they would bring us back to the Home in two weeks. But what she'd really planned on doing was getting a Florida judge to grant her the legal right to keep us in Florida and not take us back. Her meeting with the judge was part of that plan.

I was anxious to get done at the courthouse so we could go do something. We had decided to go to Fort Meyers Beach to swim that afternoon after the hearing. After that, we were going to stop and look at the school we would be attending in the fall. I was thinking about all that when an officer came over told us it was our turn to see the judge.

Walking into the courtroom, I could hear Grandmother talking. From the sound of her voice, I wasn't sure she was going to get her way. On the other hand, she was a persistent woman. I hear that's not all that unusual for Methodist women. They tend to be doers.

The judge was resisting, but I'd heard this woman's determined voice before.

"But lady", the judge was saying, "I don't have any say-so in this matter. My hands are tied."

His words, however, did not seem to deter our grandmother. Speaking loudly enough for everyone in the courtroom to hear her, she told the judge that these two kids were in serious danger if they went back to Illinois.

"You don't have a say-so in Illinois, but you sure do here. I want an order of protection for these children and I want it now."

Our grandma had been through a lot, and she was tough. She knew what was right and she knew how to fight. She was not the kind of person who would back down from anyone.

I remember saying to myself that day, "This is why Dad hates her so much. She isn't afraid of him."

A few moments later, Grandmother walked out of the judge's chamber with a signed paper in her hand. Without saying a word, she folded it up and put it in her purse. We were staying.

Chapter 19

School and Racial Tensions in Florida

Today marked my second trip to the Yacht Club. Doing the back-stroke in a crystal clear swimming pool was not at all like swimming in the less than sparkling rivers back home. "Back home" was slipping farther and farther from my mind with each passing day. Florida was home now, and I loved it.

And of course, to a fourteen-year old boy, the cutie pies sitting around the side of the pool in their swimsuits were nothing to sneeze at. I was sure this one girl, the one I had, in my expert judgment, deemed the prettiest one, was looking at me. You can bet I never missed a chance to look back. Grandmother said that boys my age should not be interested in girls, that there would be plenty of time for that later. But try telling that to an adolescent boy surrounded by girls in swimsuits.

With my most mature voice I'd explained to her that I'd already had two girlfriends and had kissed more than that. She responded by saying, in no uncertain terms, that I was to keep my mind fixed on other things. I would like to say that I heeded her wise counsel, but of course that would not be true. At that age, my mind kind of went where it went when it came to that subject. (In all honesty I should mention that by this point I had been sexually active for some time, but I wasn't about to tell my grandmother that.)

My grandparents went all out at making a home for my sister and me. They even purchased a new house for the four of us to live in. They were not wealthy people, but they made whatever sacrifices were necessary to provide for Susanne and me. Grandpa even mowed lawns and took on some landscaping jobs to make ends meet. I loved them, but at the time, I did not appreciate the many things they did for us.

Across the street from the house was a canal, and if you hopped on a boat you could follow it all the way to the Gulf of Mexico. The canal was almost like being at the river. I spent a lot of time there, but was instructed not to go swimming because of the coral. According to Grandfather it would cut my feet all to shreds. He was right, too. A few days later, I got a deep cut on my foot.

With my grandparents, everything had a rule. I loved them, but more than once I reminded my grandmother that I was not my dad. I assured her that she didn't need to watch me so closely. But I was lying and she knew it. She always suspected that I was up to something. That woman could spot a lie or sniff out a pack of smokes in a heartbeat.

Back home, I had fished most of every summer for years running. I was pretty good at it. I'd caught and eaten lots of carp, blue gill and catfish, but for some reason I couldn't catch a single fish out of that canal. I tried for weeks, using every bait I knew to use, but I couldn't get a single bite. One morning, I watched a neighbor who was standing out on his dock. His fishing technique was completely new to me. The first time I saw him, he was pulling in a large gillnet. It was literally full of fish.

I ran over and asked if I could help. There were all kinds of fish in his net. He explained that he left the net out all night and the fish would swim into it while he was sleeping. Because they couldn't swim back out, they would be waiting for him the next morning. He also explained why I hadn't been catching any fish the way I was going at it. He suggested that I get a spear.

When we finished taking the fish out of the net, the man sent me home with ten large fish that he called Jacks. Grandfather was excited to see them. He called Grandmother and she came out with the camera to take a picture. We took turns holding them up and posing for the camera. That night we had a really good fish supper. Eating fresh fish made me feel right at home.

After supper, Grandmother put a fresh baked pie on the table, then informed us that we would be going shopping the next morning for school supplies. After that, we would take a tour of the junior high school we would be attending in a few weeks. Yes, I was still in junior high, even though I was a year older than most junior high kids. I was a year behind because I'd been required to take the third grade twice.

When summer was officially over and it was time to head back to school, I was surprised to find myself excited about it. That first morning, when our bus pulled up to Cypress Lake Junior High, I hurried to get off and get to my locker. Because of our tour two weeks earlier, I felt like I already knew the place. The thing that was strange but still kind of cool about this school was that all the lockers were outside. There was a covering overhead in case it rained, but still, having the lockers outside made it not seem like school at all.

Everything went fine the first day. I met the teachers, got my schoolbooks, and played some ping-pong during lunch break. But there was something not quite right. There was a buzz and weird sense of uneasiness in the air. As it turned out, a bunch of black kids were being bused in from North Fort Meyers the next day to attend our school. "Busing," they called it. They said it was some kind of court ordered desegregation policy. I really didn't get why this was such a big deal to everyone. It wasn't to me.

Back in Danville, Illinois, my partner in the County Home was black. We were good friends and race just wasn't a thing. He was the guy who went with me looking for my dad that night. And he was the one who stood in line with me, waiting to feel the sting of the director's paddle for sneaking up to the girl's dorm. His sister was as sweet as she could be, and in fact, I kind of had a thing for her for a while.

At any rate, the talk among the kids was all about the blacks coming to our school the next day. I thought it was stupid the way they were talking. It seemed as dumb as the rule that the boys and the girls had to sit on different sides of the bus. No matter how I felt about it, though, there was no mistaking the fact that something was in the air. And it was something with which I was very familiar; fear. Fear mixed with hate.

I stepped off the bus that next morning and headed into the building. I noticed that the other students were all lined up with their backs to the wall on both sides of the hallway. Everyone was talking, but with lowered voices, almost whispering. Gathered en mass at the far end of the hall was last year's football team. They all had on their school lettermen's jackets and were giving each other high fives, talking about how they had beaten the black school's football team the previous year.

The jock crowd was making sure everyone knew that there was no room on the team for any of the new students. I stood there watching and listening to everything. Sure, I heard the tough words they were saying, but the looks on their faces said something else. They were afraid.

I stood quietly for a few moments, then I asked this one kid, "What are you scared of?" The whole team turned as one and looked at me. One of them answered with a tough guy voice, "Not you."

I walked away to avoid a confrontation, but turned back over my shoulder and countered with, "See you later, brother."

Out front, one bus pulled up, then another, and another. There were four buses total, all full of black students. The new kids stepped off the buses and made their way toward the door. It was clear to me as I watched them enter the building that the new kids were feeling the same emotions that I saw in the white kids – fear and uncertainty.

I was pretty sure that most of those new kids didn't want to be there either. They were all just unwilling pawns caught up in a game the politicians and judges were playing all over the South at the time. As the new kids started down the hall, everything became quiet. You could hear every footstep as the black kids shuffled along, most of them directing their eyes toward the floor.

It was a volatile atmosphere. There was fear mixed with still more fear. A strange place. Different looking people. Different clothes and haircuts. I think everyone recognized that one loudmouth could make the whole scene break out into open violence. It was pretty intense.

Without stopping to think about what I was about to do, I started down the hall toward the new kids, cheerfully calling out to them, "Hey, how you doing? Welcome to your new school. Give me five, brother. Hey how you doing lady? Come on in."

I was a one man welcoming committee. Black kids smiled at me. Some high-fived me. And, just like that, the ice was broken. The white kids standing along the sides of the hall started moving toward their classrooms. The tension of the moment was over, but for me there would be repercussions waiting just down the road.

For some reason, I decided to go out for football. I don't know why I did it. I had never played football, but there I was, standing in line doing toe-touches with the rest of the team. I really had no desire to play the game, but I didn't want to go home either. Don't get me wrong, home was fine. My grandparents were as good and caring as people can be, and they genuinely loved my sister and me. There was no doubt about that.

But the thing is, I was fourteen, and unsettled in many ways. There were so many thoughts bouncing around in my head. I realize, looking back, that I kind of had it made at the time. I had a good home. No one was beating me; I was still getting used to that feeling. I had friends now and even a new girlfriend named Vicky.

But I had a sense that something was missing. Maybe it was just me trying to sabotage my own happiness. I'm sure that's what some shrink would say. Maybe I was just missing the adrenalin rush and the excitement of getting away with something. But, whatever it was, I simply wasn't excited about going home after school.

"Hey, you, start running!" the coach yelled. He was looking at me. We had barely finished our second set of twenty-five push-ups and now we had to run laps. So off I went. I ran as fast as I could, doing my best to keep up with the others, who were already running. I was not in shape, but I was determined that I wouldn't be last.

When practice was over I was beat. Standing in the shower, still out of breath, all I could think about was eating and going to bed. My body had never been pushed like that and it wasn't liking it one bit. But I hadn't come in last in the running. Winded or not, that was the important thing.

I don't know what it was with me and school work. Sitting in a classroom listening to a teacher was about the most boring thing I'd ever had to do. It wasn't that I didn't like learning. My problem was, I just couldn't retain the material. I listened and did my homework, but it just wouldn't stick. And every time we had to take a test, my mind would go blank. Everything I'd learned got lost in some filing cabinet somewhere in my head. Unfortunately, my grades reflected that.

It wasn't that I didn't have a good mind, but my mind could not focus on one thing for long. I couldn't concentrate. My thoughts would fly from one place to another like lightning.

A day after I'd joined the football team, I was sitting in class looking at the teacher, doing my best to listen, when the kid next to me leaned over and whispered, "Don't come to practice today or I will kick your ___."

"What are you talking about," I asked him. I really had no idea.

"I don't want you or your black friends on my team," he replied.

So the rest of the day, all I could think about was that after school I was going to be in a fight. I couldn't shake it. I wasn't scared of the guy, but I really didn't want to get in trouble. I didn't want to take a trip to the office and have a sit-down with the principal. Grandmother had already warned me about that. I didn't want to be in trouble with her and I knew I would be, if she found out that I had been in a fight at school. She still had the impression that I was just like my no account dad and I didn't want to prove her right.

Nonetheless, I decided I would go to practice just like other days. Some kid who thought he was tough wasn't going to stop me.

Getting dressed in the locker room before practice, other players kept prodding me, saying things like, "You're going to get your ____ beat, if you walk out to the field. Go home and take your friends with you, you _____ lover."

The racism I'd seen on everyone's faces the day the blacks showed up at our school was still very much alive. And I was now the enemy and the focus of their hatred. I had "betrayed my kind" and befriended them.

It seemed odd that the white players wouldn't say anything to the blacks themselves about playing, but instead focused their anger on me. Oh well, I had no regrets about not hating black people for being black.

I took my time getting dressed, hoping to avoid trouble. I was the last one out of the locker room. Being last would only mean a lap. Fighting and getting in trouble could result in me being sent back to the County Home up north.

When I walked outside, there was no one waiting outside the locker room door. So far, so good. But when I turned the corner to go to the field, there was Darin Megan, anxious to go at it. The white players had formed a circle and Darin was standing in the middle of it, waiting for me. He was ready to fight. He was bouncing up and down on his toes like a boxer anxious to get to it. The other guys were cheering him on.

"Come on, you!" he sneered at me. "I'm going to smash your face, you ____ lover. Go home! I don't want you on my team."

The circle of guys blocked the way to the field, so other than turn and run I had no choice but to walk through them. But instead of going down the middle, I walked to one side, hoping I could go around Darin and maybe avoid having to fight him. But the guys moved in and the circle got tighter, leaving me no way out. There was no way to avoid fighting this guy. I was trapped. I felt the anger building up inside me.

Without any warning, I rushed Darin and knocked him to the ground. I wrapped my left arm around his neck, held him tight, and started pounding the snot out of him with my right fist. The strange thing was, it wasn't Darin's face I was smashing. I hardly knew the guy. And I certainly didn't hate him, even if he was a punk. The face I saw that afternoon belonged to a certain dark and evil woman from my past. I hit Darin over and over. I hit him hard. I hit him until he started crying. Then I punched him some more. I unleashed my hatred and bitterness on that poor kid.

Finally, I let him go and stood up. When I looked around, everyone was gone. Suddenly I felt bad about what I had done to poor Darin. I hadn't wanted to fight him. He was the one who'd pushed it. But still, I didn't like the guilt I was feeling.

I stood there feeling sad, guilty, and very much alone in the world, wondering how everyone at school would treat me when they learned that I had just pulverized one of the stars of the school's football team..

Junior high can be a difficult time for a lot of kids. It sure was for me. And to make matters worse, in a few short weeks, the courts were going to make me and my brothers and sisters relive our entire nightmare.

Chapter 20

The Lie Detector Test

E ventually, our younger brother Kenny joined Susanne and me in Florida. He was with us when the call came in. I could tell from the way Grandmother was looking at Grandpa that the call was about us. Turned out it was the social worker. She'd called to tell us that the court had ordered Susanne and Kenneth and me to return to Illinois. We had to show up for a custody hearing in two weeks.

By that time, school was out for the summer, so we wouldn't be missing any classes if we took the trip, not that we really had a choice in the matter. It would be nice to see John and little Frances. I hadn't seen them since that morning when the police and the State came and took us all away.

I liked living with my grandparents, but I had not exactly been a good kid. Truth be told, I was very much out of control. Enough so, that before we left for Illinois, my grandparents told me that I would not be coming back to Florida with them after the hearing. I couldn't blame them for coming to that conclusion. I had been living two lives. Around them I was a normal kid, even likeable. But when they were not around, I was smoking and leaving the house in the middle of the night and going on crime sprees with my friends.

Shoplifting was pretty much a daily routine. Then at night, we broke into people's cars and stole their stuff. We stole anything of value we could find. Of course I couldn't bring the stuff home, but I would sell it at school or wherever, and tell Grandma that my extra cash came from tips I got at my part time job.

The thing is, there wasn't a thing in the world I actually needed. I just liked the action and the thrill of breaking the law and getting away with it. Hiding in the darkness, casing an area to see if there was anyone around, then when it looked like the coast was clear, striking and getting away. It was all rather addicting. Kids on the prowl do a lot of damage and hurt a lot of people just for the "fun of it." I know we sure did.

That kind of stuff was nothing new for me. I had been committing petty crimes for years. I craved the adrenalin rush, the pure excitement of getting away with something. I recall a night when the police almost caught me, but I hid in some shrubbery. It was a close call, but I got away with it. Talk about a thrill, though. Police looking everywhere for me. I could see them from my hiding place, but they couldn't see me.

After that night, I convinced myself that I was too smart and would never get caught. I was certain that I could do this my whole life and get away with it. Most career criminals develop that mindset, you know. They can't imagine getting caught, so it "can't happen." Until it does.

I was too smart to get caught. I was too clever and too sneaky – right up until the night I found out otherwise. I was prowling cars, like I'd done many times, when the police appeared out of nowhere and caught me red-handed. They handcuffed me, put me in the back of a patrol car, and took me to the police station. Then they called my grandparents, who drove to the station and picked me up. Probably due to my grandma's intervention, I was never charged. But that doesn't mean there were no consequences.

Grandma had never stopped telling me, "You can't pull the wool over my eyes, Chuckie. I knew your father all too well."

I always argued with her, up one side and down the other, but that night when the cops caught me and hauled me in, I knew the gig was up. I was embarrassed and sorry, but mostly sorry that I'd been caught.

I couldn't see it at the time, but Grandma was right. I was turning to the bad. It was like that Merle Haggard song, "Mama Tried." Only instead of Mama, it was Grandma. There's a line in the song that says, "Mama tried to raise me better, but her pleading I denied. I have only me to blame 'cause Mama tried." Well, I was only fourteen, but that's pretty much where I was in life.

A few days later, we headed back to Illinois to keep our court date. Shortly after we arrived, we found ourselves sitting in a hallway in the courthouse, waiting for our hearing. I didn't see my dad anywhere, but I knew he was around because I'd heard someone tell my grandmother that Charles was just down the hall. As usual, I had mixed feelings about seeing Dad again.

The social worker assured my grandparents that "Mr. Dudrey" would not be allowed to see any of us, at least until after the hearing. Eventually, a man came out and instructed me to follow him. Grandmother said that it was all right to go and assured me that she and Grandpa would see me in a little while. The rest of the kids waited there in the hallway.

The man led me to a small room and asked me to take a chair. He explained that the machine on the table was a polygraph machine. He said some people call it a lie detector, because it can tell if you're telling the truth or not. He hooked me up to several wires. He wrapped one around my chest and then clipped something to my finger.

"I am going to ask you some questions," he said. First of all, I want you to tell me "No," when I ask if your name is Charles." I did as I was told. Then he asked me some other "nothing" questions. "These are to establish a base line," he explained. "Now relax and breathe normally."

Then things got serious. He started asking me questions about everything that went on at Church Street. Did I see this? Did I see that? He mixed in a few questions designed to find out if someone had told me to give the answers I was giving.

He mostly asked me things that I had already talked to the caseworker about. He asked me about my dad and about my sister. He wanted to know if Barbara had burned my little sister's arm with cigarettes and if I saw her do it. I answered, "Yes" to both questions.

"Did Barbara force your sister to eat a jar of peanut butter mixed with a box of salt?" I assured the man that this had indeed happened.

"Did she force you to eat food that she had urinated in?" he asked. I said, "Yes, on several occasions."

"Did Barbara beat you with a two-by-two?"

"Was the food in the kitchen kept locked up so you wouldn't have access to it?" I kept answering, "Yes."

After I'd answered question after question about the abuse, going clear back to dad ramming my head into the wall and causing brain damage, the examiner got to the hard stuff. He wanted to know about the sexual abuse. There had been so much of that, and so many kinds of things that often it was painful to even answer. Unfortunately, the answer was always, "Yes."

I should point out that for all the evil Barbara had done to us, she had never sexually abused any of us. She was a crude woman and did lots of perverse things in front of us, but she never touched us in that way. That was just Dad, and for one of the other kids, Grandpa Dudrey.

The questioning went on for quite a while, but finally, it was over and the man led me back to where the others were waiting in the hallway. Then, one by one, each of my brothers and sisters were led away to undergo the same kind of examination, even Frances, who was only seven or eight years old at the time.

When the polygraph examinations were finished, the next step was for all of us to go before the judge. But by then it was lunchtime. The judge ordered us not to talk with one another or to anyone else about anything we had been asked or anything we had said in our polygraph exams. Then he said he would see us all again in a couple of hours.

Before adjourning, the judge told Dad that he was to have no contact with us until further notice.

"Do you understand me, sir?" the judge asked my dad rather sternly. Dad answered that he did. I noticed that his voice was not so strong or defiant as I was used to hearing.

We left the courthouse and went out for what would be my last meal with Grandmother and Grandfather for some time. As you might imagine, the mood at lunch was somber. All of us kids had relived some terrible things that morning. Plus, for me there was the fact that I would not be going back to Florida when the hearing was over, due to my rotten behavior and my getting caught by the cops and embarrassing my grandparents.

Eventually, it was time for us to head back to the courthouse. When we walked into the courtroom, I saw Dad and Barbara sitting a short distance away. Barbara looked at me with the same look of hate I had seen a thousand times. I thought to myself, *I should have killed you, you nasty* _____. But I didn't say anything. I just gave her a sarcastic smile as we made our way to our seats. The truth about her had finally been brought out into the light of day, or at least put on the record.

Being in her presence that day brought back that old mindset, wishing I would've killed her that night. My hatred had not been diminished by the passing of time. Maybe it was all of those bad memories the polygraph exam had forced me to relive. Either way, she could have dropped dead on the spot and I would have just walked around her. The one thing Barbara had taught me to do was hate, and that day I had plenty of it, all for her.

We all stood up as the judge entered the courtroom. Then the lawyers for both sides went forward and talked with the judge for a moment. When they'd finished, the lawyers returned to their places and the judge announced his decision.

"The children will remain in the care of the State until further notice. All records in this matter are to be sealed." Then, with a crack of his gavel the hearing was over. Apparently what had just taken place was only a custody hearing and did not involve any criminal charges.

The attorneys' conference with the judge just before he'd announced his decision resulted in Dad being allowed to say goodbye to us kids after the hearing. Our visit with him was brief and was supervised by the social worker. Dad's younger sister, our Aunt Shirley, was there too.

We met outside, beside Dad's car. He told us how much he loved us and how much he missed us. That was about it. It was odd, though, that while he was saying he loved us, his body language and the look in his eye said this whole thing was our fault, apparently for telling on him and Barbara. In other words, we could still be living with them, if we hadn't blabbed.

After Dad told us he loved us, no one spoke. It was kind of awkward. Barbara broke the silence with a simple, "Let's go." Dad got in the car and the two of them drove away.

For several years, we had been led to believe that Dad and Barbara were married, but apparently they weren't, not until just before the hearing. That was just one more lie in their tangled web of deceit.

As they turned the car around in the parking lot and drove away that day, Dad didn't even look back. Later I learned that Barbara had had given him an ultimatum. It was either her or us. Dad chose her. Perhaps that's why he didn't fight to at least get supervised visitation rights.

Grandmother was angry that day, when Dad drove away. She didn't like it that he was allowed to walk away from the courthouse a free man. But it wasn't over. Too much awful stuff, illegal stuff, had come out in the hearing and the polygraph exams for the law to simply ignore.

The district attorney had to review the polygraph results and maybe even convene a grand jury before issuing an indictment. Proceedings like that sometimes take time.

It turned out that a short time later, Dad was in fact indicted on two counts. The charges were first degree indecent liberties and aggravated incest. But by the time the indictment was handed down, Dad had left the state and moved back to Minnesota. He was smart enough to make it as difficult as possible for the state to prosecute him. Moving to another state left a set of jurisdictional matters for the authorities to resolve.

Eventually, the two states and Dad's attorney worked out a plea agreement, wherein he would serve one year in jail in St. Paul for child neglect. It wasn't much, but at least there was some consequence for him. Barbara on the other hand was never held accountable for the things she did, at least not in this life.

After the hearing, the five of us kids were again split up by the State. We went our separate ways, never to be a family again. I've never understood why the State does that, splits up families, but that day was, by and large, the end of us as a family unit.

Susanne, who had suffered unspeakable abuse on Church Street, and as a young girl had been a slave to Barbara, went back to Fort Myers, Florida with our grandparents. She had scarcely had a life before we escaped from Church Street. I later learned that Susanne did not like living with our grandparents, as I did, so according to her, she intentionally got herself pregnant so she would be sent back to Illinois. She stayed in foster homes there until she was eighteen.

John was adopted by a Seventh Day Adventist family and moved with them to Missouri. After he came of age, he moved back to Minnesota and he and I, usually at my urging, occasionally went on crime sprees together. I don't think John ever got past what he went through as a kid.

After the custody hearing, Kenny went back to Florida to live with our grandparents and Susanne. By that time, however, Kenny had developed some of my bad habits. So, Florida didn't work out so well for him either. After a couple of years, he ended up back in Illinois in a foster home. From there Kenny was eventually adopted out. After he grew up, he came back to Minnesota, where I was at the time, and we pulled some jobs together.

Looking back, I have to say that our grandparents did their best to help us kids. They went to great lengths and made many sacrifices, but we were all pretty messed up by the time they came back into our lives. I would see them again, after many stints in jail and prison cells, but I will tell you about that later.

I have to take some blame for the paths John and Kenny took. I wasn't exactly the best influence on my brothers back then. I could blame the things we did on bad genes, but I think we just made a series of very selfish, stupid decisions, with me usually leading the way.

Little Frances, still today, has almost no recollection of what happened to her at Church Street. That's probably a good thing.

It is probably safe to say that Barbara reserved her worst torture and abuse for Frances and Kenny, maybe because they were the youngest and most vulnerable. I don't know if Frances repressed her memories, or just mercifully forgot the hell she went through at Barbara's hands, but to this day, she refuses to talk about any of it.

Frances was adopted by the first foster family that took her in after the custody hearing. I love my baby sister. But sadly, I have never seen her smile. That fact pains me still today.

As for me, I was headed for a new chapter in my life. I was off to another foster home; one I should have stayed at.

Chapter 21

Riots, Hippy Chicks and the War

I didn't go straight there, but eventually I ended up in the home of Jack and Betty Myers. Not all foster parents are like the Myers. They were truly great people. Every child they took in was treated with love and compassion, and I was no different.

On two conditions, the Myers allowed me to take a job working full-time at a restaurant. I had to keep my grades up and I had to save half of each paycheck. To help me with that, Betty opened a savings account for me. The principles Betty Myers taught me about money stayed with me for the rest of my life. I got to the place where I actually liked handing my paycheck over to her, knowing that she would take good care of my money. Eventually I even started buying U.S. Savings Bonds. I liked the idea of spending thirty-seven fifty for a fifty-dollar bond. That seemed like good math to me.

As for working at a real job, to my surprise I actually enjoyed washing dishes and bussing tables. I was making some honest money, which was a new experience for me. For a high school sophomore, I was doing all right. There were plenty of cute waitresses at the restaurant and I got along with them all. The manager said he liked my energy and since I was fast at the dishwasher, he was going to move me up. Soon, he said, I would be working beside him at the grill.

Jack and Betty Myers had been taking in foster children for many years and were well suited for the job. They had two children of their own, plus one adopted daughter. By the time I met them, fifty or more needy kids had passed through their home. Mrs. Myers was a stay-at- home mom. Mr. Myers was a fireman and also worked for the

University of Illinois. As a fireman, he worked twenty-four hours on and forty-eight off. He gave me permission to visit him at the fire station where he worked, and occasionally I did.

The fire station was only two blocks from the University of Illinois, which was where the action was in our town. I had become an avid bicyclist, and would ride my ten-speed over to see Mr. Myers at work and then go to the university and hang out with the hippies and anti-war crowd. Those guys spent a lot of their free time protesting the war in Vietnam, though I had no idea whether they were right or wrong about any of that.

School was a breeze for me. Okay, I'm not suggesting that my grades were good. They weren't. But life was good. I got along well at school. I had money in my pocket because of my job. And I had a new girlfriend. Terri and I only had one class together, but I would run to see her after every class and walk her to her next one. Sometimes we would meet somewhere in between and hang out for a few minutes.

I was warned more than once about kissing in the hallway, and holding hands. But the hippies had indoctrinated me well on that subject. I would just tell the teachers that what the world needed was more love. If you try, you can probably imagine me, straining to sound serious when saying that. And for some reason the teachers let it go at that. Maybe it was just the times we lived in, or maybe it was because two of our teachers were engaged and were often caught kissing between classes.

On the evenings when I didn't have to go to work, I was either bowling or playing pool, and when I got a chance, hanging out with the babes. I didn't have to break through to be accepted on campus because I already knew several of the college girls from working with them at the Howard Johnson's.

It seemed like everybody was protesting back then, whether it was the Vietnam War or civil rights or free speech stuff. Everywhere, people were carrying signs that read, "STOP THE WAR, GIVE PEACE A CHANCE."

I confess that I was more interested in the hippie chicks with their long straight hair and faded bell bottom jeans than the things they were protesting. I noticed right away that almost all of them smelled like patchouli or grass, and sometimes both.

The hippy guys seemed to have their own set of issues. They talked about the war a lot, or heading to Canada to escape the draft. And it seemed like there were nonstop protests against the presence of military recruiters on or near the campus. When the news started reporting that the war was spreading to Cambodia, the protests turned violent. There were flag burnings. The ROTC lounge was fire-bombed, and two more fire-bombs were discovered in Altgeld Hall. It was pretty intense.

Then that May, a large group of protestors at Kent State University clashed with National Guard troops and things really got out of control. Guardsmen used tear gas in an attempt to disperse the protestors. Rocks were thrown, and by some accounts the troops felt threatened when hundreds of protestors apparently attempted to surround them. Shots were fired and four students were killed and another nine were wounded. Two of the four killed weren't even protesting, but were just walking to class. Two of them were girls.

Students at the Illinois campus, where I hung out, were outraged. The protests heated up and the atmosphere on campus became truly intense.

There were protest signs everywhere, calling for peace, but all I saw was anger.

If there was one thing I couldn't understand about the protestors, it was the animosity they directed toward the young guys coming home from Vietnam. Most of vets had been drafted against their will, ordered to fight the Viet Cong in the hot, humid, snake infested jungles of Southeast Asia, and in so doing suffered unspeakable emotional and physical hardship. Then when they came home, they were often met by angry protestors calling them murderers and child killers. It was awful.

Not all of the angst was about the war. On most weekends, there were race riots on the north end of town. People were forced to stay on their "own side" of the street. It was the same kind of fear and hatred I had seen between blacks and whites in my junior high school down in Florida. Blacks were lined up on one side of the street and whites on the other, and they were all just one smart-mouthed remark away from going at it.

That year, after winter came to an end and spring arrived, I started feeling restless. I still believed the Myers were about the best people I had ever known. But my young mind was moving a thousand miles a minute and I had to change something about my life, anything. It was like I couldn't be happy when things were going okay. Maybe I was unhappy with being happy. Whatever it was, I had a strong desire to travel, to get out on the road and go someplace.

Undeterred by logic and unencumbered by maturity, I went to the bank early one morning, cashed in all of my savings bonds, and withdrew all the cash from my savings account. And without saying a word to Jack or Betty or anyone else, I packed my bags and caught a Greyhound headed north. I owed the Myers more than just up and disappearing without a word, but I didn't give much thought to such things back then.

For the first time in my life I was now totally on my own. There was no one to tell me what to do or to threaten me. I liked that feeling. I settled back in my seat and got comfortable for the long bus ride to Minnesota. I had no real plan, other than I would maybe look up my old man and see what he had to say for himself.

Chapter 22

Uncle Ron's Help

Pulling into the bus station in St. Paul brought back a stream of happy but sorrowful memories of the time I'd had there with my mother a decade earlier. So much had changed since then and I couldn't help but wonder how different my life would have been if my mother had lived.

I found myself missing Mother all over again. I hadn't let myself feel those feelings for quite some time, but there I was, thinking it would be wonderful if I could just see her again, even if for just one day, or even one hour.

As a runaway, I had no place to go and no schedule to keep. Before I knew it, I found myself walking up to the same counter where Momma had bought me a cup of hot cocoa before we boarded the bus for Rochester and the Mayo Clinic. I wondered for a moment if my dear, sweet momma would even recognize me now. I had changed as much inside as out. I felt a twinge of guilt at that thought. The changes on the inside had not all been for the better.

I thought about how my mom might look today. My brief glimpse of her lying in her casket at the funeral leaped to my mind. I recalled some woman at the funeral that day letting out a loud scream, shocking everyone in the otherwise quiet room. The lady thought Mother had opened her eyes and looked at her. Actually it was just the reflection of her own eyes in Mother's glasses, but her reaction sure gave everyone quite a start.

I was jarred from that memory by a man over the loud speaker announcing, "Rochester, Winona, Des Moines and all points south, gate two." That was our bus. For a moment I was seven again, and fought back a tear.

I walked around the bus station for a few minutes looking for a telephone. I was in Minnesota now. No one in the world knew I was there. Everything I owned was in a flight bag on my back, except for the almost two thousand dollars' cash hidden in my pants. I didn't have a plan for the future, but I had money and I was free.

I knew that my dad lived somewhere nearby, but I hadn't decided yet whether I wanted to see him. On impulse, I did the next best thing. I went to a phone booth and looked up my Uncle Ron's phone number. I dropped a dime into the slot and dialed his number.

Uncle Ron was my dad's brother. He had been in my life for as long as I could remember. Uncle Ron was the one who came to my aid when I started convulsing from the brain injury I suffered when Dad rammed my head into that wall stud. Ron probably saved my life that night. If it wasn't for him, I probably would have choked to death on my own tongue.

Uncle Ron also watched us kids sometimes back when Mother was still alive, and he was someone I trusted. I hoped he would be glad to see me after all that had taken place. I wasn't sure how much he knew about the abuse or if he knew that we had been taken away from our dad. I guessed I would find out soon enough.

Ron answered the phone after one ring. He seemed excited to hear from me. That was encouraging. In a surprisingly short time after we hung up, he arrived at the bus station to pick me up. During the drive to his house I shared some of what I had been up to for the past few years. He seemed interested, and we talked all the way to his house.

Right away, my uncle and his wife Jan went to work making me feel right at home. They set me up with my own, fully furnished bedroom in their basement.

Ron was a respected counselor and job coach, and he took it upon himself to teach me some job skills. I felt a sense of pride when people at his work would say, "Oh, you must be Ron's nephew."

The vocational training Ron gave me was the first time I could remember actually liking school. One afternoon, he said he thought it would be wise to contact Family Services in Illinois and let them know where I was and that I was all right. He went ahead and made the call. He also contacted the social services people in Minnesota and asked them to step in and help make it legally okay for me to stay with him.

He said he wanted to make sure I didn't get into any kind of trouble with the authorities. At seventeen, I was after all, underage.

Looking back, I'm pretty sure my uncle was really looking out for himself, ensuring that he wouldn't get in trouble for harboring a runaway. Plus, there was the matter of the cigarettes. Uncle Ron kept a carton of cigarettes in the refrigerator, and one day they went missing. I smoked, so naturally he accused me of stealing them.

Okay, I was a thief. There is no getting around that. I stole a lot of stuff. But I didn't take my uncle's cigarettes. I told him I hadn't touched them, but he didn't believe me. It might be safe to assume that the matter of the missing cigarettes, as much as anything, contributed to my uncle's decision to call the authorities and let them know where I was.

While I was staying at Uncle Ron's, my dad popped in from time to time. I wasn't all that excited about visiting with him, but I felt an obligation to at least be social when he came around. I really don't know why. The last two times I'd seen him had not been all that positive.

We talked when he stopped by, but I had an abiding sense that I could never trust the man again. I was uncomfortable around him and I'm sure he felt the same way. The first time he showed up, I walked over and gave him a hug. I assumed it was expected with us not having seen one another in years. But when I put my arms around him his entire body went stiff. He hugged me back, but it was about as awkward as a hug can be.

One afternoon Dad picked me up from Ron's house and took me for a drive. He showed me old haunts and places where we used to live. All afternoon, though, I kept sensing that he had something on his mind. Finally, he pulled into a parking lot in the housing projects. The Mount Airy Housing Project wasn't exactly the best place in the world to live. It was basically a ghetto, but that's where my dad was living.

When we walked into the house, I had immediate flashbacks of Georgetown. The way the place looked, the way it smelled, even the sounds. And there was Barbara. She looked just like I remembered, unkempt and no teeth in her mouth. I was surprised to see that her brother Walter was living there, too.

Barbara and Dad now had four kids together; two of whom I had never seen before. The two new ones were born after Georgetown. Biologically, all four of them were my little half brothers and sisters. Yet the only thing I felt for them was pity. The second from the oldest was the baby girl Barbara was pregnant with that night in Georgetown, when I ran to get help instead of pushing her down the stairs. At least the child was alive and had a chance in life. She might live a miserable life, or she might turn things around and overcome her upbringing. That would be at least partly up to her.

Barbara didn't look at me at first. When she finally turned to speak, it was about the dinner she was making. At that moment, I saw two things in her eyes. The first was loathing. The second was fear. Barbara was afraid of me. Just my being there was exacting a toll on her. It was written all over her face. I found some comfort in that.

Apparently I was there for dinner; not that Dad had mentioned it. I soon found myself seated at the table with the kids and being handed a bowl of perhaps the only thing Barbara knew how to cook, my least favorite meal in the entire world. While I ate, Barbara yelled at the kids for this or that. Meanwhile my dad retired to the living room to eat alone in front of the television. I was not invited to join him. Sometimes I wondered back then if the man even had a soul. Who would invite their own son, someone they hadn't seen in years, to their home for dinner and then go eat in another room?

I couldn't wait to get out of that place. After Dad had finished eating, he showed me the machine gun he kept in a closet. It was impressive. I had never seen a real, fully automatic machine gun before and was surprised that he was allowed to have one. Actually, he probably wasn't, but there it was, nonetheless. He told me how he had come to have the gun. I didn't say what I was thinking, but I was pretty sure that the source was mob related.

On the way back to Uncle Ron's, we did something that my dad probably saw as a bonding experience with his son. He spotted a nice ten-speed bicycle that no one was guarding and stopped the car and let me out. I grabbed the bike and rode it down the street and around the corner to where Dad was waiting. We tossed the bike into the trunk of his car and took off. Now I had a nice, almost new bike, and some other kid didn't. You know, that incident kind of defines my relationship with my dad. We were "thief" and "thief's son."

The result of Uncle Ron's call to the social services department in Illinois was not what I had hoped. He'd promised me that he would do his best to talk them into letting me stay with him, but whether he did or didn't, the Illinois authorities forwarded a court order to Minnesota and had me arrested as a runaway.

They had me standing before a judge that same afternoon. That was the very first time I had ever stood before a judge completely on my own. The hearing was about as brief as such things can be. Without any discussion the judge slammed down his gavel and decreed, "Back to Illinois with him."

I was led to a holding cell while the deputy looked for a policeman to transport me to the airport. I didn't know what was waiting for me back in Illinois, but I was sure I wasn't going to like it. Now that they knew that I couldn't be trusted to stay where they placed me, it was likely I would be placed in a more restricted environment.

Eventually, two police officers arrived to drive me to the airport. I immediately disliked the one in the front passenger's seat and hoped he would not be the one flying me back to Illinois.

We arrived at the airport and headed for the gate. When we were finally allowed to board the plane, the cop who'd stayed with me turned and said politely, "You have a good flight, Charles."

Then to my total surprise, he turned around and walked off the plane. It didn't seem real that a runaway would be placed on a flight without any supervision whatsoever. My mind began to think of the possibilities this new arrangement afforded me. First, I had some lunch; then I ordered a drink. The stewardess brought me my drink, which was exactly what I had ordered, minus the booze. Oh well, I'd tried. But I was not going to let that get me down. I had never had a margarita before anyway.

As the plane was making its approach to land in Chicago, my heart started beating faster. Would there be someone there to meet me and walk me to my next plane? What if there wasn't?

I walked off the plane and slyly looked around. I didn't see any official-looking person scanning the passengers for me. I started hoping. Doing my best secret agent impersonation, I stuck close to a group of people I had been talking to during the flight, trying to look like I was with them. It turned out that none of my covertness was necessary. There was no one waiting for me. Apparently it was my responsibility to catch the connecting flight to Champagne/Urbana, like my ticket said. Seriously? Like that was going to happen.

I searched the monitor for departing flights, looking for one headed back to Minnesota. There was one scheduled to leave in less than hour. I found a seat in the terminal and retrieved a hundred dollar bill I kept hidden under the inside sole of my shoe. I took my unused ticket and my hundred dollar bill up to the counter and got me a seat on a plane headed right back to where I had just been.

I don't know what genius assumed that a runaway would go back to face some new judge because some other judge wanted him to. But whoever it was, in my case they had made a slight miscalculation.

Chapter 23

Hiding Out in the Pacific Northwest

Regardless of the weather, it was, in a manner of speaking, a little too hot for me in St. Paul. The authorities didn't take too kindly to me skipping out on the ticket they had purchased to return me to Illinois, so they had a judge issue a warrant for my arrest. They sent officers to my dad's place and Uncle Ron's. But I was too smart to be anywhere they might reasonably be inclined to look.

Strange as it may sound, I called my dad and he and Barbara gave me a ride to northern Minnesota where I hid out in Duluth with my great uncle. Uncle Ed was a big, barrel-chested man who had lost one of his arms in the Philippines during World War II. I stayed with him for a couple of weeks, but life at his house was much too rigid for me. I had cash and wasn't inclined to stay for long at any place I didn't like. A few days later, I was seated on another bus; this one headed for the Pacific Northwest.

A few years back, Grandma Dudrey had moved into a small house outside of Morton, Washington. Morton is a little logging town at the foot of Mount Rainier in the Cascade Mountain Range. I had been there with a cousin four years earlier. The two of us had spent the summer swimming and fishing in the Tilton River. The terrain around Morton is rough. It's mostly steep, heavily forested mountains and foothills. I fell in love with the rugged wildness of the area on my earlier trip and had always wanted to come back. The present seemed like a good time to do that.

Sure, I was a runaway, wanted by the state of Illinois. I really didn't care, though, as long as they didn't catch me. The fact that they were looking for me made the adventure all the more fun. I was still pretty much addicted to the drama and excitement of getting away with something, and being on the run from the law only fed that.

But something else was going on inside of me. I was a sad, empty kid who spent a lot of his time worrying about his life. I wanted to know what was going to happen to me. How were things going to turn out? I found myself wondering how different my life might have been if I had stayed with the Myers or just continued my flight back to Illinois like the judge had ordered.

When I showed up on her doorstep unannounced, Grandma Dudrey was more than a little surprised to see me. I was surprised, too. My grandma had a boyfriend, or more accurately, a fiancé.

Grandma and Bill tied the knot while I was living there. They got married in the city of Chehalis on Christmas Eve of 1971. Strange as it may sound, I was the best man at their wedding, and my great-grandmother was the maid of honor. I wish I had a photo of that little group because the wedding party spanned four generations.

It turned out that Bill was a fine man, and he clearly loved Grandma. It was fun to hear him call her "Sweets," and I could tell she liked it when he did. They seemed to be a happy couple. Bill seemed to be a lot better man than her first husband had ever been. She deserved that.

Morton, Washington was a small town and everybody knew everybody else. Before long, I was out and about, meeting most of the kids in town. I had already been more places and done more things than most kids my age, so I guess that made me kind of interesting. Whatever it was, I got a lot of attention. I spent every day shooting pool and listening to the jukebox. And every so often I would step out back and smoke some grass with anyone who had some.

All my hanging out at the University had paid off, because I could roll a joint with one paper without tearing it. That also made me cool. I had no idea at the time that marijuana was slowly but surely digging its hooks into me, and I absolutely would not have believed it if you had told me. Eventually pot would all but define me, but that was years down the road.

I didn't particularly want to work in the woods or the lumber mills, like most of the locals did, but I found a part time job working for the lady who owned the second hand store in town. I liked having new cash money on me at all times, because that meant I didn't have to tap into the cash I had stashed away. I called that stash my "running cash."

I was still wanted by the law back in Illinois, but only as a runaway. I knew that once I turned eighteen there was nothing they could do to me anymore, and my eighteenth birthday wasn't that far off. I hadn't really done anything in Illinois, except leave without their permission. Well, that's only legally true. I had done lots of stuff that I could have gone to jail for. If it was all added up, I could have gone to jail for a long time. But I hadn't been caught and the law didn't know what the law didn't know.

As for being a runaway, the more I thought about it, who were those social workers and judges to tell me anything? In my mind I was old enough to do what I wanted and if they didn't like it, so what. I was free and on my own and doing better than I ever had. I liked Washington and thought that someday I might live there for good. All I needed to do for the time being was to lay low and stay off the radar.

So I spent my days playing pool and listening to the jukebox. I liked singing along with Janis Joplin to, "Me and Bobby McGee." My newest favorite song was Smoky Robinson's "Tears of a Clown." Folks probably got tired of me playing that song all of the time.

Before long, though, that same restless spirit rose to the surface and I started feeling the itch to get moving. One day, out of the blue, I decided to go back East. I would find myself a place to live and get me a job. I was bored with life in Morton and needed to hit the road. I just had to.

So, with only a little warning, I said so long to everyone I knew in Morton and caught a train headed East. I loved traveling and being on the road, and in my own mind already considered myself to be quite the man of the world.

I was sitting in the train's dining car one morning when I started playing my life over and over in my mind. I fiddled with my sausage and eggs and pondered the possibility of perhaps never settling down anywhere, but just living a life on the road, roaming from town to town.

It suddenly occurred to me that what I was really running from wasn't just the law. It was something else. It was real and powerful, and it would not let me rest. But I just couldn't put my finger on what it was.

When I got back to Minnesota, I did something I can't believe I did. I moved in with my dad in their little place in the projects. I stayed there for five or six months. I hated being around Barbara, but it was a place to live; and I dealt with her simply by working at odd jobs and being gone most of the time after work.

Finally, I turned eighteen and was a free man. I was officially an adult. That meant I had to register for the draft. I went down to the post office in St. Paul and filled out my selective service papers. As I was leaving the post office, I ran into a man outside who happened to be a Marine Corp recruiter. That guy was impressive. I mean, I had never in my life seen such a fine specimen of sheer manliness. We talked for quite a while and before long I'd decided that this guy was the kind of man I wanted to be. I wanted to be a Marine, one of America's finest, so I signed up for the United States Marine Corp.

To my complete and utter dismay, I was rejected due to an elbow injury I had sustained on Church Street. I was devastated, so devastated in fact that I got on a bus and went to Washington D.C. to talk to the Corp's head guy to see if I could get him to let me in.

When I arrived at the Pentagon, I was met by another perfect specimen of manhood who immediately demanded to know what I was doing out of uniform. I told him why I was there, and he forthwith took me to talk to a Sergeant Major, who patiently explained that there was nothing the Commander of the Corp would do to help me.

I went back to Minnesota dejected. My dream had been shattered. Not yet completely deterred, I continued to hang around the recruiting office in St. Paul and talk to the Marines there. Eventually, one of them took me aside and told me how I might get in. He referred me to a recruiter in Fargo, North Dakota who might be able to pull it off. Sure enough, he did.

I got all of the paperwork filled out, but kind of fudged on one question, which asked if I had ever enlisted before. I answered no. I was at basic training for about a month and then got called into the office where I was informed that I was being discharged because of my elbow injury. It was a general discharge, but was related to my less than honest answer to that one question.

In the coming chapters you are going to see where my life went next, and it's not always a pretty picture. But the Marine Corp episode is another one of those forks in the road where everything in my life could have gone in an entirely different direction had this or that worked out differently. I have often wondered what my life would have been like had the Marine Corp let me stay.

Over the following weeks, I spent part of my time hanging with Barbara's brother Walter. One day, on an impulse, we decided to hitchhike to California. That is a story in itself, but I will just say, we made it there, got jobs working at a Shakey's Pizza, and stayed for about six months before heading home. The next time I made it to California the officials would not let me leave quite so easily, but we will get to that later.

When Walter and I got back to Minnesota, I learned that my dad and Barbara had separated. Dad was now managing some apartment buildings in St. Paul, a couple of blocks off "the strip." The strip was where all of the action took place in St. Paul. Wanting to be where things were happening, I rented myself a seventy-five dollar a month place right in the middle of it all. It was a ground floor, one-bedroom apartment with a private entrance and a porch. It was a pretty nice place, actually. Moving into my very own apartment, my first, made me feel like a real adult.

I immediately went to work furnishing the place. I also purchased my very first vehicle, a pick-up truck, and started putting it to use hauling stuff for rich people. During daylight hours I drove around the upper class, well-to-do parts of town soliciting work hauling people's unwanted junk to the dump. Before long, my little business was doing well. Everywhere I went, I looked for an opportunity to haul something for cash money.

Richer people throw away a lot of good stuff, so I used some of their perfectly good "junk" to furnish my apartment.

After a while, I decided to save some cash on the dump fees, which were a major part of my overhead. I started unloading my truck behind some old buildings on the other side of town. One day, when no one was looking, I dumped a load of junk onto a vacant lot. The thing was, I had just picked up the junk from the backside of a business only a few blocks away. I thought I was pretty smart pulling that one, until some guy who'd seen me dump the stuff started chasing me in his car. I drove like a crazy man through alleys and side streets, doing my best to lose the guy. But that do-gooder citizen wouldn't give up. He stayed close behind me, honking his horn and flashing his lights the entire time. He must have been watching too much TV, thinking he could catch a pro like me.

I flew across a couple of intersections against the lights and finally put an end to the chase. He apparently wasn't having as much fun as I was, because at one point I looked in my rearview mirror and saw two of his hubcaps rolling down the street.

"Chump," I shouted into my rearview mirror, "Mind your own business." It honestly never occurred to me that this "chump" was in the right and what I was doing was wrong. I don't want to leave you with the wrong impression. I did have a conscience of sorts. There were things I wouldn't do. But I had a way of compartmentalizing my conscience and separating out the things I was willing to excuse from those I wouldn't or couldn't.

In my opinion, I had a legitimate business operation going. I was in the "trucking business." But with the price of gas going up to fifty-six cents a gallon I had to cut some costs. Saving on dump fees was not enough. I needed to improve my bottom line even further. So I resorted to an old trick I'd learned from my dad – the siphon hose. I'd filled a lot of cans of gas from the company truck for dad when I was a kid and the same trick would work for me now. Armed with a siphon hose, I had all the free gas I wanted. I just had to steal it.

I had this all figured out. I would go out early in the morning, fill up my gas cans from any vehicle that was available, and be set for the day. Who cares about those chumps who went out to their car that morning to head off for their real jobs, only to find an empty gas tank? I didn't know those people, and besides, the way I saw it, paying for gas was for suckers.

The thing was, I might steal from one guy and then see someone else who needed something and buy it for them. I never knew what was going to stir up some compassion in me, but some things definitely did. So I guess I still had a soul. And a conscience, too. Mine just wasn't all that trustworthy.

Chapter 24

Quaaludes, Arsenic, and Suspicion

I first met Poppy in the county jail. He had wavy brown hair that went to his shoulders and the build of an athlete. He was what you might call a scrapper. I was in the joint for a probation violation, purely a technicality of course. I got caught drinking while on probation. That's part of a bigger story that I'll tell you about in just a bit.

I had been reading about Poppy in the local newspapers for weeks. He was well known among the criminal element. "Man Arrested for String of Safe Jobs," the headlines read. I guess even the best of them get caught sometimes.

Poppy had been hitting businesses all over the state, prying open safes or cutting them open with a torch. It just so happened that I was making bail that very afternoon. Poppy heard I was getting out and pleaded with me to make some phone calls for him, once I was on the outside, and help him get out, too. I told him I would, on the condition that we would get together and make some money once he got out.

I should tell you how I ended up in the jail where I met Poppy. A year earlier, I had been arrested for credit card theft and sentenced to five years in prison. The court ordered my sentence set aside, on the condition that I complete a community corrections program. That was a pretty easy decision to make. The program was new and had been created as an alternative to prison for first-time offenders. I qualified.

In my defense, I must tell you that I wouldn't have been charged in the first place if I had not decided to take the fall for my dad and his new girlfriend, Susan. I did a scam with them, and rather than rat them out, I took the fall when our scheme fell through.

Susan was a two-time widow. After the death of her most recent husband, she'd continued to receive credit cards in the mail. They were always in the name of her late husband and the temptation to use them was apparently too great for her. She had only been married to the guy for a short time when he died and left her a home and a farm.

When Dad met Susan, he was still with Barbara, and he left the one for the other. I was of the opinion that Dad made a good decision leaving Barbara, no matter what the reason. I say that, ignoring the fact that Dad had four children with Barbara and left her to fend for herself. But at least when it comes to appearance and hygiene, he definitely traded up. Susan (not her real name) was good looking, could carry on an intelligent conversation, and actually had some class. And she came without the body odor and filthy mouth.

Dad seemed pretty committed to being with Susan. He would drive the seventy-five miles to Susan's house every night after work, and then make the return trip back to St. Paul the next morning.

One weekend, Susan invited me to come along. She said she had a younger sister she wanted me to meet, and we could all go dancing together.

It was no secret that I was a self-proclaimed criminal. Since moving back to Minnesota I had been wheeling and dealing and robbing and stealing. I never lost my love for the excitement and fast pace. My senses were honed by now, so I could spot trouble or a threat before it got too close. I could scan a room or a crowd of people and immediately spot what was going on. That is a learned skill, I think. At least it's one that can be developed. Players almost always have it. Successful con men have it, or they learn it. And so do good cops and detectives.

One day, Susan showed me a handful of unused, unsigned credit cards. I'm sure Dad put her up to it, but it wouldn't have mattered to me either way. I instantly responded with, "You bet! Let's do it." Keep in mind that at this time I had never been to jail or prison.

Dad and Susan were as confident as I was about the game we were going to play. At least that's what I thought at the time. Maybe, in reality, they were afraid of getting caught, so they arranged things in such a way that I would take all of the risk. That's probably what Dad was doing when he had me carry the "empty" salt bags with stolen stuff in them out to the truck, back when I was eleven. If I would have been caught, the blame would have fallen on me, not him.

At any rate, I made it clear that I would not implicate either of them if anything went wrong. Hearing that, they seemed excited about the plan. Every time we talked about it, I assured them I would never tell, but would take the hit if I got caught. Honestly, I had no idea what I was talking about.

But with those formalities out of the way, I blurted out, with some excitement, "Let's sign the cards and go shopping."

I had fun shopping. It made me feel like a big spender. Dad would wait in the car. Susan and I would go into the store and fill the cart with all the things we had talked about buying. We were furnishing her home, so there were lots of things on the list. I used those fraudulent cards to buy lamps, toasters, binoculars, furniture and artwork. You name it. If they could use it to furnish a house, or just wanted it for some reason, I bought it.

When we got up to the checkout, I would go into my memorized script, then take out my card and pay for the merchandise like I had been doing it all my life.

Then I would thank the cashier, telling them to have a nice day, and meet Susan at the door. By the time we got to the car with the merchandise, I was so full of myself that all I wanted was to do it again. We had a game going and I loved the drama. I suggested that we continue using the cards until the stores wouldn't accept them any longer.

At the next stop, Dad and Susan went shopping. They filled the cart with the things they wanted, then walked out to the car and told me where in the store they'd left the cart. I went in, retrieved the cart, and went up front and paid for the merchandise. We kept this up for weeks, covering two states.

I was the only one taking any serious risks in our little scam. I was the one presenting the cards and assuming someone else's identity. All Dad and Susan had to do was keep the stuff I scammed off the store. That was their part.

One night, while Susan and I were shopping, a man from the store's security team approached me and instructed me to follow him. He took hold of my arm, which told me that this was no customer service meeting. Susan was standing a little way apart from me, but was looking my way, so I discreetly gave her the signal to leave.

The store detective walked me toward his office upstairs, interrogating me as we went. He demanded that I tell him my real name and tell him whose card I was using. Just as we were about to enter his office, I said that I needed to use the restroom, and to my surprise he said it was all right. I went in while he waited outside. But as soon as the door started to close behind me, I turned around and ran back out.

Leading with my left shoulder, I slammed my weight hard against the door. The impact of the door hitting him almost in the face knocked the surprised store detective to the floor. I ran out the emergency exit and down the fire escape without looking back. I ran as fast as I could. I found a motel and used the payphone to call a cab to take me to where Susan and I had agreed to meet up, if something went wrong.

Good plans make for a good job. That's what I told her when she arrived to pick me up. She wasn't so sure. Actually, she looked frightened. She asked me if I was scared, and I assured her that I had been doing this all my life and liked the action. After talking with my dad about how things had gone down, we decided that it might be best if I left town for a while. So, the next morning, I went to the airport and caught a flight south.

Florida was as nice as I remembered. I rented a car and drove around for old times' sake. I drove past some of my old hangouts, and the house I used to live in with my grandparents. They had moved back to Minnesota a few years after the custody hearing in Illinois. Seeing their old house reminded me of just how much I loved that sweet old couple. They were such good people. So different from me. That last thought hurt. I wasn't liking who I was becoming, but I shrugged it off.

I hung out near the Gulf Coast for a week or two, then decided to look for a way to make some money. I found a job at a grocery store, then moved in with some friends I knew from going to school there. I was doing pretty well, all things considered. From time to time I would think about the scam I'd pulled up in Minnesota and smile. I was pleased with myself for getting away unscathed.

I wasn't outgrowing my tendency to think of myself as a spy or secret agent. Sometimes I would dream of being "The Saint," or the guy from the Johnny Rivers' song, "Secret Agent Man," always living the life of danger.

I knew I wasn't really doing the kind of stuff those guys did. But I was getting used to the criminal life. It made me feel alive and free. And I liked hanging out with people I chose to think of as friends, even if they weren't. I also liked hanging with cute girls. And if I needed some cash, I just went out and got some, fast and easy.

One day, I received word through the grapevine that my dad wanted me to call him. I found a pay phone and dialed his number. We didn't talk for long. He'd called to let me know that the State of Minnesota's Bureau of Criminal Apprehension had a warrant out for my arrest. They had proof that I was the one who had charged several thousand dollars on those credit cards. They'd told Dad that if I would come back and turn myself in, they would go easier on me than if they had to find me and arrest me.

Of course Dad reminded me of what I had said about not implicating anyone else, if I got caught. I assured him that I would do as I'd said. I shook my head when he said that, thinking that my old man was weak. He didn't have loyalty to his own son, even when we were partners in a job. As for turning myself in, "They'll have to find me first," I whispered as I hung up the phone.

But I stayed in touch with Dad; we spoke on the phone from time to time. Eventually he told me that he thought it might be best if I just came on back and dealt with this thing. He promised to post bail for me, so I wouldn't have to sit in jail awaiting trial.

I thought about it for a couple of days and then for some reason decided to take my dad's advice. To my surprise, when I got back to Minnesota and turned myself in, the detective wanted to talk to me about things a lot more serious than credit card fraud and identity theft.

"So tell me about your relationship with Susan," he asked. I was being questioned at the jail. I had been under the impression that my interrogation was going to be about the credit card scams.

"How long have you known Susan?"

"Did you know her husband Carl? Did you know that his death is being investigated?"

"Tell me about Robert, Susan's husband before Carl. Did you know him? Have you ever heard anyone talk about his death?"

I couldn't tell them a thing. I had no idea what any of this stuff had to do with anything.

"Did you know that they both died suddenly? Did you know that both of their deaths took place within less than a year?"

I knew that there had been some kind of investigation into the death of Susan's late husband, but I didn't know any of the particulars. I certainly didn't know that they were investigating the death of another husband who had died less than a year before the last one.

"Tell me what you know about arsenic?" the detective demanded. "Have you ever known anyone to have any?"

Now that was an interesting question. It made me stop and think about other things that had happened.

What a coincidence. Their questions about Susan's two dead husbands reminded me of my mother. That afternoon that I'd gone to Dad's place in the projects for dinner, Dad, Barbara, and her brother Walter had all been there. Those three were the same three who were at our house the morning my mother was shot and killed. And now the cops are investigating two more people who had died suddenly. It sure seemed like a lot of people around my dad and his friends ended up dead, like I almost did that morning at the County Home when that kid shoved my dad's gun in my face.

I was slowly drawing conclusions about my dad's role in my mother's death. Speculation was beginning to mature into outright suspicion.

The detective continued, "We think Susan had something to do with the death of both of her husbands."

"We wanted her to take a polygraph test," he told me, "and she agreed. But she came in so high on Quaaludes that the test came back inconclusive."

This was all sounding eerily familiar to me, kind of ringing some bells. I didn't say a word to the detective. That wasn't my style. But I actually did know something about arsenic. Dad had a vial of it in his safe! I had seen it. And Quaaludes, too.

I knew Dad and Susan definitely had access to Quaaludes from the night they drove me to Duluth when the authorities were after me for being a runaway. I had gone to the bathroom at the Chinese restaurant where we were all having dinner. When I came back to the table, I took a sip of my coffee and noticed something right away. I recall saying, "Those Chinese sure make some strong coffee." I woke up the next morning still in the car. I don't know why Dad or Susan slipped a Quaalude into my coffee, but I'm sure they did it.

Whatever the detective's end game was, he seemed intent on finding something on Susan. He was trying hard. Well, try as he might, he wasn't going to get anything from me. I wasn't a rat. I had made a deal not to talk to the cops, so I wouldn't.

Of course there were things I didn't know at the time I'd made that promise. I hadn't been told, for example, that Susan was suspected of killing two husbands to get their money and property. No one had told me that the parents of Susan's second husband had threatened to have his body exhumed and checked for poison, or that she had signed the farm over to them to avoid a murder investigation. That hardly sounds like the actions of an innocent person.

"You know," the detective continued, "if you had permission to use those credit cards, we can't charge you with anything. Did Susan help you use them? You can make this all go away right now if Susan gave you permission to use the cards."

"No," was all I said.

I ended up pleading guilty to credit card fraud and being sentenced to five years in prison. But like I said earlier, I got off with probation and community treatment because that was my first offense. Not much later, however, I got caught drinking, which was a violation of my probation. I got a few days in jail for that, which is where I met Poppy.

A couple of days after I was released from County I raised some bucks and got Poppy bailed out, too. Now he owed me. The way I saw it, my short stay in the clink turned out to be a stroke of luck. That's where I met Poppy, the man I hoped would take my career to the next level. A man with his experience could teach me how to move up to more serious stuff.

It wasn't long before Poppy and I were pulling jobs together. Poppy was anxious to pay back the bail money I had raised to get him out of jail. He said that meant we had to raise some fast cash, and I liked the sound of that.

It was funny how the man worked. He would sit on the toilet, browsing through the phone book looking for a business that might have a safe. Car dealers and restaurants were always good targets. After spending an hour going through the Yellow Pages, Poppy decided that we would hit a car dealership on Saturday night. That was when the safe would likely have the most cash in it. The banks were not open on weekends back then, so Saturday night or Sunday were the best times to hit certain businesses.

We broke into the office of a dealership that weekend. We immediately went to work with hammers and pry bars, peeling back the safe's steel walls. We were working up a sweat and making quite a bit of noise, when suddenly we hit a tear gas wall-liner in the safe. That was quite the shock. When the gas shot out, it caught us both right in the face. Our eyes burned and we started choking and gasping for air.

Fortunately for us, there was no alarm attached to the safe, as would likely be the case today. Not to be deterred by a little tear gas, we took turns running back and forth to the door for a breath of air. We continued working on the safe, holding our breath to avoid the gas.

Finally, we broke through. We grabbed the cash, stuffed it into our bag, and took off. With our bag of cash and our safe cracking tools in hand, we ran as fast as we could across the field behind the lot. We'd left our getaway car, a rental, on a back street where no one would spot it. Poppy was as high as a kite that night, so his girlfriend was waiting in the car to drive for us.

On the way back to town, we were laughing about the tear gas and enjoying the sheer exhilaration of getting away clean. But we almost didn't.

All of sudden, we saw bright flashing lights coming up behind us. We had no idea why we were being pulled over, but my heart started pounding. Our heavy hammers and big pry bars were all in plain sight in the back seat. If the cop, by chance, looked back there, he wouldn't miss seeing them. Plus, Poppy had a bag of weed and 150 hits of white cross speed, a powerful "cocaine like" amphetamine, under the front seat!

We decided that we had better get our stories straight, in case this was just a routine traffic stop and had nothing to do with the job we'd just pulled. We quickly made something up, then sat back and tried to look as calm and innocent as possible.

After talking to Poppy's girlfriend, the officer shined his flashlight in the rear window and saw our tools. He immediately ordered me to get out of the car and step around back.

He asked what the tools were for, and I calmly told him that we had spent the day helping a friend tear down a shed and were just heading home. Then he told Poppy to join him, while I climbed back into the car. He asked Poppy the same question and our stories matched. Our ruse worked perfectly and the cop let us go. That was about as close as we would come to getting caught – until the next day.

Before we split up that night, we made plans for our next caper. Like someone addicted to a narcotic, we needed our next rush of adrenalin before the high from the last hit wore off.

Chapter 25

Prison and the Con Job

"Someone saw us! Someone saw us!" I whispered loudly. Poppy dropped the torch and started for the door. We had almost cut through the safe, when someone looked in the window of the tractor dealership and saw the bright glow of the torch in the comparative darkness. Whoever he was, he was staring right at us.

This was not how it was supposed to work. It was Sunday morning and all the local farmers were supposed to be in church. So much for that theory. We had no choice but to make a run for it.

The thing was, we still had the cash from the previous night's job at the car dealership. We didn't need to do another job so soon. We just couldn't resist the temptation.

I kept thinking as we ran that maybe we should have planned the job a little better!

Be that as it may, we'd been spotted and now there was no time to waste. Out the door we ran, racing for the car. I revved the engine on the new, green Ford Fairlane, slammed it into gear and headed for the freeway. I was feeling pretty good about making it this far without seeing a cop. But still, my heart was pounding pretty hard. A voice kept screaming in my brain, "Get away before you get busted! Get as far as you can! Blend in with the flow of traffic."

Just ahead was the Minnesota state line. If I pushed it, we would be out of Iowa before anyone spotted us. The traffic on the freeway was pretty light. I glanced down at the speedometer and saw that I was doing over a hundred and the needle was still moving up.

"Whew! That was close," I shouted over at Poppy. I glanced up at the rear view mirror. Still clear. All I needed was to be sent back to jail. My probation officer didn't like me much and would not mind seeing me locked up again. She was a tough egg and putting me in prison would get me out of her hair.

To be honest, getting spotted by that passerby back at the tractor store really scared me. I was not accustomed to being seen while pulling off a heist. I was too good for that to happen, or so I thought.

I was just thinking that we had gotten away clean and starting to feel bad about not getting any cash, when I looked out my side window and spotted a police car pulling even with us on my left. The two of us were speeding along side by side at well over a hundred miles per hour.

The cop was talking on his radio and glancing over at me, looking me straight in the eyes. I didn't like the look on his face. I pushed the gas pedal to the floor, hoping more speed might separate us. It didn't work; he stayed right beside us.

I glanced over again and saw that the guy had one hand on the steering wheel and a shotgun in the other. The strap was wrapped around his forearm and the barrel was pointing right at my head.

I heard his voice come over a loudspeaker. "Pull over," he demanded. "Now!" There was a no nonsense, no messing around tone to his voice.

Frantic, conflicting thoughts flashed through my head. I can't outrun him. I definitely can't outrun his radio. We're caught!

I instantly started feeling sorry for myself. It wasn't a good feeling. I knew what it felt like to get fingerprinted and booked. I knew the sound of a steel door slamming shut behind me. I knew all about the boring daily routine and the lousy food. But I had never been in for a long stint. But with me being out on probation, this time they would give me serious hard time.

But what could I do? I was out of options. I glanced over at Poppy and mouthed the words, "We have to pull over." He nodded grimly. The look on his face said he knew the gig was up. It was either pull over, or get shot or run off the road.

I slowed down and pulled over to the shoulder. We sat there for a few minutes, waiting for the cops to come and arrest us. They seemed to be taking their sweet time about it. Part of me was steaming, mostly mad at myself for getting caught. The other part of me was dealing with a heavy helping of self-pity. An hour earlier I had been a fast moving, "too clever to get caught" smooth operator. Now it was becoming clear that I was just another loser.

I definitely didn't want to get shot, so I kept my hands on the steering wheel, up high where they could be seen. Suddenly, the wait was over and there were cops everywhere around us. They all had guns, some handguns, some shotguns; and they were all pointed at us.

Poppy and I did as we were told and got out of the car slowly. We placed our hands on the top of the car, me on one side and my partner on the other. They handcuffed us and shoved us into the backseat of different squad cars.

Yes, sir, Poppy had sure shown me how to hit the big time!

Half an hour later we were sitting in a holding cell waiting to be booked. I told Poppy I thought I was in trouble this time, really big trouble. He said he knew it. We were both feeling pretty grim. We sat in the holding cell for a long time, waiting for something to happen. Eventually a guard came in and handed us both a paper bag. It was lunch. A baloney sandwich on white bread with mustard and a little wilted lettuce. Mine looked like someone had sat on it. There was also an orange and a doughy sugar cookie. I wasn't much in the mood for eating, so I left mine sitting on the bench. Eventually I ate the cookie.

I had only known Poppy for a month. We'd met in jail and here we were again, sitting in a cell, waiting to be charged by the State of Iowa with burglary. We should have been satisfied with last night's safe job, the one at the auto dealership. We netted some good cash. But no, we wanted more. We'd hardly slept the previous night because we were so anxious to rush out and do another job. Like a gambler who thinks he's always going to win, we rolled the dice, betting everything we had on the outcome, including our freedom.

It was fun living in the fast lane, pulling a wad of dough out of your pocket anytime you wanted to pay for something. But now it looked like we were going to get more than we had bargained for. I wasn't feeling so great anymore. I knew there would be no talking my way out of this one. This time Dad wouldn't show up with bail money. There would be no special first offender treatment. This time I was going to prison.

I didn't talk during the drive to the State Men's Reformatory where I would serve my sentence. In fact, I could barely think. My mind was numb. I had lived in the fast lane, craving the thrill and excitement of pulling one over on everyone else. And now I was going to prison. I had made all of the decisions that had gotten me into this mess. I knew that. But I just didn't think they would catch me. Not ever. I couldn't even imagine that a day would come that they would lock me in a cell for several years of my young life. Yet here I was, sentenced to five years behind bars.

Poppy was already at the prison when I got there. He had pled guilty sooner than I had, a month sooner in fact. When I walked in the front gate, he was waiting for me. He had already settled in to his new life. He had already hooked up with some partners and done what long term cons do, accept that this is just the way things are. Poppy was making the best of it. Good for him. But I was pretty sure it would take me a while to adapt to prison life.

Poppy and I were what they call "fall partners," meaning we took a fall together and got sent up together. He told me he would see me in the chow hall later and would make sure I got some smokes. He handed me a partial pack for the time being, and when I looked inside I saw that one of the smokes was a joint. Nice! Maybe this place wouldn't be so bad after all.

Some of the guys I saw when I walked in the door, were men I had met back at the county jail. Several of them had told me back then that they had been to this facility before and that the place was pretty laid back. They were right about that.

My cell was small, of course, but it was freshly painted. I liked that. To a kid who had spent years sleeping in a closet growing up, sleeping in a cell wasn't so bad. Even though Dad couldn't bail me out this time, he sent word that my television set would arrive in a few days. And he said he would bring me my guitar in a few weeks. Not every facility allows inmates to have their own TV and guitar, but this one did, so I started making myself at home.

It may sound a little odd, but I went into prison with money. We didn't get any cash from the tractor dealership, but I had my cash from the safe job we'd done the night before. Somehow the cops never connected the two. So with lots of money on my books, I could go to the canteen and buy just about anything I needed.

Some prisons keep you locked up most of the time and let you out only to eat, or for work, or for exercise time. But this prison had open-yard. So, when I wasn't working I could come and go pretty much as I wanted. I planned on learning my way around quickly and making contacts. I was pretty good at networking, so before long that I was smoking weed every day. I made some friends, found some partners, and started doing some serious wheeling and dealing.

Oh yeah, I also went to the weight yard and gave that a try. I discovered that I liked pumping iron. I got some bodybuilding tips from the guys who worked out every day. That afternoon, I visited the canteen and bought vitamins and protein supplements, and they really worked. I started bulking up and found that I liked the confidence that being strong and hard bodied gave me.

To my surprise, the food in the chow hall was great. On Sundays, we had either steak or ham. It was hard to complain about that. And if you had cash, you could buy a lot of things to make life on the inside less dreary. Well, you didn't actually have to have cash. The currency of the common man in prison is smokes. It's amazing how much you can buy with a pack of smokes. In fact, everything on the black market was priced in cigarettes. You were still better off with real money, though. Hard cash was worth five to one, sometimes more, which meant that I was in pretty good shape.

Maybe eight months in, I was reading in the law library one day that I could appeal my conviction. The book I was reading said that, in the meantime, I could get out of prison on what was called an appeal bond. The procedure outlined in the law book said that when your attorney files the appeal with the State Supreme Court, the Court is required to set a bond. All an inmate needed was ten percent of the amount of the bond and he could walk out the prison door a free man, pending disposition of his appeal.

My mind immediately went to work. I started writing letters to friends on the outside, asking for money. In less than a month, I had raised the bail money and was out of prison. I knew my appeal had no hope. My lawyer told me so. I had, after all, pled guilty. But it would be great to get a break from prison and then come back and finish the sentence when it was more convenient. What a deal!

Walking out the door, I could hear my buddies yelling, "Don't forget us, man... send me some money... send me some pictures of babes... find some girl to write to me." Some things never change. I assumed I would see those guys again soon enough, but for the moment I was free and helping them was the last thing on my mind.

I had been out on bond for about three weeks when I bumped into Earl. I'd met Earl when he was a volunteer counselor at the community corrections program I was assigned to for the credit card jobs. Earl and I got along well enough back then. We'd even smoked some weed together. So it was easy for us to strike up a conversation.

We talked for an hour or two, then agreed to meet again the next day. Earl said he wanted to talk over a possible job that we might be able to do together. He said he was glad he had run into me, because I'd be the perfect guy for the task he had in mind.

Earl said he had heard that I'd been sent to prison, but told me he wasn't surprised that I'd found a way out. I chuckled later about how odd it was that I had spent the afternoon with one of my former counselors, discussing doing a job together. Oh well, I was out on bond and going back inside anyway, so why not pull a caper or two while I had the chance.

A few days later, Earl and I rented a car and headed out of state to run our game. I was excited about the prospect and kept running over different ideas in my mind for how we'd pull it off. For our plan to work, I would have to make a phone call and share some damaging and embarrassing information with the person who answered the telephone. I was confident that I could do my part. I rehearsed the lines over and over until I knew exactly what I would say and how I'd say it.

I found a payphone and dialed the number. I told the guy on the other end that I knew what he had done and that there were those who would be greatly disappointed in him if they found out. I told him that calling the FBI wasn't a good idea because I had copied the stuff I had on him, and it would all be delivered to his boss and his wife if something happened to me. All he said was, "How did you find out?"

That was my first blackmail job, but I told myself that I was already pretty good at it. The guy was obviously nervous, judging by the sound of his voice, so he would likely pay up with little more than a whimper.

We set up the drop for later that night. I parked where I could watch our mark through the window where he worked. I never let him out of my sight all day long. At one point I even stood beside him in the checkout line at the drug store. He had no idea who I was or that I was the guy putting the screws to him. The poor guy had to be wondering how I had gotten my information. That question must have haunted him all afternoon. But just to be safe, I stayed close to him all day long. He had no idea that his blackmailer was sitting at the table across from his when he ate his lunch at Denny's.

The whole plan went off like clockwork. The fellow left work and went straight to the bank. He was inside for no more than ten minutes. He came out and got into his car and drove straight to the drop spot. He did exactly as he had been instructed, then drove away. I watched from a distance as his car entered the freeway onramp.

Earl and I waited anxiously in a bar across the street from the drop site. We passed the time shooting pool. From there we were we could keep an eye on the money and see if our mark returned or if the cops showed up. We watched for hours. When we were confident that it was safe, I crossed the street and picked up the bag of money.

Minutes later, my partner and I were on the freeway and headed out of town. We had pulled it off. I felt that old exhilaration, the thrill of being a smooth operator. It was the same high that in the past had faithfully landed me behind bars, and most assuredly would again. But, not that day.

Chapter 26

A Flight to Texas

E arl and I had made a clean get away and were driving toward Minneapolis. Now that we had our blackmail money in hand, my highest priority was to put some distance between Earl and me. I told him to drop me off at a hotel along the freeway. He pulled into the parking lot and we split up the money without getting out of the car. A few thousand bucks each seemed like a nice little haul for so little work.

I told my partner that we would talk in a few days, and he took off to return the rental car. I stood outside the hotel and waited for him to drive off. As soon as Earl was out of sight, I went inside and called a cab. I wanted more distance between us. I didn't want Earl to know where I was or where I was going to be staying.

You never know when someone is going to roll over on you. Sometimes they don't need a reason. They just do it. There was no way of knowing what was going on inside the head of a counselor who would pull a job with a former client. So taking my loot and getting away from Earl seemed the prudent course.

At the airport, I purchased a one-way ticket to Corpus Christi, Texas. I don't know why. It was just a faraway place. The flight was scheduled to depart early the next morning, so I had some time to kill. I took a cab to a different hotel and checked in for the night. I used the name Phillip Walker, paid cash, and ordered a four-thirty a.m. wake up call. As soon as I closed my eyes, I fell asleep and slept hard.

The moment I walked off the plane in Corpus Christi I decided that I liked Texas. At the airport, I rented a new Ford LTD and headed out in search of a hotel where I could lay low for a month or so and let things cool off. The mark had paid the money and no cops were waiting at the drop site, so chances were there would be no consequences for us. But better safe than sorry. We had blackmailed a pretty sizeable amount of cash from the guy, so you never know. He just might have backtracked his actions and contacts and somehow figured out how my partner had come across the information we'd used to make him pay up. And, getting to Earl could lead to me.

The bellman showed me to my room. It was nice. I thought to myself, *This sure beats prison*! My suite featured a large living room and a bedroom toward the back. I had a private balcony overlooking the pool and I could see the front desk from there. If someone came looking for me, I might be lucky enough to spot them before they got to my room. Just to be safe, when I checked in, I paid the rent a month in advance so I wouldn't have to spend unnecessary time in the lobby.

I had decided that it might be a good time to put everything behind me and start a new life in Mexico. I would have to think about that. I kind of liked the sound of my new name, Stewart Thomas. With a new name, I could live any place I wanted and no one would be the wiser.

I spent a lot of time that month in my sunglasses and swim-trunks, lounging beside the pool. I decided I liked this kind of life, that it suited me well.

For the moment, Minnesota, Iowa, judges, and prison all seemed far away, unlike a bunch of bad memories I desperately wanted to forget, like Church Street. The trouble was, I had little to do every day but sit and think. Sometimes I sat there by the pool and watched my entire life pass before my mind like a silent movie on fast-forward. My dad bashing my head into the wall. The sex abuse. I could never escape the pain and humiliation of that. The beatings. The County Home. Jail. Prison. More crimes than I could remember. Most of my memories were bad ones, and they were ruining my vacation in the Texas sun.

Close to fifteen years had passed since my mother was killed, seven since I had lived with my saintly grandparents in Florida. Now, here I was, living the good life sipping tropical drinks by the swimming pool of a nice hotel, yet haunted by the feeling that my life was little more than a tragic train wreck. Where would I end up? What would my mom think of me if she saw me right then and knew the things I'd done and the choices I'd made? I was pretty sure I knew the answer to that question.

And what if Earl flapped his mouth about the little caper we'd just pulled? I was out of prison on bond when we did that job. If the court ever found out about that one, they would really throw the book at me.

I told myself that it wasn't really that big a deal. It wasn't like we robbed somebody at gunpoint. The guy just paid us for our silence. Besides, the fool shouldn't have let anyone know what he had done. He did, so he had to pay up some money. It wouldn't hurt him. He had plenty of it. Well, for all I knew.

I was always conducting these internal debates and always managed to somehow rationalize the things I did. Sure, I knew that I crossed the line from time to time. But I was generous with the money I took. I bought a Christmas ham for some poor people or helped a friend if they were down and out. And I always bought drinks for folks when I was at the bar. In my estimation, those things made me a pretty good guy, compared to some.

Still, I knew my life was missing something. I just didn't know what it was. I had enough cash to get me through for quite a while. There were beautiful women sitting around the pool in their swimsuits, the tequila was good, and I had plenty of weed. What more does a guy need?

I think part of what was haunting me was the fact that this was not the kind of action and adventure I had dreamed of as a boy. I was a good guy in those dreams, doing daring things that a hero would do. There was no threat of jail or prison in my youthful fantasies. I knew that if kept living the life I was living, it was very possible that I would end up spending my life behind bars.

Finally, the boredom of lounging around all day, day after day, got to me. I decided it was time to make a call or two and find out what was going on back home. I was very careful about how I proceeded. I gave the person I talked to a little misinformation, so they wouldn't know where I really was. That way I could gauge the situation before revealing anything pertinent about myself.

The first person I called told me that Earl, sometime after he had dropped me off, was involved in a serious car accident and ended up in the hospital with a broken collarbone and a broken shoulder. One arm was in a cast and he had also broken his left leg. Apparently, Earl had been in a coma for three days before coming out of it.

Then he told me the bad part. He said that while Earl was in the hospital, they gave him some Sodium Pentothal for the pain, and while he was under its influence he started talking and saying things like, "Chuck, we never should have done it."

Apparently the FBI was told about Earl's ramblings. Great! Now the feds wanted to talk to me. That's all I needed. I hated uncertainty, so I gave the whole thing a couple of day's thought, then decided to hop in my rental car and drive up north to St. Paul.

I had a friend in town named Foster. I hadn't seen him for a few years so I gave him a call. He invited me to stay at his place while I was in town. Foster and I had met while I lived in that apartment on the strip in St. Paul. I'd even dated his niece for a while. His family referred to us as the "salt and pepper" team because she was black and I was white.

Foster's mother once told me that if we were in New Orleans, I could get myself killed for dating a black girl and running with Foster. She explained with a knowing look, that it wouldn't be a black person who killed me either; it would be my own kind.

No matter, Foster and I had been partners and friends for a long while and and I was looking forward to seeing him. Plus, I had missed St. Paul and was glad to be back.

A few nights later, Foster and I went out on the town with a couple of friends. We went to all the places we used to go, and at first the night went off without a hitch. We were shooting pool at a club and winning some money when out of nowhere the club's security showed up and told us that we had to leave. Their excuse for kicking us out was Foster's shirt. Apparently it didn't meet the dress code. Yeah, right! As if we didn't know the real reason. My friends were black and even though it was not the Deep South, they were not welcome to mix with the whites in that club.

Foster was kind of a tough guy. He was involved with some of the seedier activities in town, including prostitution, but to me he was a friend and a fun guy to hang out with.

I tried to calm him down and ease the embarrassment by telling him about the time in New Mexico when I was given plastic utensils and a paper plate while everyone else in the restaurant was served with real plates and silverware. I was the only white person in what was apparently an all-Mexican restaurant. I told Foster that I was a little embarrassed about the kind of attention I got, but stayed and finished my dinner anyway.

As we were getting into the car, I thought of the perfect way to make Foster forget the bad experience we'd just had. I let him drive my car up and down the strip a few times so all his friends could see him driving a new Ford LTD. We turned the tape player up loud and played some James Brown. We both started singing, "I Feel Good," as loud as we could, keeping time with the music. Foster liked that. It seemed to make the bad stuff fade away, at least for the moment.

We headed for another club, one where Foster and I had spent many an evening drinking, shooting pool and just hanging out. It was called the Metropolitan Club. We rang the bell on the door. Three big black guys answered and spoke to Foster.

"You are welcome to come on in," they said. Then they rolled their eyes toward me and continued, "But he has to go." Foster told them that I was all right. He explained that I had been there several times before. But they didn't budge, so we left.

Foster was not happy. He started apologizing to me for the way I'd just been treated. But it cut both ways, I told him. In one night, we had both experienced discrimination, once at the hand of whites and once at the hand of blacks. The two of us were proud of our friendship, knowing that we had broken the color barrier. So we shook our heads, got in the car, and went to pick up our dates for the evening. It probably looked odd to some, but my date was black and Foster's date was white, a really good looking blonde gal, named Kathy.

The four of us partied and danced most of the night, then decided to get some food and call it a night. We pulled up to a burger joint before going back to the house. Our plan was to eat, take the ladies back home, then sleep all day. While we stood in line waiting for our order, two men started making a big deal about us being mixed couples and saying that we should keep to our own kind. I decided to ignore what they were saying. I figured they'd been drinking and were just running their mouths. Foster, on the other hand, had had enough of the harassment. While I paid for our food, he went to the car. I thought he was just walking away from what could have been a fight.

All of a sudden, Foster jumped out of the car with a pistol in his hand and started shooting at the two guys who had been giving us a hard time. I grabbed the women and ducked for cover as bullets whizzed through the air around us. Foster emptied the clip and started to reload when a security guard appeared out of nowhere and drew down on him, yelling, "Freeze!" Caught with an empty weapon, Foster did as he was told. The guard threw cuffs on him and held him until the police arrived.

I motioned for the women to get in the car with all due haste. Then the three of us drove off before we attracted any unwanted attention. There wasn't anything we could do for Foster at the moment. I dropped his niece off at home, but I had no idea what to do with his white, blonde haired girlfriend, Kathy. With Foster in jail, she had no place to stay.

Chapter 27

California Run

The last thing I needed while I was out of prison on bond was to be associated with any kind of gunplay. I was seriously afraid of that kind of heat, so I decided to get out of town for a while. I headed for Fargo, North Dakota. As I mentioned earlier, that's where I had earlier joined the Marine Corp, or tried to.

Kathy had no place to stay, so she went with me. I called from Fargo to see what had happened to Foster. His mother told me that her son was still in jail and would stay there at least until his court date. I asked her to give him a message from me and hung up the phone.

Foster's girlfriend Kathy was a looker, the kind of woman every guy notices. We stayed in North Dakota for a day or two, then decided to head for California together. Kathy didn't say much about her background and I didn't ask. Besides, we were just traveling partners.

To be honest, I didn't bother telling Kathy what kind of mess I was in. No reason to unload all of our dirty laundry on each other. Just for the record, I later learned that Kathy too was using a fake name.

Somewhere in the middle of Montana we spotted two young guys hitchhiking. Their little cardboard sign said they were trying to make it to California. We decided to stop and pick them up, just for fun. They told us they had just graduated from high school and were making the "trip of their dreams." My first reaction was that California was a long way for two young kids like this to travel, especially hitchhiking. Then it dawned on me that I had made the same trip when I was their age, with Barbara's brother Walter.

I'm sure those two kids didn't know what to make of Kathy and me. We were driving a brand new car, had all the weed we wanted, and were living like two people with a lot of money. Neither of them could stop staring at Kathy. She was a knockout blonde and knew it. She enjoyed the attention they were giving her and played along with their game.

I thought it was kind of funny. Kathy wasn't really my girl, so what did I care if she flirted with these two kids just for fun. I couldn't help but think that, down the road, these two would have a pretty good story to tell their friends about their dream trip to California. I was pretty sure Kathy would get better looking every time they told it.

Eventually we made it to California. Standing on the beach looking out over the ocean, I liked the feel of the sea breeze blowing in my face. I hadn't thought about my troubles for a few days now, but as often happened when things got quiet, those thoughts began to return. I started having heavy duty, bare wire conversations with myself again. On top of that, I felt a serious migraine coming on. Deep cogitations tended to do that to me.

Kathy came over and stood next to me, unknowingly diverting my attention from the troubling thoughts. She had starting acting differently toward me the last day or two, like she was my girl. She was always hanging on me, laying her head on my shoulder or holding my hand. I wasn't sure if it was for real or if she was performing for the boys' benefit. Either way, I was finding her on my mind way more than I wanted. Kathy was Foster's girl. That made her off limits. It was best that I remember that.

We had made it to California just as we had planned, but once we were there I wasn't quite sure what to do next. Our hitchhiker friends didn't seem to be in any hurry to part ways with us, so for no particular reason we continued hanging together.

I decided that I would like a little time to myself, so I called the two kids over.

"Why don't you guys go down the beach and hang out with Kathy?" I suggested. They both stared at me with surprised looks on their faces, glanced at one other, grinned sheepishly, then took off in her direction. That made me laugh. They had the same puppy love expression on their faces that I'd probably worn when I'd looked at a certain high school English teacher I had once considered to be the most beautiful woman on earth.

After a while the three of them came back to the car and we got back on the freeway. I was doing my best to keep up with those speedy southern California drivers when out of nowhere I saw a highway patrol car come up behind me. I was going the same speed as everyone else, so, not wanting to look suspicious, I kept moving with the traffic and didn't slow down.

As you might imagine, a guy with my kind of history gets nervous when there's a cop car right behind him. I glanced in the rearview mirror, signaled, then switched lanes and took the next exit. He did too. He stayed behind me for quite some time before eventually turning on his lights. My heart, which was already pounding, started racing. I was being pulled over.

I told myself to keep cool, that this was just a routine traffic stop and nothing to worry about. If I would just act normal, everything would be okay.

I signaled and pulled over to the side of the road. The tension in my gut was all too familiar. I had been here before. The officer came to the driver's window and asked me if I knew why I had been pulled over.

"No sir," I replied. I handed him the driver's license I had. It was a pretty good fake. He took it and walked back to his squad car.

The boys in the backseat didn't know what was going on with me, but I knew that this was going to go one of two ways. If my ID passed, I would be all right. At least that's what I thought. If it didn't pass muster, I was going to jail.

We were sitting there, waiting for the officer to come back with my license, when another cop car pulled up. All of my instincts told me that this was not going to end well.

I told the guys in the back that if they wanted to get out of this unscathed, they needed to sit still and do whatever the cops told them to do. The next thing we knew, there were officers with shotguns surrounding us. I had been through this routine before, but I have to tell you, it's not something a guy ever gets used to. The hole in the end of a shotgun barrel is large and rather ominous looking when it's pointed at your head.

The cops ordered me out of the car and onto the ground. One officer held a gun on me while another handcuffed me, telling me in that cop voice that I was under arrest. I looked over and saw that Kathy was in handcuffs too. I didn't know if this was about the blackmail job or something else, but whatever it was, these guys meant business.

I told the police that the boys were hitchhikers and not with me, so they treated them well. Even with that, for a while the four of us were all lying face down on the side of the road in cuffs. For a normal person that would be a once, or never in a lifetime experience, so no matter how this ended for them, our hitchhiker friends would have some story to tell their friends.

Eventually I was told what the arrest was about. If I had just bothered to call the car rental company in Texas and extend my rental time, I would not have been picked up in California. But when I never showed up with their car and never bothered to call and check in, they reported it stolen. I couldn't really blame them for that. If I had been thinking a little clearer, none of this would have happened and I would have wound up in Mexico living it up. Instead, I served ninety days in the Los Angeles County Jail on federal interstate theft charges and got five years' probation.

After serving my time in California, I headed back to Minnesota. When I got there, there was a letter from my lawyer at my dad's house. The court had decided that my appeal had no merit. There was really no surprise in that.

I had enjoyed my six-month vacation, while it lasted. Well, except for the three months I'd spent in a California jail. Seeing no real alternative at that point, I checked myself back in at the prison to finish my sentence and get that out of the way.

I had lots of stories to tell the guys once I was back inside. Inmates with no lives of their own like to live vicariously through the stories they hear from guys who have recently been on the outside.

Before long, I got a job working in the prison furniture shop. The foreman was a nice enough man and we got along well. His name was Bill and I'd heard that he was some kind of minister on Sundays. Bill and I discovered that we shared an interest in honeybees, so we spent a lot of time talking about that and I ended up liking the guy. Bill had a lot of stories to share. He talked about God sometimes and made references to the Bible from time to time. He kind of reminded me of Grandfather Mausolf, my mom's dad. He too was always telling stories about God and Jesus, and talking about religious stuff. I listened and was respectful.

Some of the other guys in the shop were rude to the guy. They didn't care for the things he talked about. As for me, I kind of felt sorry for him for getting picked on so much. But if the harassment bothered him, I couldn't tell it. He seemed completely unfazed.

Kathy started writing to me in prison. The police had let her go shortly after we were arrested. My name was the only one on the LTD rental agreement in Texas, so they had no evidence that Kathy was involved. The name on the rental agreement matched my fake driver's license, so it took the cops a while to discover that I was not that guy. Eventually, however, my fingerprints gave me away.

Anyway, Kathy kept me up to speed with what was going on back in Minnesota. The two of us had become pretty good friends on our adventure out west so it was nice getting mail from her. It's nice getting mail from almost anyone when you are locked up. Well, usually.

One day I got a letter from Kathy and opened it with my normal anticipation. But the first thing I read was that Foster had been shot in the head at a bar. The letter said he had stepped in to break up a fight between two people he knew. One of them pulled out a pistol and shot Foster six times. One of the bullets struck him in the head and the doctors were not sure he would make it.

Bad news in prison is often worse than bad news on the outside. In prison you feel especially helpless about things happening on the outside because there is usually nothing you can do about it. You are stuck in your own little world, which consists of surviving another day and hopefully getting another pack of cigarettes. Bad news makes you sit and think until you find in it a new reason to feel sorry for yourself.

Then one day I got a surprise, some really good news. The Iowa parole board had decided to release me early. I was anxious to get out of that place and on with my life, so I started making plans. I hoped to start over in Minnesota with no one looking for me. That would be great. I already had a part-time job lined up and I was thinking about buying a mobile home. All I wanted to do for a while was lay low and mind my own business. I had had my fill of trouble with the law.

There was, however, one part of my release that I was not looking forward to. I would have to have an immediate meeting with my old parole officer, the same lady who was in charge of me back when I was on probation for the credit card scam. I was sure that woman lived just to make my life difficult.

Chapter 28

Helen and a Baby Girl

Shortly after I got back to Minnesota, I found a job working at a gas station, and after some searching, a house trailer that would suit my needs just fine. The trailer was pretty nice for the money, so I bought it, cleaned it up, and began furnishing it. Dad and Susan helped me add some fresh paint and drapes. The trailer park was just a few minutes' drive from my work, so I had no complaints.

My brother John came over one evening with some of his friends. He brought his new girlfriend along. We turned on some music and the bunch of us had a house warming party in my little singlewide trailer. Life seemed good and thoughts of prison began to fade from my memory.

My home was actually pretty comfortable. I had some money saved and was feeling good about how far I'd come. But, for the life of me, I couldn't shake the feeling that my life was a dismal failure. I told myself that having your mother murdered when you are a little kid would mess with anyone's mind. But I knew there was more to it than that.

I was at home one night, watching TV alone, when it occurred to me to give Helen, this gal I used to know, a call and see what she was up to. When she answered, I asked if she wanted to get together to talk about old times and maybe go out or something. She accepted, and that weekend we went out. Helen started talking about when I'd dated her sister. She asked me if I thought her sister was prettier than she was. What could I say? Apparently she was satisfied with my answer because we went to dinner and a movie that night. That was it, nothing else. I drove her home afterward, and didn't talk to her again for about a month.

Then one day, she and a friend of hers showed up at my trailer. Out of the blue, Helen wanted to know what I thought about her becoming my roommate and moving in with me. I asked what she meant by "roommate," referring of course to sleeping arrangements. We cleared that up and she moved in with me the next week.

Helen was a little homemaker and immediately put some feminine touches on the trailer, making it downright homey. It was pretty much like being married. I would come home for lunch every day and then every night we would have supper together. We would smoke some weed, drink a little wine, and listen to my only record, Meat Loaf's album, "Bat out of Hell." We knew every song on the album by heart.

One impulsive weekend, not long after my twenty-seventh birthday, we decided to take a road trip to Illinois and get married. We let some people know what we were going to do, and they planned a celebration party for when we returned. Our plan hit a major snag when we had a big blowup while we were on our way there. We decided to call the wedding off and just head home.

The not getting married part didn't bother me so much, but I had driven hundreds of miles in a snowstorm with a woman who'd made me so mad I could have busted her upside the head, just like I'd seen my dad do to my mom more times than I could remember. The mouth on that girl! I couldn't believe the things she said and the way she acted. It was almost like she wanted me to slap her or something.

I thought about leaving her and her mouth at a truck stop and driving off, but I felt sorry for her and kept driving. All she did after that, for mile after mile, was stare out the window. I was sitting behind the wheel, sulking and steaming, when it slowly dawned on me that there was a hurting and troubled girl inside this woman sitting next to me.

That was hardly the first time I'd found myself feeling sorry for someone else who'd had a hard life. I knew what it felt like to be hurt and abused. It was kind of confusing being a tough guy with a tender streak that just kind of showed up uninvited from time to time and messed with my head.

Eventually, we calmed down and continued on our way back home, still single of course. We hadn't been home ten minutes when the telephone rang. It was one of our friends congratulating us for getting married. I didn't tell him otherwise. I had barely hung up the receiver when there was a knock at the door. When I opened it, a whole bunch of people flooded into our little trailer. The marriage celebration party was apparently still on.

Helen and I exchanged glances, shrugged our shoulders, and without mentioning the fact that we didn't actually get married, joined the festivities. Our little masquerade continued completely undetected by any of our friends, and then that June, the two of us sneaked off, found a judge, and tied the knot officially.

The following October our daughter Jacqueline was born. We barely made it to the hospital in time. I drove like a mad man, honking the horn and driving through red lights. Our little girl was born fifteen minutes later, which was cutting it a bit close.

Our daughter was a cutie pie, and for me it was love at first sight. I couldn't get enough of holding her. The day we brought her home from the hospital marked the beginning of a really happy time for me. Every night and on weekends I spent hours holding my little girl, kissing her and loving her. With the birth of our daughter, Helen and I started a new chapter in our relationship; we started making plans to move into a bigger house in the spring.

Things were looking pretty good, but that was only because I couldn't see the dark clouds forming up ahead.

Chapter 29

Under Arrest–Again

Not long after we moved into our new house I began to notice that Helen and I couldn't get along unless we were either smoking weed or had people over. There were still struggles going on inside my head and sometimes the battle would rage for days. There were good times, for sure, and I loved our baby girl immensely. But, eventually I would find myself angry and resentful at the thought of living the rest of my life with a wife I couldn't stand.

Helen was always talking smack and doing her best to start a fight. That made me want to leave. Having a child together, however, complicated things, so I wasn't sure what to do. I finally came to the conclusion that I'd married Helen more because I felt sorry for her than because I loved her, or even liked her.

I sometimes smacked Helen upside the head to shut her up, but it never worked. She just kept blabbing. I know, it wasn't right to hit her, but we were in a situation that neither of us knew how to handle. We were both just acting on instinct and in my case, probably following the example my dad had set. There was no telling where this messed up relationship was headed, except that it probably wouldn't end well.

One day, I spent the afternoon with my buddy Rich in the back room of his liquor store. We were reloading pistol shells. Rich had a nice little setup going. He sold booze up front and guns in the back. The funny thing was, the same federal agency was in charge of both. Rich had a license to sell liquor and a federal firearms license so he could sell guns, too.

I would kid Rich about how much he had "the man" all up in his business. Neither of us had any love for the Bureau of Alcohol, Tobacco, and Firearms. Both of us were under the impression that all they wanted to do was take away our guns. If you've ever seen the poster that says, "Alcohol, Tobacco, and Firearms Should Be a Convenience Store, Not a Government Agency," that pretty much describes our philosophy regarding such things.

The way we saw it, with the Contras losing to the commies in El Salvador, it wouldn't be long until we would need to defend our homes from the Communist hordes coming north. Yeah, I know, that was a little nuts, but if they did come, we were definitely ready. We had been buying guns and ammo for quite some time. Plus, in our storage we had several gas masks, extra clothes, and enough food and water to last for a few years.

As for weapons, I had a forty-five semi-auto handgun with hollow points and a 12-gauge shotgun with double-aught buckshot for close encounters. Oh, and a .223 mini fourteen for targets further away. Let 'em come, was my attitude, 'cause we were ready.

Rich had just been to a gun show where he had picked up some British practice ammo. He thought we could reload them after they were fired. Never mind the fact that the Brits used these shells on the practice range, and once they were fired threw them away. Rich brought home a few thousand rounds. That meant we could shoot a few rounds to test them, and if they worked out, we would have a lot more bullets to add to our supply.

That particular day, I stopped off at the house just long enough to say hello, hold my daughter for a while, have a sandwich and wash it down with a cup of coffee. I got my forty-five out, slid it into my waistband, and with some shells in my pocket went outside to do some target practicing. I walked about fifty feet and placed a target in the firing range. As I turned to walk back to the shooting area, I noticed that there was something unusual going on up the road.

Rich's tavern and gun shop was just up the road from my house, and I could see what looked to be something like thirty cops getting ready to raid the place. They appeared to be getting into position, so I knew that something big was about to go down. It occurred to me that maybe I should get in the car and drive by, and if possible warn the people in the tavern of what was about to happen. Before getting in the car, I ducked back into the house, took my gun off and put it away, then emptied my pockets of the cartridges I was carrying. I grabbed my keys and headed for the car.

Our house sat about sixty feet off the highway, and there were railroad tracks between the road and our home. I crossed the tracks, but as soon as I'd turned toward the highway, three or four police cars with lights flashing surrounded me, blocking me in. Cops stepped out from behind bushes and trees. Talk about déjà vu all over again. Once again, I found myself surrounded by cops, all of them with guns pulled and pointed right at me.

I was shocked. There was a small army of law enforcement personnel intent on apprehending me. Frankly, I had no idea why the police would come after me with such a show of force. I couldn't think of a single thing I had done.

One of the officers approached my window with a shotgun pointed at my face and yelled, "Get out of the car!"

Another came from behind the car on my side. He was carrying a revolver and looked ready for action. I saw him approaching through my rear view mirror. When he got close, he too started yelling, "Get out of the car, hands up! Don't move! Out of the car, now! Show me your hands! Show me your hands!"

I wasn't sure what to do. I didn't want to get shot. The problem was I had my foot on the brake so the car wouldn't move, but it was still in drive. My hands were in the air so the cops could see them, but if I took my foot off the brakes to get out of the car, it would immediately start rolling forward. People get killed for nothing in situations like that. I knew that, and was most definitely scared.

Under my breath I whispered, "Stay cool, Chuck. Don't move a muscle. Just wait. Don't get yourself shot by some trigger happy, rookie cop."

When the cop with the shotgun leaned in and put the gun right in my face, I meekly told him that the car was in gear.

"Out of the car," he yelled even louder. The barrel of his shotgun was frighteningly close to my head. I wasn't sure what to do. I knew of more than one guy who had been shot by a nervous cop even while he was trying to cooperate.

"The car is in gear!" I yelled back. Speaking calmly hadn't worked, so this time I let the panic I was feeling come through.

Fortunately, another cop opened the passenger side door and reached in and turned off the engine while the officers on my side kept their weapons trained on me.

"Don't move or I'll blow your head off," one of them yelled.

Sheesh! Calm down, boys. All I'm doing is cooperating.

As soon as the engine stopped, the officers dragged me out of the car and unceremoniously threw me to the ground. Instantly four or five officers jumped on top of me and one held his pistol against my ear.

"Don't move! You're under arrest. Where are the guns? Where are your _____ guns? Where are your automatic weapons?"

I didn't answer the officer's questions about the location of my guns, so two of them grabbed me by the arms and pulled me to my feet. They thoroughly searched me, and then all but threw me into the backseat of one of the patrol cars. As the car started to pull out onto the highway, I looked back. There was my little girl in her mother's arms. My little Jacqueline was crying uncontrollably. It felt like my heart was being ripped from my chest!

An hour or two later I was lying on a bunk in a jail cell staring at the ceiling. Depression hung over me like a dark cloud. I hated my life. I really hated my life. And I hated myself. In the past hour, all of my dreams and plans had gone down the drain, right before my eyes. I would lose my new home. I would probably lose my baby girl. That was the hardest part. I felt so bad for little Jacqueline. She looked so frightened.

There was no one to bail me out of this one. Even if I could get bail, and I doubted that, Dad would not want to come anywhere near this situation. I was certain that my parole officer had already had her fill of me, so there would be no help there. There was simply no way she was helping me get out of jail. It looked like I was going up the river for the long haul. I drifted off to sleep that night feeling sorry for myself, wishing I was anyplace but where I was. Inmates do that a lot.

The jailers kept me in a cell by myself for three weeks, which got old really fast. I asked to be moved, but all I ever heard back was, "Wait and see."

I had a pretty bad view of guards to start with. In my mind, guards were wannabe cops who couldn't make it as real cops. They still thought they were something, though. Big men at work, and then when they went home they slapped around the old lady and the kids. That was my opinion back then. That's all I'm saying. Lots of inmates think the same way, right or wrong.

To make matters worse, there was this guy down the hall in another cell, yelling all day long, pounding on the walls and carrying on. Seems there's one or two bad eggs like him in every jail. It's like they spend their days and nights making sure nobody else gets any sleep. I intended to deal with him when I got a chance.

I hated jail and all of the games the inmates and guards play, but there I was again, right smack in the middle of it again. Of course I had no one to blame but myself. I was a felon and yet had guns and bullets all over my house. A felon possessing one shotgun shell, even without a gun to fire it, can go to prison for five years. Actually, it's a state and federal crime, so if the feds are the ones ringing you up, you can get ten years.

I had ignored the law. I had flaunted it, actually. So this was my mess and no one else's. That's the part that hurt the most. I did this.

The depression set in full strength. I missed my baby girl. I wondered if little Jacqueline missed her daddy. I suspected I wouldn't see her again for a long time, if ever. I wondered how long it would take for her to forget me completely.

After a few long weeks, they moved me into a cellblock with other inmates. At least I could play some cards to pass the time, and have room to walk around. From my new cell I could stand on the bars and see the street. I could see cars and trucks passing by, and people walking around free. How I longed to be out there. I hate sounding like an emotional baby, but sometimes being alone in a cell has its benefits. You can cry and bury your face in a pillow and no one is the wiser.

One night, I was completely overwhelmed by the hopelessness of my situation. It was all more than I could bear. I pressed my face into my pillow to muffle the sounds and sobbed like a baby. I cried uncontrollably. My pillow was soon soaked with snot and tears. I forced myself to take only short breaths. My chest heaved up and down and my stomach ached with the pain of trying to hold it all in. I was overcome that night by a powerful, dark depression and the weight of just how sorry I was feeling for myself. Toward the end of the outburst I could feel a powerful migraine coming on.

No one must see or hear you doing this, Chuck. Inmates can spot weakness. Don't show any. Shake it off, Chuckie Boy! Shake it off!

Finally, I got a hold of myself. I stood up and went over to my little sink and washed my face. I walked over to the door and looked out, trying to see if anyone had heard me sobbing. It looked like I was in the clear, the best I could tell.

A few days later, late in the middle of the night, the jailers brought in three new inmates who had been assigned to our cellblock. Those punks were up all night long shuffling and banging decks of cards on the steel tables. It was all but impossible to sleep. I rolled over twice and asked them to keep the noise down. That didn't work. Later on they started wrestling and engaging in other rowdy horse play. By that time, I was really ticked, but I decided I would wait until morning to deal with them.

I'd had enough trouble sleeping with the battle that had been going on in my head for the past few weeks and these guys were sending me over the edge. All night long I lay there, thinking about how I was going to deal with these guys come morning. Trouble was brewing for those punks – they had no idea.

As soon as breakfast was served, I walked over to the table where they were sitting and demanded, "Which of you punks kept me awake all night?" No one answered.

I asked one more time and got the same result. So I busted one of them upside the head. I took his breakfast and walked over to the other two sissies and took theirs, too. I was definitely feeling cranky. Then I told them that they were evicted and to get out of my cellblock. They ran to the door and started banging loudly and calling for the guard.

The guard came to the door and asked what all the noise was about. They told him that they were kicked out of the cellblock and needed to move now. I thought it was kind of funny when the guard answered, "You boys stay in there with Chuck and don't bother me anymore." They were significantly more thoughtful after that.

To my surprise and delight, Helen came to visit me and brought little Jacqueline with her. I can't express the joy I felt when I got to see and hold my little girl again. That child was the light of my life. Helen seemed genuinely happy to see me, too, so it was about as good as a family visit can get.

Helen came back several times during the four months I sat waiting for my trial. Those visits meant the world to me and helped break the cycle of depression I was trapped in. I started hoping again.

My felon in possession trial lasted four days; in the process, my attorney fees drained away all the money I had saved. By the time the jury went into deliberations, I had been sitting in jail for four months. Now I just wanted it to be over. I had been there long enough. I hated jail and everything about it. I was sure I would be found guilty, so I might as well get to prison and face the music.

The night before the verdict came in, I had this dream that felt amazingly real. In the dream my dad and some of the guys came crashing through the gates and broke me out. I was going to make my escape across the Mississippi River and then hop a freight train heading south. I was going to head down to Central America and join up with the Contras.

As soon as I woke up, the reality of my situation jumped up and climbed all over me. No one was going to save me. In fact, it was downright ridiculous to think my dad was coming to my rescue. The only time he had ever helped me was when I went in for the credit card scam, and he probably only did that because he was afraid I might rat on him and Susan if he didn't.

My lawyer came to see me while the jury was still deliberating. He told me that the longer the jury was out the better my chances were of being found "not guilty." At that time, it was nearly ten o'clock at night and I was starting to feel pretty sure of myself. Every few minutes after that I asked the jailer if he'd heard anything about my case. All he ever said was, "The jury is still deliberating."

Good, I thought. I'd beat the rap. I was sure I'd be out of there soon.

No sooner had that thought crossed my mind when the guard came to my cell to get me.

"The jury is back with a verdict," he said.

A guard took me to the courtroom at eleven-thirty that night to stand in front of the judge and learn my fate. My hope was running high. The judge asked the foreman if the jury had reached a verdict.

The foreman stood and replied with a clear, unapologetic voice, "Yes, your honor. We find the defendant guilty as charged."

I was sentenced to 46 months in the state penitentiary.

Chapter 30

State Prison

T he walk up the concrete steps to the Stillwater state prison was the longest, most painful walk of my life. I was handcuffed with my hands behind my back and had shackles around my ankles. The stainless steel cuffs hurt. They were too tight and dug into my wrists. As I climbed the steps, a guard walked beside me and held my arm, otherwise I'm sure I would have fallen.

I can think of few things more humiliating than being out in public dressed in jail garb and having to take tiny steps because of leg shackles. The pain I felt that day actually had little to do with the shackles and cuffs. It was more the hopelessness and despair that came with knowing that I was going to do 46 lonely months of hard time in a really tough joint.

The prison that I would call home for the next three or four years looked like a dark, foreboding castle out of some medieval movie. The walls were constructed of cold gray granite. Large iron bars adorned every window. Once I was inside, the heavy iron door slammed shut and the steel locking mechanism slid noisily into place behind me. I felt that sound all the way down to the depths of my soul. I knew what that sound meant. I was once again being caged like an animal.

Voices in my mind were laughing at me and ridiculing me. The fear that I'd felt in the past, when walking into a new prison or jail, climbed up on my shoulder and whispered in my ear. "Look straight ahead, Chuck. Don't look anyone in the eyes. Stand up tall. Don't let them see your fear. Fear is weakness to them. Walk like a man."

I stood in the middle of the center turnkey with thick glass surrounding me. The door behind me led to freedom. The one in front led to the inside of the prison. Behind the glass, guards were looking over my papers. There was still hope.

Maybe this was as far as it would go. They were going to discover their mistake any minute and let me go. I wasn't hurting anyone with my guns. They know that. They wouldn't really lock me up for three years, at taxpayer expense, just for having a few guns.

My heart sunk and all hope faded when the gate in front of me opened. Two guards, who from the look of them would rather have been somewhere else, led me to the inmate receiving area and began processing me into the institution. I hated the look of the place, the smell and the sounds. Everything was loud and noisy. My emotions were running wild, but I did my best to remain outwardly calm.

Processing completed, I was given prison issue clothes, a new pair of government made shoes, some toiletries, two towels, and a set of sheets that were so thin from wear that I could literally see through them. From there, I was led down a long hallway to my cellblock.

The cellblock they put me in housed three hundred plus men. I walked past cell after cell, all the way to the far end of the block, then up two flights of stairs to the place I would call home for the foreseeable future. The door opened and I was told to go inside. The door closed behind me. As the guard turned to leave I asked him, "What's next?"

"Next? There is no next," he said. "Make yourself at home."

The cell was filthy. The sink and toilet were plugged and the floor looked like it had not been cleaned in a very long time. Fortunately, there was a broom and cleaning supplies waiting for me in the cell. Without even bothering to sit down on my bunk, I went to work cleaning my "house." About the time I finished, a porter came to my cell door to deliver a sack lunch. I had arrived too late for chow that evening, so this would be my supper.

I was actually glad that I didn't have to leave my cell that first evening. When the lights went out for the night, the place became very quiet and somber. I lay there, alone in my thoughts. Eventually, I buried my face in the pillow so no one would hear me and began to sob quietly.

There would be no phone calls, and no one coming over to the house to visit. There would be no little Jacqueline to hug and kiss. It was just me and this hard bunk and four grey, dirty walls.

Before I eventually fell asleep, my grandmother's words came back to me, something she'd said more than once when I lived with her and

Grandpa down in Florida, "You made your own bed, Chuck. Now sleep in it." Her words had been wiser and more prophetic than I'd realized.

When you're locked up, the first few nights are the hardest. It takes a while to accept the reality of where you are and the hopelessness of it all. My eyes were wet a lot. My nose needed blowing most of the time. But if I was going to cry like a baby it was critically important than no one hear me. More so than in county jail. This was the big house. This place was hard core.

I eventually got used to the routine and settled into my new digs. With that, time started to move a little faster. By the time I'd been in for six months, I had become about as comfortable as one could get while locked up. I had a television and a stereo in my cell. From time to time, I cooked my own food in my cell, using the coffee pot. I only did that when I wasn't up to going to the dining hall to eat slop with a bunch of thugs and losers – like me.

I landed a sweet job working in the prison tractor shop, which made the time pass faster and even gave me a little extra money. On top of that, I hooked up with some guys and was able to enjoy some extracurricular recreational substance abuse.

One particular morning, some of the boys and I were going to spend the rest of the day tripping on some blotter acid. So I locked my cell door with a padlock and headed out for breakfast with my buddies. Out of nowhere some guy walked up beside me and called me a punk snitch.

I recognized him as a guy from a halfway house I'd been in some time back. I didn't give it much thought at first. The guy had been a sissy back at the halfway house and no doubt was one here, too. I knew he was a punk because I had punched him in the face back then for running his mouth on me. Maybe he needed some more. I could do that, if necessary.

After chow, I was headed back toward our cell hall when one of the guys from our group came up and whispered in my ear, "You have to kill that punk that called you a snitch, or you have to move out of the cell next to mine. You can't even walk with us until you kill that punk!"

Just like that, this became no small problem. It was something I had to take care of today. In prison, word travels fast. Being called a punk and not doing anything about it meant you were indeed a punk. Well, I wasn't going to be anybody's punk, so I started making plans.

I stood in my cell, waiting for morning count to end. They were always counting us, several times a day. If anyone was missing they would quickly know and the whole place would go into lockdown. I stood with my hands on the bars of my cell door, thinking that only two hours earlier I'd been doing okay. Now I was stuck with having to kill a man for running his mouth on me.

Inside, my guts were tight. I didn't like the position I was in. Pounding this punk wasn't a problem. Hanging out in bars and running with tough guys like I had, I had punched out my share of big mouths. The thing was, my personality was actually kind of polite. Sometimes I was even kind. Then invariably some guy would mistake my politeness for weakness and make a move on me. When that happened, I would have no choice but to let loose on him and bust his head. Then after it was over, I would feel that somehow the whole thing was my fault.

There were two rules at the group meetings in the program where I had met this guy: No violence, and no threats of violence. That was why guys like him would sometimes get away with running their mouths. They always had the group leader or some authority figure protecting them.

The more I thought about it, the more I actually wanted to bust this punk's head. But the thing was, I had to find a way to do it and not get caught. I wasn't going to kill him. If I wanted to kill somebody there were others on my list way ahead of this guy. In any event, I had to do something and it had to be rough enough to make the point, or I might be next.

When the buzzer sounded after count, I moved quickly to get into position to take care of business. I had to be careful so no one suspected that I was about to make a move. I walked out into the main flow of people and waited. There he was on the other side of the hall, not too far away. He was acting like he was some kind of tough guy. Sometimes cons act like that just to bluff others away from them.

I picked up my pace until I drew up beside him. When he turned to see who was walking so close, I swung my fist and nailed him squarely in the nose, hitting him as hard as I could. Then I went down on top of him and pounded his face into the floor two or three times. The whole thing lasted less than five seconds.

I was on my feet and back into the flow before the guards made it to where the guy was lying. He was bleeding all over himself and crying like the sissy he was. A guard helped him to his feet.

Run your mouth on me, punk. How does it feel, big mouth? You better call your momma.

The guy knew better than to be a prison rat. Snitches don't fare too well behind bars. More importantly, none of my friends said anything about me not killing the guy. I had taken care of business well enough to satisfy my honor, so with that, it was once again okay for me to hang with them.

I should make something clear. Prisons like Stillwater are a very scary place. Look the wrong guy in the eye and he might let you off with, "What you looking at, punk." Or he might smash you in the face. If he's a lifer with nothing to lose, he might stick a glass or plastic shiv in you and break it off so you can't pull it out, then stand there and watch you bleed to death.

Cons are in prison for a reason, and some are downright scary dudes. Cons get raped. They get beat up real bad, sometimes by one guy and sometimes by a gang of guys. Cons mug you on your way back from the commissary and steal all of your stuff.

When people have nothing to lose, they are sometimes more dangerous than a caged animal. And they are creative in the ways they attack. I remember a guy who broke up some of the disposable razors we were all issued and inserted pieces of the steel blades under his fingernails. Then when he got close to the guy he was after, he reached out and slashed him hard across the face, leaving five severe gashes across the guy's cheek, nose and mouth. It was a bloody mess. It's probably safe to assume that the guy carried those scars for the rest of his life.

Incidents like that are why it's so important that when you accidently bump into someone, you quickly apologize and make it clear that you meant no disrespect. Respect is a big thing in prison. Disrespect can cost you money or a shake down, or it can get you beat down or worse.

Probably the last two things you'd want to be called in prison are a snitch or a child molester. Life expectancy for either can be fairly short. The convict code is what it is, and best you learn it quickly, lest you die of ignorance.

Let me just say that I learned quickly enough not to let my guard down, and leave it at that. People died while I was there. Trust me, I could tell you stories, but you probably wouldn't want to hear them.

All humility aside, I could hold my own in a fight, but it was my personality to be more of a schemer and a dealmaker who avoided confrontations, when possible. Once it became known that I could be a scrapper when I had to, I had some respect.

About a year into my "visit," I got lucky. Somehow, I landed one of the most coveted jobs in the joint, working at the canteen and commissary. I loved it. With control of so much coveted stuff, I saw opportunity knocking. All I needed was a plan. In this prison, like all the others, the currency or medium of exchange was anything of value. Cash money was worth five or ten to one, but cigarettes, coffee, and stamped envelopes were prized commodities. People used those items to trade, and there I was working in the Fort Knox of the prison.

I was in charge of case after case of cigarettes and coffee stacked clear up to the ceiling. All I had to do was figure out how to get my hands on some of it. One evening I came up with a plan. What I came up with required a partner on the trash crew, so I found someone who could hook me up with a solid contact.

The next day I was sitting in my cell watching TV and smoking a joint when someone walked up to my cell and told me to look over the railing. He said someone wanted to talk to me. So I wouldn't look like a punk that people could boss around, I took my time going to the rail. When I finally looked over, I saw my soon-to-be partner, Chief Lacy.

The man they called Chief was a big man. He was tall and ugly, with lots of dark tattoos. He had been a guest at this prison for many years. Chief motioned with his eyes for me to come down. On the way down I whispered to myself, "This is one scary looking dude."

I had heard about this guy. Word was, Chief was one of the most feared and respected men in the institution. Supposedly he was in the joint for kidnapping some guy and then killing him by skinning him. He was a nice enough fellow, if you never crossed him. But underneath beat the heart of a stone-cold killer.

Prison is a noisy place, with people talking and yelling all the time. There's always noise over the loudspeakers announcing lock down, lock out, chow line, or sick call. It's the times when there is no noise that make you nervous. For example, when someone is going to be killed or has just been killed, prison becomes eerily silent. If there is a suicide by hanging or someone dives head first off the top tier, killing himself, it tends to sober everyone up for a few moments, and for a while, quiet reigns.

Evening lock down on the other hand is almost always quiet. If there is too much talking, other cons will yell out, warning you to shut up. Sleep passes time better than anything else and cons do not like having their sleep disturbed.

Holidays tend to be quiet, as well. During the holiday season, cons get emotional, missing families and loved ones. You always have to be careful about accidentally pushing some inmate's buttons, but much more so during the holidays.

As for the Chief, I knew who the guy was and how to talk to him. That's not to say that I wasn't a little nervous the whole time. But the two of us eventually came to an agreement, and before long we were doing business. After a while I had to admit that I kind of liked the dude. The cons feared and respected him. When he walked down the hallway, cons instinctively moved out of his way. But me, I was the man's "friend," so the more other cons feared him, the safer I felt.

Twice a week, when the trash was set out from the canteen, some of the bags weren't actually trash. They contained the loot I had set aside. Chief would take it from there. While the guard was driving the trash truck to the next stop, Chief would find the stash and hide it until the end of the day. Then he would bring it into the cell hall where we would store it.

We had so many cartons of smokes that we had to have other people keep them in their cells for us. The same went for coffee and envelopes. We were "prison rich." A month later, we expanded our network when we worked out a deal with a guy on the lower galley who ran a two-for-one store from his cell.

The lower galley guy was a real prison entrepreneur. He could sell you just about anything you wanted, and he cooked the best fried ham and cheese sandwich in the joint. How could he cook sandwiches in his cell, one might ask. Well, he had the ham and cheese smuggled to him from the kitchen and he cooked them on an iron he'd ripped off from the laundry.

A lot of the people in prison were players on the outside, so if you took your eye off them for a second, or assumed they couldn't possibly do something, they would find a way to take advantage of the opening you'd left them. As for me, I was a player, too. I had found a way to make my life on the inside more comfortable than it otherwise would have been. Well, for the time being anyway.

There were other advantages to working in the canteen. On paydays, the line to buy stuff was long. Sometimes, inmates would have to wait in line for hours to spend their monthly pay. I knew who the leaders of the gangs were and I made sure that they never had to stand in line and wait. As soon as I saw one of those guys enter the area, I would push their order slip to the front so they were in and out fast. I played every angle I could, and the favors were repaid in kind. In exchange for my favors, the gang leaders made sure I had access to plenty of the stuff that is not supposed to be in prisons.

A lot of people are surprised to learn that many of the "products" you might only find in a dark alley or on a street corner in a sketchy neighborhood are often readily available in prison, if you have a way to pay for them. Corrupt guards and supply vendors routinely smuggle drugs to inmates as a way to supplement their incomes. New inmates entering prison swallow capsules or baggies of drugs to get them past guards during intake. Once inside they swallow shampoo to make them throw up the bag.

Larger portions of illegal narcotics are bagged and inserted in the rectum and "removed" in the privacy of the cell's toilet. If you're careful, you can also smuggle things in from the visitors' room, passing them when guards aren't watching. Sometimes when there is a line going back into the cellblock after visitation, an inmate farther back in the line, who hasn't been searched yet, will deftly toss contraband forward to an inmate who has already been searched and thereby slip it into the prison, right under the noses of the guards. Cons working the laundry can easily pass stuff to other inmates when their clean laundry is returned to them.

There are lots of ways. Sometimes you just find the right guard and bribe him outright. Other cons will tell you which guards are willing to cooperate for a price. If a guard catches you smuggling something in, he might keep it, or chances are, turn right around and sell it back to you or some other inmate. Let me just leave it at this: Hard drugs are common in prisons and probably always will be.

One day, an inmate came to my cell and told me that Michael Cain wanted to see me. This was a big deal. Cain was the guy we called the "mayor" of the joint. He was the top dog, the leader of the biggest gang. If Michael Cain ordered something, it was a done deal. This man could call a strike. He could call a riot. If he wanted someone killed, all he had to do was give the word. And for some reason the man wanted to talk to me.

That's all I needed to hear. When, with some trepidation, I arrived at his cell, I saw that there was another guy there, too. Cain looked at the other guy, a member of his group, and asked him, "Is this the guy?"

The fellow nodded and said, "Yes."

Cain told the fellow in a voice that left no room for questions, "Dudrey here is my canteen man. Don't ever look at him again or come to me with a problem concerning him."

I was more than a little surprised and also perplexed. I learned later that I'd said something to the guy when he was in the canteen line; he didn't like it and had decided to drop some weight on me. That situation could have worked out less favorably for me, but that day in his cell, the boss of the joint set the guy straight. I was the Mayor's canteen guy and was not to be messed with.

I returned to my cell that day feeling like I had it made. And for an inmate locked inside the four walls of a prison, I kind of did.

Things on the outside, however, were not so good. Helen divorced me while I was in the clink. I think she just decided to move on. I had been in for well over a year, and it was almost Christmas again. In all that time, I hadn't seen my little girl even once. Helen had completely ignored the court's order, which required her to bring Jacqueline to visit her daddy at least once a month. I grew increasingly bitter about that.

After a while the anger grew until I started to hate my now ex-wife. She didn't answer my letters. She was never home when I called. None of our friends knew where she was. And she was keeping my child from me.

The more I dwelt on the subject the more enraged I became. One moment I cared for her and the next I hated her. It's really easy for feelings like that to fester in prison.

Week after week I tried to make contact. I wrote letters. I called people. In my desperation I even tried a prayer one night. That didn't work either. Instead, I fell asleep that night with a splitting headache.

Depressed, I began spending more time than usual in my cell, wallowing in self-pity. My dad and his wife didn't write. They did, however, come to see me one time. That's one time in the three years I was in. Then when they did come, they kind of ruined the gesture by complaining about the money they had to spend on gas for the drive.

I think Dad was still a little perturbed and maybe a little embarrassed about the last time we had seen each other. We had met at a gas station to talk over some stuff, and for some reason he raised his voice and started talking down to me. Something clicked in my head that day and the way I perceived him changed forever. I stood up to him, toe to toe, and made it clear, for the first time in our relationship, that I was prepared to knock his head off right then and there. Who did he think he was anyway, yelling at me in front of my wife?

I saw my dad scared that day, and more importantly, he knew that I saw his fear. I wasn't a kid anymore. I wasn't the little Chuckie he could beat on and push around anytime the mood struck. After that day, I guess I should have been surprised that he visited at all.

With New Year's Eve coming up, I decided to make some hooch so some friends and I could do some serious celebrating. I was cooking it up in my footlocker and it was starting to smell pretty darn good. As you might imagine, I had some concerns. First, I hoped the plastic bags would hold up. All I needed was for one of them to burst and spread half-cooked hooch all over the floor of my cell. More than that, though, I was worried that the man would smell it, or find it in a shake down. That would not be good. I decided, however, that the reward of some good hooch was worth the risk.

Yes, sir, I said to myself, if I pull this off, my friends and I are going to get totally blasted on my raisin jack. On top of that, my mule had come through and we had a big sack of weed and some acid. New Year's Eve would be a night to remember. I had everything planned. There would be no stopping me now. I was back in my "feeling good about myself" mode. At least for the time being.

One morning in late December, I locked my "house" and headed for the canteen to put in my hours. It was a slow day, so I played a few hands of spades with some guys, smoked some weed, and zoned out. Anything that passes time in the joint is a good thing to an inmate, and that's all we had in mind that day.

I was shuffling the cards and about to deal a new hand when a guard showed up and told me to report to the captain's office in the security center. Walking down the long hall, I felt a tight knot forming in my gut. I suspected that my brew was perhaps smelling a little too strong to go unnoticed by the powers that be. I hoped that was not the case.

When I walked in the door of the security center my heart sank. I was busted! Lying there on the floor of the security center was my footlocker.

I got thirty days in solitary confinement. That was a tough price to pay for one night of partying that didn't actually happen. You know, a seasoned inmate learns to adjust his way of thinking, just to survive. Prison, he says, oh well. You can make the best of a bad situation. But solitary confinement is another matter altogether. Solitary is just plain ugly. There's no TV, no smokes, and no dope. There is nothing to do all day long except stare at the floor, sleep, eat, and stare at the floor and sleep some more. Sometimes you stare at the wall for variety, and studiously memorize every crack. But that's all there is to do. Oh, and take one shower a week.

It goes without saying that I hated my time there. I was cold. I didn't have enough to eat. And I missed my cell with all the comforts of home. I was beginning to hate prison even more than I had before. I did my best to sleep all day long to pass the time. But when I would sleep all day, I would lie awake at night thinking about my life and the mess I had made of myself. When I was asleep I would dream. I had dreams about the outside, mostly dreams about the bad things associated with life on the streets.

It will drive you crazy thinking about life on the outside while you're in prison. Staring at the ceiling, I directed my anger and hatred at those on the outside who had let me down. Of course there was my dad and his wife. Some piece of work they were. I took the heat for them a few years ago, which cost me some county time, and yet they had come to see me only once. And my ex-wife, she could have crawled in a hole and died as far as I knew.

And where was my daughter? More than anything, that was the one question I wanted answered. I missed that little girl so much. I had to see her. I had to get out. There had to be a way.

Maybe I could go into treatment. Man, I hated the thought of treatment. Sitting in a circle with a bunch of cons whining and taking turns yelling at one another. No way! The way I felt right then, if I went to treatment I would have just punched someone out and been sent back to solitary.

The main thing about solitary is the complete aloneness with one's self. There is no place to run or hide from you. The loneliness often turns to rage and plans for revenge. Sitting there alone, stewing in my own juices, I decided I wanted to find Barbara and kill her when I got out. She deserved to die for what she had done to little Frances and Kenny, and to me.

Deep down, I knew that when I got out of prison I wouldn't actually find her and kill her. I wasn't a killer, except in my heart sometimes. Besides, I knew that, all things considered, I was the only one to blame for being where I was. For the time being, it just felt better to hate people and tell myself that I would deal with them when I got out.

Chapter 31

Treatment and Did Dad Have Mom Killed?

When I was released from solitary, I broke down and signed up for treatment. Cooking hooch in my cell had cost me my plum assignment at the commissary and all of the benefits that came with it, so it was time to try something new.

Treatment sessions on the inside are not like going to an Alcoholics Anonymous meeting on the outside. Convict-on-convict group meetings can get pretty rough.

"You have to change! You have an image problem. If you don't stop and listen to what people are telling you, you will end up right back here in prison. You won't be on the streets a month!"

The second time I attended, the group yelled and screamed at me for over an hour.

"Take a look at your self! What makes you think you've changed? You actually like prison, don't you, convict?"

The group's goal was to break down my defenses so I would stop and look at myself, and hopefully change my way of doing things.

But I was in no mood to get lectured by a bunch of loser cons, so I yelled back, like a caged lion staring them down. I gave as good as I got.

To their taunts I replied, "Shut up, punk! Who do you think you're yelling at? Who are you to tell me anything? You're in prison too, stupid!"

When I laughed at them, all they did was mock me right back. The rants flew back and forth for weeks. They blasted me and I returned fire.

Truth be told, most of the guys in the group genuinely cared about me. This was just their style of intense group therapy. I didn't feel like crying in front of these people, so I bowed my neck and fought back. If these guys thought that screaming at me was going to shake me up, they were wrong. I wasn't some weak punk! And yet, deep down inside I desperately wanted to change my life. I wanted to change who I was, but it was just not in me to do it.

Perhaps that was the one thing I walked away with from those sessions. It was not in me to do it. Pure and simple, I did not have the ability to change. At least not yet.

The treatment program was a live-in community at St. Cloud Men's Reformatory. I was transferred from Stillwater to St. Cloud midway through my sentence. Every day, I would spend twelve hours sitting in lectures, studying topics like Transactional Analysis. To my surprise, I really enjoyed the teaching and could relate to and understand what the instructor said. The program's curriculum was based on the theories of a man named Eric Burn, who had authored some pretty famous self-help books, like "I'm O.K., You're O.K." and "Games People Play."

One day, I was sitting at my old fashioned school desk listening to the lecture and taking notes. The speaker was saying, "As children grow, between the ages of birth and six years of age, they begin a decisional process with their parents and the outside world. It's called Scripting."

He went on to explain that a script is an ongoing life plan that is formulated in early childhood. Under parental influences, the script directs a child's life as he grows and matures, affecting even the most important aspects of the person's life. This means that sons usually learn how to be men from their fathers, or from substitute fathers, and daughters learn how to be women from their mothers.

That made sense to me, but it became a bit hard to accept when he went on to explain that men would most likely turn out like their fathers. That was about the last thing I wanted to hear. After all, I was pretty sure I hated my father. By this time, however, it was pretty obvious that I had indeed turned out like my father in many ways.

I'm not sure my dad had much of a conscience or any real desire to change the kind of man he was, so in that way I think we were quite different. But in other ways, I was definitely following in his footsteps.

Anyway, I soaked the stuff up. I particularly liked the study of "Game Analysis." It's complicated and technical to explain, so I won't try. The way the instructor put it, a game was "an ongoing series of complimentary, ulterior transactions that led to a well-defined predictable outcome." That sounds heavy, but my experience on the streets had already taught me this. I simply had never heard it put into technical terminology. This was how, as a criminal, I had been able to predict things people were going to do. I watched what they did, remembered it, and then took advantage of what I had observed, striking at the opportune time.

This is also why I had become convinced that my dad was responsible for my mother's death. The one time I had asked him about it, he, of course, denied it. But I knew he was lying. How did I know? In another matter, when I knew for certain that he had done something, when I confronted him, he denied it in the same way, with the same exact demeanor, displaying the same tells. In other words, I had learned how my dad responded when he was lying about something I was certain of, and therefore could tell that he was lying when he denied his role in my mother's death.

Plus, my dad always had this one personality flaw. He needed to make sure that at least one person knew that he had gotten away with something he'd done, no matter how bad it was. He was incapable of keeping his bad deeds totally to himself. He had to tell someone.

One time he showed me a nicely framed coin collection that had supposedly been destroyed in a fire. The owner had collected the insurance money, and my dad got the coin collection for assisting in the insurance fraud. He showed it to me one day, because he just had to brag a little about what he'd gotten away with.

The worst example was when my dad gave me a certain gift. A symbolic one, I believe. The look in his eyes when he handed it to me told me as much as the gift itself. What was this special gift? An exact replica of the American Arms 22 caliber pistol Dad's friend used to shoot my mom that morning in our kitchen. My dad had arranged the murder of his own wife, the mother of his children, and just had to make sure I knew that he'd gotten away with it. If you had seen the look in his eyes when he handed me that weapon, you would understand why I am saying this.

If I learned nothing else in treatment, I at least learned how to read people like my dad.

Finally, my third spring behind bars arrived. I would be released from prison soon. I was seriously looking forward to getting out and starting over – again. By this time, I had a new attitude and finally hoped to do something positive with my life.

The final days before a convict is released pass very slowly. It's like a child anticipating Christmas. Leading up to the big day, you start hoping again, and that makes everything both better and harder at the same time.

In my case, it wasn't a perfectly clean release. They had shaved ten months off of my time, but I had to report to a halfway house for a while. I wasn't overly excited about that. I had enough of living with people with character and personality disorders, and with lunatics and anti-social nutcases. But better to deal with them on the outside than inside prison walls.

More than a few times, after an encounter with some particularly scary dude, I'd whispered under my breath, "This guy should never get out of prison."

Some people don't believe in prisons or long sentences. They think everyone can be reformed and turned into good, useful members of society. Not me. I'm glad there are prisons and long sentences, because some of the guys I met on the inside should never walk free among normal people, especially women and children.

But, if entering a halfway house was a condition of my parole and getting out of prison early, I could handle it for a few weeks.

My last day, I was called to the front office. There was a sheriff's deputy waiting to serve me with a restraining order. I was ordered not to have any contact with my ex-wife.

How ironic. She'd had an order to bring our daughter to the prison to see her daddy once a month and had never done that even once. And now that I was getting out, she had a judge restrain me from seeing her, which meant I couldn't see my little girl. For the time being, all I could do was accept the reality that I was forbidden to see my own daughter, a little four-year-old girl I loved and had never harmed.

The halfway house was everything I expected it would be, and I just went with the flow. I knew I could do this. I could finally see light at the end of the tunnel.

One night, I was sitting alone going through the telephone book, looking up old friends, when I stumbled upon the name of an old girl-friend's sister, Sandy. I'd always thought she was rather good-looking, so what was there to lose? All she could do was tell me to get lost. And I was already pretty lost. The phone rang and a girl answered. A real girl. "Hello Sandy, how have you been? This is Chuck," I began.

"Chuck who?" she asked. So I reminded her who I was, to which she replied, matter-of-fact, "I don't know you."

"Oh, you must have a boyfriend or something. Sorry, I must have the wrong number." With that I hung up.

Chapter 32

Life with Sandy

I was sitting looking through the phonebook a few nights later, when it occurred to me to try Sandy again. I kind of liked her voice, and maybe tonight her boyfriend, or whoever he was, wasn't there now. It was worth a try.

Sandy answered the phone. "Sorry I bothered you the other night," I began. "This is Chuck. How have you been?"

"Who are you and who do you think I am?" she responded. I tried to explain our connection, but after a few minutes of small talk I slowly began to realize that I had in fact dialed the wrong number. This girl was not who I thought she was. In fact, I had no idea who she was.

We decided that that didn't matter to either of us, so we just started talking. It's a good thing it wasn't long distance, because we visited for two or three hours that night. We talked about our lives, places we had been, and whatever else popped into our minds. Later on, after I hung up the phone, I realized I was feeling pretty good. Funny how the prospect of a new love puts a spring in a fellow's step. I went to sleep that night happy, simply because I knew that I would be talking to Sandy again the next night.

We talked every night for three weeks. We both looked forward to the time we spent together, even if it was only on the phone. Then one night I suggested that we should meet somewhere. I suggested that with me being a stranger, perhaps she should bring her brother along the first time we saw each other in person.

"You wouldn't care if I did?" she asked.

"No," I said. "And have him bring some of his friends, if that would make you feel any better."

We arranged to meet the next night at McDonalds. I had no idea what the girl looked like and vice versa, but still, I was so excited that I couldn't sleep. As it turned out, she was a decent looking girl and we hit it off as well in person as we had on the phone.

Two weeks later, when I was successfully discharged from the halfway house, Sandy asked me to move in with her. So I did.

It was summertime when we started living together. I got a job working construction with a man I had met while I was living at the halfway house. I had to get up very early every morning and drive thirty miles to work, spend the day working in the heat and humidity, and then drive back home through rush hour traffic. I did this for six months and in spite of the hardships, I decided that I liked the building trade. The boss paid me the most money I'd ever made working a real job, a lot more than I'd made washing dishes and bussing tables back at the Howard Johnson's.

Plus, the boss was a good guy. He and I got along nicely. But talk about a workaholic! The guy worked construction all day, then played in a rock and roll band half the night. I don't know how he did it. There were nights when I'm sure he didn't get any sleep at all. His being in a band was cool enough, but it was his carpentry skills that I admired most. He taught me how to build things and I really liked the feeling that gave me. I loved the hard work and having my freedom. Things were going well at home, too. With life definitely looking up, thoughts of prison began to slowly fade from my memory.

One day during my lunch break, I called the house. Sandy said she had a really exciting idea and wanted me to hurry home after work. All she would say was that she had a great idea and it included us driving to North Dakota for the weekend. "Fine with me," I said, and went back to work.

That afternoon was especially hot and humid. A major thunderstorm passed through, bringing with it flash flooding. It rained for about two hours straight, the hardest rain I had ever seen. I was on my way home when the traffic on the freeway came to a sudden stop because the highway was under water. I sat at a standstill for two hours, waiting for the water to go down. In those days, there was no way to make a phone call home when you were stuck in traffic, so all I could do was hope that Sandy had seen the weather on TV and knew why I was late.

Finally, traffic started moving again. I made it to the house a little after seven. I was shocked by what greeted me when I walked through the door. Sandy had become totally unglued. Apparently she had made plans for us to go to North Dakota and get married. In fact, her friends were already headed there and would be waiting for us to arrive. Of course, this was all news to me.

"What took you so long to get here?" she screamed. "Why didn't you call me? I wanted to surprise you. I wanted us to go to North Dakota and get married this weekend. Now it's too late." Then she flopped herself down on her belly and started pounding her fists and feet against the floor like a spoiled two-year old. The grown woman that I had been living with had a full blown temper tantrum right there in front of me, crying, yelling and screaming, the whole shebang.

I didn't mean to laugh at her, at least not out loud. It just came out. Her behavior was the most childish display I had ever seen. As soon as I started laughing, Sandy jumped to her feet and started pounding my chest with her fists, yelling, "I hate you, I hate you. I wanted to get married."

Maybe I was being too logical, but would an adult shout, "I hate you, I hate you. I wanted to get married,"?

I was completely awestruck. I definitely never saw that coming. Just then, the telephone rang. What a welcome interruption! This little drama had gone on for an hour already and I was never happier to hear a telephone ring.

It was Sandy's mother on the other end. She asked me if her child was there.

I said, "Who?"

"Oh, that's what we call Sandy at home, 'our child.' So tell me, are you guys getting ready to go to North Dakota?"

Call me an idiot and I won't argue, but Sandy and I went ahead and got married. Don't ask me to explain why I married her after having witnessed her tantrum, but I did.

Four months later, I was sitting on the deck of a cruise ship, relaxing on our honeymoon, of sorts, and waiting for the waiter to bring me another Rum Punch. I liked the rum and for a while enjoyed the punch too, until the headache came. Sandy was sun bathing and working on her tan. She was always working on her tan or buying another swimsuit.

The temper tantrum was months behind us by that time and I had put it out of my mind. I was seriously hoping that things would work out for us. Sandy was really a nice girl, most of the time, even though our getting hitched had gotten off to a pretty shaky start. The wedding was conducted by a judge, and my brother John was supposed to be the best man. Problem was, John didn't show up, so Sandy's sister stood in his place. This should have been clue number two, but I ignored it.

Ironically, my brother told me later that he just couldn't go through with being my best man with me marrying someone that he was certain I should not be marrying. It would have been nice if he had told me that at the time, not a month later.

Anyway what was done was done, and there I was sitting in the warm Caribbean sun, smoking weed and sucking down Rum Punch. Life couldn't be all that bad.

Suddenly, something dawned on me. I had for a second time married a recovering alcoholic. I started playing the amateur psychologist. I reasoned that I had managed to find another needy woman, someone who had serious unresolved issues with her father, and then got as close to her as I could. I wondered if maybe I was drawn to that type because I had some of those same issues myself.

We talked about psychology when I was in treatment. Our group leader called this an "unhealthy symbiotic relationship." Was it love that got me into this, or was it me fulfilling some need to take care of people, to rescue them and thereby rescue myself? My head was starting to hurt again, and this time it wasn't the Rum Punch. I decided that I hated psychology.

When Sandy and I got back home, things went okay for a while. Well, there was this one road rage incident. Traffic on the freeway was heavy that day. It was warm and Sandy was driving. I had my arm out the window and was tapping on the top of the car, keeping time to the music on the radio. Unbeknownst to me, some guy behind us had become angry about something. He pulled up alongside us and stared over at me. I nodded at him and motioned with my hand for him to go ahead. He apparently took that wrong. Maybe he thought I was flipping him off or something. Whatever it was, he got angry and started following us, honking his horn and flashing his lights.

We ignored him. Eventually, we got off the freeway so we could take a side road to get around the traffic. The guy followed us. We drove around for a while until we lost him, or so we thought. After we parked, I sat there in the front seat, cleaning my fingernails with a pocketknife. All of a sudden, the guy who had been following us approached my car door and started swinging his fists, trying to punch me in the face through the open window. Instinctively and totally in self defense, I shoved the knife at the guy's shoulder to force him back. The knife went in, and when he jerked, it slid down his chest, leaving him with a pretty nasty cut. It was purely a defensive move on my part, and I did it without thinking, but he was definitely injured.

Getting stabbed in the shoulder took the fight out of the guy. He took off, and Sandy and I went on about our business. The next day, the police called and wanted to hear my version of what had happened. They said the guy I stabbed had to get something like thirty-two stitches. The officer also informed me that they had several witnesses, who said they saw the guy walk up and attack me, unprovoked, so I wasn't going to get into any trouble. But, he explained, they still wanted to talk to me in person.

"Well, it sounds like you already have everything you need," I replied. I hung up the phone, and never heard any more about it.

If I left it at that, you would have a somewhat lacking image of Sandy. There was more to our relationship than I have told you. The more my wife learned about my "former" life of crime, the more she wanted to get into that game, just for the excitement, I suppose. Sandy and I committed several crimes together.

If I was hitting a safe or breaking into the change machine at some laundromat, usually across the state line, Sandy would sit where she could listen in on the police scanner and keep watch for any heat or trouble approaching, and then warn me on our two-way radios.

When I would do safe jobs, I would come back with cash, savings account passbooks, gold coins, jewelry, all kinds of stuff. Sandy looked innocent enough to fool most people, and that came in handy. One time she walked into a bank with a savings account passbook I had stolen and withdrew $3,500 cash from somebody's account with no I.D.

One time we rented a U-Haul truck using fake I.D. To buy some extra time, we told the rental company that we were using the truck to move to Florida. Instead, we parked it behind an appliance store and set Sandy up where she could keep watch. After the store closed on Friday night, I broke in. From the inside, I opened the big door in back and loaded the U-Haul full of washers, dryers, microwaves, and stereo equipment.

We drove the truck to where my dad lived, in another town, and sold all of the stuff to him for cash money. Then we wiped the truck down to remove fingerprints, and parked it back in front of the rental office like good, responsible customers.

Dad kept some of the stuff we sold him, but gave the appliances and stereo equipment to his kids for Christmas that year.

Sandy was the youngest of three and was somewhat of a tomboy. Living with me, she discovered that she craved the drama of the criminal life. Looking back, I can only say with some regret that I wasn't much of a positive influence on her life.

These stories also reveal that even though I was out of prison, I was nowhere near turning my life around. I was doing things that, if caught, could have sent me back to prison for several years. Of course I was telling myself that I wouldn't get caught.

Some months later, Sandy and I started remodeling our house. I was putting my newly acquired construction skills to good use adding on another bedroom. One day, I was busy putting up some drywall in the back of the house, when Sandy came back to where I was working. Out of the blue, she changed the radio dial to another station. It was annoying, but I didn't give it much thought. Then she came back a little later and unplugged my extension cord.

I got the feeling that something was about to come to a head. I knew Sandy was upset that I had taken a new job with a bail bondsman. She didn't like my being away from home as much as the job required, and we had been arguing about this for weeks.

Without saying anything to her, I turned the radio station back to where I had it, plugged the cord back into the outlet and continued to work. A few moments later, Sandy came out again. She was holding the power cord in her hand. She looked at me with an odd expression on her face, then unplugged the cord again.

"What are you going to do?" she demanded. "Come on, you sissy. What? Are you afraid of me?" She stood there mocking me, daring me to react

I told Sandy to knock it off or I would give her something to think about, and went back to work hanging drywall. My little threat was merely an attempt to make her go away and leave me alone. I assumed she had gotten the message, because she went back to the other room, slamming the door behind her.

By that time, I had had enough. Sandy's bizarre behavior had gone on for far too long, and I just wanted out. I didn't agree with the whole divorce thing, but I had come to the conclusion that things were not going to end well for us. Sandy was far too needy. She really was the "child" her folks had raised her to be, and if she was still needing a daddy, I was declining the assignment.

I was about to continue with my mudding and taping, when out of nowhere two cops came up behind me. They grabbed me by my arms and tried to put handcuffs on me. I didn't know who they were or why they were there. Taken completely by surprise, I resisted them. The next thing I knew, there were two more cops. The four of them jumped on me and knocked me to the floor.

"You're under arrested for domestic abuse," one of them shouted.

"What are you talking about?" I asked.

"You made a threat against someone in your house. You're going to jail."

I had no love for cops to begin with, but this made me downright angry. I had not done anything wrong, unless you count thinking about it.

"I'll be out before the ink is dry, tough guys," I shouted back.

Unfazed, they threw me into the back seat of a squad car and off we went. Two days later, I was sitting across the desk from my lawyer. I told him straight out, "I want out now. I have had enough of this nut case."

My attorney told me that I had a significant amount of money invested in the house and that we should try to recover some of it in the divorce. I told him that I didn't want anything from this marriage, except to be free from it, and that as soon as possible.

I was still seething with anger over the fact that cops had come into my house and knocked me down like I was some punk, even though I hadn't done one thing wrong. I had seen their kind before, cops anxious to stretch their muscle anytime they got the chance.

Of course, I had no idea what Sandy had told them or how much she had embellished. Back then, I rarely put myself in the shoes of law enforcement. All I knew was I had been thrown to the ground by cops more times than I could remember. I had had shotguns and pistols pointed at my face at least half a dozen times. So, let's just say that me and the cops were not on good terms and I was not about to give them the benefit of the doubt about this fiasco.

When I was released from jail, my attorney told me that a judge had already signed an order prohibiting me from going back to the house to pick up my belongings without a cop being present. I decided not to bother. I walked away from the house and all my stuff and never looked back. All I had in life, at the end of that day, were the clothes on my back.

I don't know how much my own actions and attitudes contributed to that debacle, but if there is such a thing as irreconcilable differences, Sandy and I probably defined the term. Maybe marrying someone you barely know, or in my case probably didn't know at all, was not the best idea in the world.

Chapter 33

The Ten Thousand Dollar Bond

At the time Sandy and I split up, I was working for a bail bondsman as a skip tracer. I kind of fell into the job when Foster's niece was picked up for possession of crack cocaine. I posted her bail so she could get out of jail, but she skipped and left me hanging. I didn't appreciate that one bit, so I helped the bail bondsman track her down. In the process, the bondsman and I hit it off, and he offered me a job. The work sounded exciting and it paid more than my construction job, so I took it.

It didn't take me long to conclude that there may not be a more interesting job in the world than skip tracing. It's definitely not for everyone, but if you have a chip on your shoulder and consider yourself a tough guy, it's hardly boring work. A lot of what goes on in the business is borderline illegal, but the law seems to wink at most of that, because, after all, the people bondsmen are after have skipped bail and are on the run from the law.

One Monday morning, the office was unusually quiet when I showed up for work. Everyone was hustling around, but I noticed that the door to Big John's office was closed. That was a sure sign that something was up. When I passed the receptionist's desk she smiled her customary smile, then rolled her eyes back toward the boss's office to let me know that something was up, and it wasn't good. I had barely sat down at my desk when the office door flew open and the boss called me in and told me to take a seat.

"I won't lose my ten thousand," he told me. "I will not let that little punk rip me off."

Not having the slightest clue what he was talking about, I simply agreed with his premise.

"What can I do, Big John?" It was, after all, my job to make sure the boss didn't lose money. Whatever was going on, something told me that this was not going to be a short week.

"I won't have some punk from L.A. come in here and pull some game on me. I want his skin, and we won't stop until I get it," he said.

"Give me the file," I replied. Big John handed me the paperwork and assured me that there would be a nice bonus at the end of the week, if I got the job done.

The problem was pretty simple. The boss had written another bad bond. He made the "sale" and got the ten percent, but the perp had skipped on him. That meant it was up to the rest of us to clean up the mess. My job was to find the "mark" and put him in jail. When I looked over the file, the first thing I noticed was that the co-signer hadn't signed over the deed to his house. The boss had screwed up. That was the real reason he was angry. Without a signature, all we had was an unsecured bond.

In the bail bond business that is a major no-no. The defendant could fail to show up for trial and our company would be required to pay the full amount of the bail, and there was no asset to seize to recover the money. Defendants and their families post all kinds of collateral to bail bondsmen to get somebody out of jail, pending trial. We'd seized cars and boats and all kinds of other stuff when defendants skipped. In this case, however, all we had was an unsigned deed to a house, which is worth zero. To further complicate matters, we weren't even sure the "mark" had given us his real name.

I started by finding out everything I could about the co-signer. I discovered that he was employed with the Ford automotive plant. I checked further and found that he was off work on disability. As soon as I saw that, I realized that I would have to run a game on this chump. Being creative comes in handy when you're a skip tracer, especially when you have to scam a scammer.

I called the co-signer and told him that I was with Ford's insurance department. I explained that we were calling to make sure he was getting his disability checks on time. I explained that it was important to us that injured workers get what they have coming to them.

"I haven't received one single check," he replied with some indignation. He explained that he had been waiting for weeks to get paid, but all he was getting was the bureaucratic run around.

That was music to my ears. I assured the fellow that I would be in town the next day and could come by to see him, if it was all right. I assured him that I could straighten things out for him.

"Oh, by the way," I told him, "It looks like some of your paperwork wasn't signed. I'll see you in the morning, say about ten, and we will get this all straightened out." He agreed to the sit-down.

I was on a roll. I just had to get my ducks lined up and be ready for the meet. Before leaving to work my game, I ducked into the boss's office to reassure him. "Don't worry, Big John, I'll take care of this for you."

I didn't have a lot of time to put my scheme together. First and foremost, I would need some official looking papers. I headed for the State Employment Office, where they keep tons of forms in their racks, all free for the taking. I took the ones I thought I could use and headed back to the office. I sat down at the typewriter and starting filling in the spaces with the co-signer's name and other useful information that we had in the file. Then I put an X on the line where the mark would have to sign "to get his benefits."

Finally, I got a "release of property" form and a "quit claim" form from our file, and put an X on each of those, as well. Those were the forms that counted. With that, I was set. If everything went as planned, I would have the boss's ten grand secured.

I went into the office the next morning and got Big John's car keys and headed out for my appointment. John always drove an expensive car, and no one else was allowed to drive it, ever. Nonetheless, I drove off that morning in his brand new Cadillac. To pull off my scheme, I needed to look the part, and the Caddie was a nice prop. I looked at myself in the rear view mirror and noticed that I needed to cinch up and straighten my tie. With that done, I was satisfied that I looked the part.

Personality wise, I was a perfect fit for the skip tracer business. I loved what I was doing. I had only been out of prison two years, and there I was, playing the same old games, but getting paid legit to do it. How sweet was that? Plus, with the boss being a bail bondsman, I had a get-out-of-jail-free card.

I pulled up to the front of the man's house. He was waiting for me and met me at the door. He welcomed me in and offered me some coffee. I told him how sorry I was that the office had made a mistake with his file. I assured him that I was there to make sure we got everything right this time, so he could get what he had coming.

We sat down and got to the serious work of signing the papers. I really had to keep myself in check to keep from laughing. I was loving this. I began by reading some of the papers I had gotten from the employment office. They all had the official state logo at the top. I read him a couple of paragraphs about an employee's right to Workers' Compensation and then asked if he understood what I had read. He assured me that he did. I told him that I wanted to make sure he knew his rights.

Okay, it was time to seal the deal, time to get what I came for, which was the mark's signature on the two property release forms that I had cleverly mixed in with all of the others.

"Well, if we can finish up here before noon," I told him, "I'll fax these papers to the main office right away and you should get your money as early as tomorrow's mail."

That said, he signed the papers, told me thank you, and out the door I went. Everything had gone as planned. Heck, I even got a free cup of coffee. Truth be told, I didn't feel bad for the guy. He would likely never know what had happened and hopefully his employer would get his claim processed and money to him soon.

I was, after all, working for the bail bondsman, and this guy really had pledged his house as security for the bail money. All I was doing was getting a signature the boss had inadvertently forgotten to secure. And of course, I was ever mindful of the fact that it was Big John who signed my paychecks.

The mood at the office changed the moment I handed the signed papers to Big John. Literally, my work that day changed the atmosphere of the whole place. The boss started walking back and forth with a big smile on his face, waving the signed papers, telling everyone how valuable I was to his organization and that he could always count on me.

As soon as the excitement of that victory died down, I got back to work. I still had to locate the punk who had skipped on us and bring him before the judge before the time ran out.

I worked the case for almost two full weeks with not so much as a lead. Our guy had disappeared from the planet and no one was saying a word. Usually by that point, someone was talking. People who are successful in our line of work have contacts on the streets and hear things, but all we were hearing was silence.

About the end of the second week, we put the word out on the street that there was a Five Hundred Dollar reward for information that led to us finding Jonny Fred Whitman. The reward was all cash, no questions asked. Late that afternoon, Big John got a call from another bondsman in Los Angeles. The caller told the boss that our guy had been spotted there. It sounded like a hot lead, so John caught the late flight to the West Coast.

I had had some strange days working bonds, but the next day was about to take the cake. The boss called me from a stakeout in L.A. While we were on the phone, a woman walked into the office, where I was, and told me that she knew where to find Jonny Whitman. I told Big John that I had to go, but would call him back in a little while.

The woman sat down across from me and asked if what she had heard was true. Was there really a Five Hundred Dollar reward for this guy? She was holding a small baby in her arms. I told her that I hoped that she was not playing me, because I didn't have time for any bull. She asked again about the money. I assured her that what she had heard was true, that there was indeed a cash reward.

She seemed satisfied. Then she explained that she was staying in the same house as this Whitman guy, and that he would come back to the house that same night. I wasn't sure what to think. Big John was in L.A. following up on a supposedly solid lead, and there I sat with some lady who was telling me that our guy was still in town, and she knew where he would be spending the night. I asked her if she felt she was in danger. She said she would be okay, that no one would ever know that she had been to see us. I told her that if what she told me checked out, I would give her the money the next morning.

As soon as she was gone, I got back on the telephone with Big John and gave him this new information. He said to go ahead and put a plan together, just in case. So I did.

I didn't have my forty-five automatic with me that day; I didn't think I would need it. I had just purchased a .357 magnum earlier that week, and that piece was still in my desk. I decided to carry it. I carried a gun most of the time, as part of my work. As had become a habit for me, I completely ignored the fact that I was a convicted felon, and unless I wanted to go to prison, was prohibited from carrying a gun under any circumstance.

That night I parked the car three or four parking spaces from the front of the building. Dan, Big John's brother, was with me in the front seat. We stationed three more guys in another car, parked around the corner. We had arranged with the informant that she would leave the downstairs door open for us, as soon as the "mark" and the friend he was with had entered the building. Once the door was opened, we were to give her enough time to take the baby to a back room for safety reasons.

I was going to be point man, so I would enter first. As we were walking up the stairs we heard people talking and music playing. I had my firearm in my hand when I kicked the door open and yelled, "Bondsman! Everyone down on the floor! On the floor now!"

Things instantly got a little crazy. Our "mark" ran for the kitchen. I took off after him, but tripped on a rug. As I fell to the floor, my gun went off. When the shot fired, the mark fell to the floor. Dan rushed into the room just as he was going down. We glanced at each other, both of us assuming that I had shot and killed the guy. I holstered my gun and went down on one knee to handcuff him, just in case. I rolled him over, and to my surprise and relief saw that he hadn't been hit. To this day, I have no idea where that bullet went.

I lifted Mr. Whitman to his feet and shoved him out the door. On the way down the steps, some other guy made a play at me. He pulled a long syringe out of his pants and tried to stab me with it. I grabbed his arm and smashed his head into the wall. Then I gave him a bit of a beating. The way I saw it, he deserved it for trying to stab me with a syringe.

A minute later, we were back at the car with our guy in cuffs. Mission accomplished. Man, I loved this! I was so jacked up. I felt like Superman. The adrenalin was flowing hard and my heart was pounding.

I glanced up at the rear view mirror and stared for a moment at the guy in the backseat. I remember thinking, *Hey buddy, you're my paycheck this week!* That's really all he was to me. A paycheck, and bragging rights back at the office.

As soon as we got back, Dan called the boss and told him that we had caught Whitman. We were all standing around Big John's desk with the phone on speaker. A forlorn looking Mr. Whitman was standing against the wall, sulking.

The boss of course had to give the guy the what for, even if it was just over the phone.

"You thought you could out run me, you little _____? Well, what do you have to say for yourself now? Well, come on, nothing to say?"

The guy wouldn't answer and that ticked the boss off. Big John told me, "Chuck, double him over."

So he got it in the guts, not once, but twice, once for the boss man and once for me. It was kind of understood back then that bail bondsmen were sometimes a little rough with the guys who skipped bail. Skippers could cost the company serious bucks if we didn't catch them, so we kind of took it personal when one of them ran out on us.

In this case, our guy went back to jail with a little more wear and tear on his body than when he had left. Stuff like that happens.

The thing about skip trace work is you meet a lot of unsavory people, and even work with some of them. Big John's brother, Al, the guy who was with me on the Whitman bust, was a big time cocaine dealer. One time I saw a coffee table piled high with bags of white powder he was planning to move. Drug dealers are usually pretty careful people, always running one step ahead of the law, but like bail bondsmen they sometimes slip up and make bad deals.

One time, Al gave a certain night club owner four kilos of cocaine, on a front basis, then the guy didn't pay up. Al approached me about collecting for him and I agreed to take on the job. The first thing I did was bring in a partner to help with the job. We started casing the guy's club, and also his home.

The next day I got a call from a source who told me that the guy we were after would have the drugs and a sizeable amount of cash on hand that evening at his condo. My partner and I got into position, planning to slip through the security door when someone walked out. To my surprise, the mark himself walked out the door. He went to his car and returned with a flight bag.

We stayed back a safe distance, then as soon as he opened the door to his condo we rushed him. We shoved him across the room to the couch. There were two women in the kitchen. My partner ordered them to get down on the floor, then covered them with his gun. They seemed thoroughly frightened, but didn't yell out.

I had a nightstick in one hand and a handgun in the other. I whacked the mark a couple of times with the nightstick to take the fight out of him. Then I frisked him and took all of his cash. The flight bag was stuffed full of cocaine. It was all broken down into one ounce bags, ready to sell. We grabbed the bag and made our escape.

We had no sooner made it out the door when we heard over the scanner that the heat was on the way. As we headed across town, we passed a long stream of police cars headed to where we had just been. Their lights were flashing, but they weren't running their sirens.

Our little job went even better than we had planned. Al got his drugs back, and my partner and I had a good payday. Looking back, I wish I could say I was proud of that job.

Chapter 34

Jimmy the Car Salesman

The first time I met Jimmy, he was a salesman at the car lot where I purchased my pick-up truck. I remember that day well. While we were negotiating the deal, I told Jimmy, "You get the price down by three thousand dollars, and when we close the deal I'll give you five hundred cash."

Jimmy definitely liked that idea. I drove off an hour later with the truck I wanted at the price I wanted. I still remember the look on the salesman's face when I asked him, "What is it you think I do for a living?"

His response made me smile. "I'm not sure," he said, "but I could just about imagine."

I told him, "I'm a skip tracer."

"You mean you're a bounty hunter?" he asked.

I had been asked that question many times. "Some people call it that," I told him, "but in the business, we prefer to be called skip tracers."

And so began my relationship with Jimmy, the used car salesman. Jim liked my style. I think when he was with me he felt like he was playing a part in some movie. He liked the drama, and always wanted to hear about my latest arrest. Sometimes that was all he wanted to talk about. Before long we were having coffee on a regular basis.

One day when he called, I was pretty sure he had something specific on his mind. He asked if we could meet and have breakfast. "Sure, are you buying?" I replied.

When I walked into the café, Jim was sitting with some of the regulars who gathered there every morning. I always got a kick out of the way they looked at me when I walked in. Maybe it was the stories

Jimmy told them about me, but whatever it was, when they saw me walk in, they always got up and moved to another table.

I sat down and Jim poured me a cup of coffee from the pot on the table. The waitress came and I ordered my breakfast. After some small talk, I asked, "So, what's up?"

Jimmy looked around to make sure no one was watching or listening in on our conversation. Then he explained his reason for wanting to meet.

"Well," he began, "I'm having a problem with my daughter and I need some help dealing with it. Actually, it's not her," he said. "It's her boyfriend."

Then he explained how the boyfriend was slapping his daughter around. He told me he had tried talking to the guy about it, but all he got back was, "Get out of my face and mind your own business."

Our waitress arrived and set my meal down. After she left, Jim took another look around, to make sure no one was listening. The look on his face told me it was my turn to speak.

"Well, Jimmy, what do you think I can do to help you?" I asked.

Jim said he was sure I would know how to handle the problem for him.

"So what would you like me to do, and how soon would you like to have it done?"

"I want you to teach the guy a lesson, and I would like for you to do it before my birthday." Apparently his daughter was going be at his house for the party. I got the impression that he wanted his daughter to know that daddy had "friends with muscle."

"Jim," I said, "I'll see that it is taken care of, and I'll need to see that five hundred back."

We shook hands, and I reminded him of the rules. "Don't call me, and don't ever talk about it." Jim assured me he understood. He gave me the guy's name, then we shook hands again and parted ways.

As with every job, I had to do my homework. In this case that required some stakeout time to see when the "mark" was coming and going. I also needed to see what the neighborhood was like, so I could plan my escape.

When the day came, I left the car in a store parking lot, a short walk from the house. I left the keys and anything that could identify me in the glove compartment. I walked up to the front door, where I stood and listened for a few minutes, to kind of get a feel for the place. Everything looked and sounded good, so I knocked on the door. I hoped the guy I was after would answer, because that would mean one less witness who could identify me if something went wrong. When the door opened, I saw my mark, standing right in front of me.

"I think I backed into your car," I said.

The guy kind of scowled, but closed the door behind him and followed me toward where his car was parked. As soon as we got away from the front of the house, I turned on him. Before he knew what hit him, I knocked him to the ground and started pounding on him. The fight went out of him right away, but I pounded him some more, just for good measure.

"How does it feel to be beat on? Do you like hitting women, you sissy? You little punk! If you ever hit her again, I'll be back. Don't you dare touch her, you punk! You woman beater!"

After a few more punches that I knew had to hurt, I was pretty sure this guy wouldn't be a boyfriend to Jim's daughter much longer.

"Do you hear me? Do you want me to come visit you again? I'll be watching you. I know your every move. Got it?"

I got off of him and headed for my car. As I drove off, I could already hear the sirens from the cop cars. I took off my gloves and tossed them into the back floor and blended with the flow of traffic. I had worked up a bit of an appetite, and it was time to get something to eat. The way I saw it, I had just made an easy five hundred bucks.

One week later, I pulled into the car lot and started looking at some of the new pickups they had on hand. Jimmy came out and asked me if I needed some help. I told him that I was looking for a car for my daughter, which wasn't true. After some chit chat, he told me that his birthday had been great and that he had gotten everything he had wished for. "Well, good for you," I said, "and happy birthday."

Jimmy told me that he was especially proud of the black eyes his daughter's boyfriend was wearing at the party. I smiled. I could see that Jimmy felt like he had done something meaningful for his little girl. As for me, I was glad that I had been able to help a friend. Plus, I knew that if I ever needed Jim's help for something, I would have it.

A guy never knows when he might need an alibi, or perhaps a car, just for the day. Jim was in my pocket now, so to speak, and I liked that.

Chapter 35

Coke, Crank and Dealing with Punks

One day, I bumped into a guy on the street, someone I'd met while I was in the joint. I didn't trust him back then, but when I saw him on the street, looking pretty messed up, obviously from drug abuse, I felt sorry for him. I invited him to stay at my place for a spell, at least until he could clean up his act and kick the dope. That might seem like strange behavior for a "tough guy," but I did things like that from time to time.

The guy was in bad shape, and I figured it was the least I could do. Besides, I had plans to be out of town for the weekend, and having a house sitter would work out for me, as well. The guy assured me that he really wanted help getting clean. He seemed sincere, and thanked me for helping him out.

When I returned from my trip, the first thing I noticed was that my car was gone. That was odd. I was in for another surprise when I went inside. I had been royally ripped off. Everything I had acquired since my divorce from Sandy was gone. If I couldn't recover it, I would be back at square one again.

I felt the anger rising up. All I wanted at that moment was to find that punk. I was angry at him and I was angry at myself. Something inside had warned me before I left him at the house that something was going to go bad. I'd felt it. But instead of listening, I'd left the guy alone with everything I owned.

The first thing I needed to do was to find my car. After that, he and I would conduct a little personal business. How dare he, after I had shown him kindness, steal my stuff? All I could think of was beating his head in.

I guessed where my car might be. I hoofed it over there and sure enough, there it was, and the keys were in the ignition. I jumped in and drove to a friend's house. I got out and thoroughly checked the car out to make sure it was in good shape and that there was no dope stashed in it. I knew this guy and his friends used meth. They cooked coke down to make crack and smoked it. The last thing I needed was to be caught with dope stashed in my car.

If I was going to recover my stuff and give the thief a lesson he wouldn't soon forget, I figured I'd probably need some back up. So I called a friend, the guy who had helped me recover Al's drugs. So we could stay in touch and avoid a run in with the cops, I gave my partner one of my two-way radios and turned on my police scanner.

I was pretty sure I knew where the thief was hiding. We parked around the corner, then approached the house and got into position. My friend went around back, mostly to serve as a lookout. I took a position on the front porch. Leaning against the door, I could hear two people talking. Without warning, I burst through the front door. When the mark saw me, his eyes went wide and he let out a deep groan. He tried to get up from the couch, but I grabbed a television from the stand by the door and threw it at him. The TV hit him in the face and knocked him to the floor. I kicked him several times, as hard and fast as I could.

While I was still kicking the thief, his buddy came at me. I grabbed the VCR and smashed him in the face with it. That sent him sprawling on the floor. I gave him one hard kick in the face to keep him out of the fight for a few minutes. My thief used that opportunity to run to the kitchen. I went after him. I found him leaning over, trying to rip a leg off of the kitchen table, which for some unknown reason was turned upside down on the floor.

There was a wild look in the guy's eyes. It looked like a mixture of rage and fear, and probably some of whatever dope he was on. Before he could react, I kicked him in the head. The blow sent him sprawling. Then I pounced on him and proceeded to give him a good beating.

I could hear my partner trying to get in the back door to help, but the two of us were on the floor leaning against it, so he couldn't get in. I grabbed an extension cord and wrapped it around the mark's neck and held him tightly with one hand. I twisted the cord tighter and tighter until the guy's face turned blue.

Before he passed out, I asked him calmly and politely where my stuff was. Then I whispered in his ear that his time was up. Just in case he hadn't received my message, I pulled his face closer to mine, so he could see the look in my eyes.

"It's in a box in the closet," he whispered. By that point, he was almost unconscious. "We already sold the rest of the stuff."

That last bit angered me enough that I let him pass out completely before I let the cord go. He slumped silently to the floor. School was over for the day. Class was dismissed.

Just then, I heard the sound of others in the building coming to investigate what was going on. I suspected that someone had probably called the cops by now, so my partner and I grabbed my stuff, ran to my car and got out of there. Just as we turned left down the street closest to the house, a patrol car sped past with its lights on. I could only assume that he was headed to where we had just left.

Over my police scanner, I heard the dispatcher put out a description of my car. I immediately turned left again and drove to another friend's house. I parked in his garage and closed the door.

Three days later, I was sitting in my house having some coffee when my partner came running in the door. "The cops are downstairs," he said, "and they are headed up here."

There was a knock at the front door just as my friend escaped out the back window. I opened the door and there stood two cops. They told me they were there to arrest me for assault. They cuffed me, took me to the jail, and placed me in a holding cell. I was pretty sure I didn't have much to worry about. All I had done was attempt to recover my stolen property. I explained everything to the detective, from start to finish.

I told him he could go to the local Target store and pick up photos from film I had left there to be developed. I had recently taken pictures of all my property for my renter's insurance policy, but hadn't picked them up yet. I assured the detective that the photos would confirm everything I'd told him.

Three days later, he came to my cell and told me that all the charges had been dropped. He said he didn't believe everything I'd told him, because it wasn't possible that one person had kicked down the front door, inflicted so much damage on those two guys, and destroyed that house in such a short amount of time.

He went on to explain that there would be no charges, because the victims had given him false names when they filed their complaint, and could no longer be located. He also explained that the two guys I had beaten up were part of an elaborate check-writing scheme, and were wanted by the police themselves. That obviously didn't hurt my case any.

Something about being arrested again got me back into my "moving on" frame of mind. I had had enough of the fast lane and all the craziness that went along with it. So I packed up all my belongings and went to see my dad. I don't know why I always went back to my dad. I just did. I hated him. I didn't trust him. But he was my dad, and in some way he was kind of an anchor for me. I knew that nothing good could ever come from being around him, but sometimes I just felt like finding him and seeing him again.

I had saved some money and hoped to buy a small piece of land where I could kick back and take a break from it all. I wanted to do something different with my life and needed a little time, and some peace and quiet to think.

I was pretty good at the tough guy life, but something told me that it was just a matter of time before I'd end up back in prison, maybe for a long time. I had developed a dangerous, "I just don't care anymore," attitude, and I knew that could only lead to trouble.

I didn't know it at the time, but my good deed of trying to help that doper get back on his feet was going to come back and haunt me far more than it already had, and in time, would change the entire direction of my life.

Chapter 36

Meeting Diana

Afterthe episode with the addict, I got serious about finding a piece of property of my own. I wanted just the right spot, a piece of land that jumped up and said, "Buy me. You will be happy here." Sometimes it takes time to find a place like that.

One morning, I found myself standing on a hilltop looking out over the Mississippi River Valley. I felt good about this spot. I was sure it would suit my needs just fine.

The parcel had a southeastern exposure, which would work well for a garden spot. I could build a large garage with living quarters in the back. I would live there until I could build myself a house. In the meanwhile, I could use the garage to do woodworking on the side, while still making a fairly steady income at my construction job. That parcel of land would be my new home, or so I thought.

It had been over a year since Sandy and I'd divorced, and over that time span I had been able to save almost eight grand. I was doing all right, I thought. I was free to stay at my dad's place for the time being, plus I had a nice little construction job coming up that next weekend.

I had given Big John my notice at work. I was following through with my decision to leave the fast paced skip tracer life behind me. It wasn't just the potential for trouble with the law that made me quit. There was also an issue with drugs. Something about that life sucked me into using cocaine. I had never been seriously attracted to hard drugs. I smoked pot, but that was all. Somehow, though, cocaine got its hooks into me.

Coke is deceptive. My plan in the beginning was merely to sell the stuff, to be a dealer, not a user. All morality aside, I was trying to make a quick buck, which had always been my way. I would buy a quarter-ounce for five hundred and make eight hundred selling it. It seemed like an easy way to make fast money.

I gave no thought to the damage the stuff was doing to the people I sold it to. The way I saw it, that was their problem. I didn't make them buy it.

Eventually, though, I started using the stuff myself. Just a little at first, to kind of test the product so I could recommend it to customers. Pretty soon I liked it. I like it a lot, and before long I was spending all of my profits supporting my own habit.

Substance abuse is a powerful thing. A line of coke and a couple of shots of vodka, and I felt like nothing could stand in my way. My ability to think clearly and rationally kind of went out the window.

I'm not sure I can explain this, but the appeal of cocaine and my addiction to the fast paced excitement of the skip tracer profession were a lot alike. Mentally and emotionally, I was addicted to skip tracing. I loved that job. I loved it all, the pay, the action, the late night stakeouts. I wasn't afraid of the danger. Rather, I craved it.

I got out when I did, because a voice inside my head told me that I was going too fast, that I was living just one moment away from that one encounter that would land me back in the big house – or the mortuary.

Looking back, I think the thing that finally tipped the scale for me was what happened on the Whitman job, when I tripped and my handgun accidentally discharged. I was a felon in possession of a firearm, when that happened. What if I'd killed the guy? The last time I'd ignored the felon in possession law I'd been sent to prison for three years. It finally dawned on me that no matter how much I liked skip tracing, I was either going to put that life in the past or it would be the end of me.

Standing on that hilltop, looking out over the wide expanse stretched out before me, I made a life-changing decision. I decided that that was where I would leave it all in the past and make a brand-new start. I had no way of knowing that dominoes were already lining up to launch my life in an entirely new direction.

I had lined up a side job for the weekend. I was going to help set roof trusses and install sheeting to get a new house ready for the roofers. The job would only take a day or two, so I arrived at the site early to get everything set up. I had a lot to accomplish that day. I was the only paid guy on the job, and it was my responsibility to direct the rest of the crew. I was pumped and ready to get the show on the road. None of the other guys were construction workers, but rather just friends of the owners or people who owed them favors.

By the time the "crew" got there I had the layout all marked and ready. I started pulling up the trusses and placing them in position, so the other guys could nail them into place. That kind of work is not especially hard, but you have to be careful and pay attention or someone can get hurt, not to mention the fact that nothing that follows will fit, if the trusses are not in the required position.

The project went reasonably well that morning and before long it was time for our lunch break. I was concerned that some of the help had already started drinking beer, or judging by the look of them, they hadn't stopped from the night before. It was hard to tell. Either way, I was of the opinion that power saws, working on a roof, and drinking booze don't mix.

I said something to one guy, but I didn't come down hard. I hadn't recruited these guys, so it wasn't my place to send them packing.

The owner of the house had warned me in advance that she was going to introduce me to a friend of hers, a girl she had been telling me about for the past few days. She'd told me, "You will really like this girl. She's pretty, and is a really nice person. Oh, and I've told her about you, too."

From my place up on the roof, I'd already spotted the girl. She'd pulled up just before lunch in her little black convertible. From where I sat, straddling a roof truss, I thought she looked pretty good. At the time, I was kind of buff from working out, plus I'd been up on the roof all morning, wearing cutoff jeans and a tank top, as was my custom when I worked construction, so my tan looked a little darker than usual. Looking back, I might have been just a bit full of myself.

When I came down off the roof, the owner introduced us. Diana put her hand out for me to shake. For some reason, I didn't take it. I think maybe I was a little intimidated by her. I said, "Nice to meet you," then smiled and went back to work. I thought about it later. I concluded that I was definitely off my game and hadn't made make much of an impression on the lady. (Diana later told me that I was right about that. She was not impressed, and in fact, thought I was a bit arrogant.)

I couldn't help but notice, even in our brief encounter, that she had pretty blue eyes and a bright smile. Plus, there was a sense of style about her, something about the way she turned her head that caught my eye. It's hard to explain something like that, but whatever it was I was kind of hooked right from the start. I hoped I hadn't blown it by not shaking her hand, but would get another chance with her later in the day.

Back up on the roof I went. There was work to do. We worked all day, setting roof trusses, and then sheeting them over with plywood. Unbeknownst to me at the time, Diana had a young son. He was eleven, and his name was William. He had brown curly hair and big inquisitive eyes. Before I knew it, the kid was up the ladder and hanging close to me. He wanted to learn how to do the things I was doing. I didn't know who the boy was at first, but the two of us hit it off right from the start.

Time flew, and before I knew, it was getting dark. I started hurrying because I wanted to finish the job that day, and knew I was getting close. All I had left to do was lay down the felt-paper and the place would be ready for the roofers.

While I worked, I'd kept track of Diana. I couldn't get her out of my mind. At one point, I saw her get into her car and drive off. My heart sank. I wasn't entirely sure that I would see her later, or ever. I even asked one of the guys if the girl in the black convertible was coming back. He told that me she was, and I felt better.

Sure enough, while I was eating some supper and having a beer, the pretty lady in the black convertible drove up. I wasn't going to make the same mistake again. I decided that I was going to make some conversation.

I wasn't, however, the only guy at the worksite who wanted to talk to Diana. This one joker had been trying to get her attention all afternoon. By evening, the guy was at least half smashed and acting like an idiot. There was an inordinate amount of unbecoming language coming out of his mouth.

Eventually, he started telling coarse jokes, the kind you don't tell in front of a proper girl. So I moved a little closer and whispered loudly in his ear, "Pal, you need to go home. Now! I don't want to turn around and see you again."

The guy apparently got the message, because he left. The others started following suit, taking their good ole boy humor and moving on. Before long I had Diana all to myself, though I must say she was not acting like she was all that interested. Finally, when I started playing my guitar and singing some Jim Croce songs that we both knew, she started warming up.

The night was still early, so we sat and visited for hours. We sang some more and then went for a walk. The evening was perfect, so we walked for quite some time, stopping and making comments about the houses we saw along the way. It was our first time together and I knew right away that she wasn't like any of the girls I'd known before.

We both went our separate ways that evening, but not until we had made plans to have lunch together the next day. I went to sleep that night feeling happier and more at peace than I had in a very long time.

Diana and I spent a lot of time together over the next couple of months. I'd met her son, William, at the jobsite, and she quickly introduced me to her very intelligent, free spirited, sixteen-year-old daughter, Stacy. The first thing Stacy said when we met was, "Aren't you the guy I see riding his bicycle all over town, and always going fast?"

"Yep, that's me," I told her, laughing. The four of us soon became a tight-knit little group. We were kind of a team, right from the start, constantly doing things together. Diana bought everybody ten-speeds and we all started bicycling. We rode all over the place.

I felt compelled, from the very beginning, to be honest and up front with Diana about the things I had done in my past, and the fact that I had a criminal record. I didn't tell her about things that had been done to me, the abuse and all that, but I came clean with her about the life I had lived on the wrong side of the law, and my time in jails and prisons. And of course, I explained that I was sincerely trying to leave all of that behind me.

Diana, in turn, shared with me how she had come to be a single mom with two half- grown kids. She explained that she had been married to the kids' dad for several years. They had operated a plumbing and excavation business together. One day, her husband was plowing snow off the railroad tracks in their hometown, when he was hit by an Amtrak train and suffered massive head injuries. He was in a coma for six months, she explained.

"Jay suffered serious brain damage, but when he came out of the coma I assumed I would just take him home and nurse him back to health the best I could. But he was not the same man. He had to learn to speak again and relearn how to walk. The walking part never fully came back.

"I stayed with Jay for more than nine years after the accident. I didn't believe in divorce and wanted to be the best wife to him I could be. It wasn't his fault that he was struggling; it was the injury.

"Hoping that he would get better, I took my husband to various rehab facilities. At one of them, he met someone else, and told me he wanted a divorce. After that, we just went our separate ways."

Diana didn't seem angry or bitter at the man. She blamed it all on the accident and made it clear that she would not have left Jay, if he had not asked for a divorce. I believed that about her. I had already sensed that Diana was the kind of person who would love someone for as long as it was possible.

It was Diana's nature to be a giver. Every morning, for example, she would go to her grandmother's to visit and help with things around the house, and do the cooking. It was obvious that her grandmother meant a lot to her.

Sometimes, I went with her. Right away I noticed the funny way her grandmother looked at me. It reminded me of the way my Grandmother Mausolf used to look at me. You know, with those eyes that can see right through you. I made sure to mention to her that my intentions regarding Diana were good. She gave me a sweet little chuckle, as if to say, "Sure they are."

We spent the afternoons listening to her grandmother tell stories about Diana growing up. Then, the topic switched to questions about me. She asked a lot of questions. She was always polite and respectful, though at times she was a bit probing. I tried to be as honest as I could, and by the end of the day I think I won her over.

Somewhere along the way, I decided that Diana should hear about my past from someone besides me. So, I brought her along on one of my visits with my probation officer. I asked my P.O. to tell Diana all about my criminal past, and she did. Diana heard it all that day. I think that helped her trust me, because what she heard from my P.O. lined up perfectly with the things I had already told her.

After that, Diana sat down with Stacy and William and told them all about me. They responded that they felt that they knew me already, and liked me, and believed there was good in me. They must have meant that, because not too long after that we were driving home from celebrating William's twelfth birthday, when I was pulled over for going a little too fast.

The officer took my license back to his car, and when he returned he said there was an outstanding warrant for my arrest. He told me that he felt bad about it, but had no choice but to take me in.

I had no idea what the warrant was about. (I will get to that shortly.) But after I was released from jail that night, thanks to fast action on the part of my bail bondsman friend, Diana told me what happened with William after I was arrested. Her story touched my heart.

"Before the officer took you away, you gave me some names to call to get you out," Diana explained. "The kids heard you say that, and as soon as we got home, William went into his room and brought out his piggy bank. He told me to use all of his money to get Chuck out of jail."

There was a warm look in her eyes when she added, "I think that's when I realized for the first time that we all loved one other, and had really become a family."

I was thirty-seven when I met Diana. She was thirty-nine. Neither of us knew it at the time, but we were about to set out on the adventure of a lifetime together.

Chapter 37

On the Run from Minnesota

O ne of the things I loved about living in Minnesota was the fishing. They don't call it, "The Land of Ten Thousand Lakes," for nothing. In my opinion, one of the toughest and meanest game fish in the country is the Northern Pike. One morning in early July, I pulled in six of them in just a few hours.

We were fishing in the Crow Wing Chain of the upper Mississippi River. It was hot and humid, even out on the lake. As hot as it was, though, there was another kind of heat on my mind that afternoon. I had a court hearing coming up in a few days, and there was a good chance it might not be pretty.

When the police officer I mentioned earlier, pulled me over to give me a routine speeding ticket, he saw that my name had been flagged with an outstanding arrest warrant. I sat in a holding cell for only about an hour before I was bailed out, but that was long enough to learn what was going on with the warrant.

Come to find out, the druggie, the guy who had ripped me off a year earlier and stolen all my stuff, had also written some bad checks with my name on them and cashed them using my driver's license. He had removed my picture from my license and replaced mine with one of his. With a few finishing touches, he'd created a pretty good piece of fake I.D. He and his accomplishes then used that fake I.D. to cash tens of thousands of dollars' worth of stolen checks, all in my name.

Someone I had tried to help had set me up to take the fall for his crime. That's a drug addict for you. It has been my experience that people hooked on drugs will lie cheat and steal, even from their own mother, to satisfy their habit. Whatever his excuse was, I wasn't about to go to prison for this guy's scam. That's all there was to it.

Now mind you, I had committed dozens of serious crimes for which I had never been caught or prosecuted. I had busted into a fair number of safes, burglarized more businesses than I can remember, and had broken into a few houses.

One time, when I had just been released from prison, I had my brother Kenny and his girlfriend follow me around all day, while I drove the truck for a vending machine company. Late in the day, when the time was right, we loaded all of the cigarettes that were left over and all of the change we had removed from the machines, a ton of change, all into Kenny's car. My brother spent the whole next day converting all that change into paper currency. We were never caught.

Still, no matter how many crimes I had gotten away with, I didn't do the phony check thing for which I had just been arrested, and it didn't sit well with me to be facing prison time for something I hadn't done. No one wants to take the hit for someone else's crime, especially when they had just decided to go straight.

It had been raining and storming the evening I was bailed out of jail, so Diana and I'd decided to spend the evening in the cabin with Stacy and William, playing board games and singing along with the radio. Deep down, I had always wanted a family like this, and I was determined not to do anything that would cause me to lose these relationships. I had fallen in love with Diana, and with her two kids. We had become a family, and that meant the world to me. It also meant that Church Street and Barbara were slipping farther and farther from my mind.

The only truly important person still missing from my life was my daughter Jacqueline. That situation did not look hopeful, so I pushed it to the back of my mind. I doubted that I would see her anytime soon, if ever. Sure, I still thought about her from time to time, and I missed her. But I was content overall, having three new and amazing people in my life.

The time came for Diana and me to talk about court, a subject we had been avoiding. I had already made up my mind that I wasn't going to jail, no matter what the court decided. The sentence I was facing could amount to several years in prison, and I knew enough to know that being innocent was no guarantee of being found "not guilty."

The hearing was coming up in a few days, so we would have to make plans in advance, if I was going to be able to avoid jail, in the event I lost the case.

I had seen my share of judges, and I didn't like any of them. Few criminals do. I had an even lower opinion of county attorneys, government lawyers who spend their careers prosecuting people. Still, in a few short days I knew I would be sitting in a courtroom with my entire future in their hands.

The way I saw it, judges sat up there in their black robes, acting like they were gods, who could do no wrong. To make matters worse, the prosecutor handling my case looked like one of those wimps that guys like me used to steal lunch money from. The man probably became a district attorney, just so he could get back at the kind of guys who used to beat him up when he was a kid.

Thoughts like those were guiding my thinking that day. In fact, it was my opinion of the justice system and the people running it that led me to the conclusion that I was not going to leave my fate in their hands.

I knew I hadn't committed the crime for which I had been charged. I hadn't written those bad checks. If I was guilty of anything, it was foolishly trusting someone who needed help, but wasn't ready to accept it. But being gullible isn't a crime, so I was frustrated and angry that I was facing prison time for something someone else had done.

Frankly, the gravity of my situation was getting to me. I was beginning to revert back to my old way of thinking. I was starting to think that maybe the only way to deal with people like this guy, people who use and abuse others, for their own selfish ends, was to dig them a hole – like I always wanted to do for Barbara.

And yet, every time I thought about what I wanted to do to people like Barbara, and to the druggie who had ripped me off, to give them what they really deserved, I found myself feeling sorry for them. Instead of getting back at them, I found myself excusing them.

When you're focusing solely on how people have wronged you, it is hard to remember all the times you have robbed innocent people, broken into their homes or businesses and stolen their stuff. Your instinct is to focus on the wrongs you've suffered, and forget the ones you've inflicted.

Notwithstanding all that, if the case before me went bad and the judge and the prosecutor were determined to send me to jail, I needed a backup plan. After talking it over as a family, we came up with a bold and creative, but rather bizarre plan for the future, our future as a family.

We had been playing monopoly that evening, so I handed Stacy the little silver boot, one of the game pieces. Then I put a blindfold on her. We laid a map of the United States out on the kitchen table and spun her around a few times. Stacy's assignment was to randomly toss the little boot onto the map.

As a family, we had agreed that where the boot landed was the place we would all move to, if I had to leave town on the run. Stacy stood there for a moment, the little boot held firmly in her fist, then gave it a fateful toss. The boot bounced and slid across the map, then came to rest on a town called Hoquiam, a city located on the Olympic Peninsula in the northwest corner of Washington state. None of us were sure how to pronounce the name of the city, but it turned out that Diana and Stacy guessed correctly.

Looking back, the whole situation was kind of funny. There we all were, standing in the kitchen of a cabin in Minnesota, our minds made up to move to Hoquiam, Washington, simply because that's where the little silver boot had landed. With that, the matter was settled.

The next morning, we drove into town. Stacy had an appointment to take a driving test, so she could get her driver's license. While she was doing that, Diana and I started making contacts in Washington. We began with a call to the local Chamber of Commerce, to see what they could tell us about the area. We called a realtor and enquired about locating a house to live in, once we got there.

We didn't have a lot of time to prepare. It was already the third of the month, and my court date was set for the seventh.

Our search went surprisingly well. Right away, we found a house we could live in "rent free." The owners wanted someone to do some remodeling for them, and that fit us perfectly. I had the carpentry experience, and working off the rent was good for our budget. Things were coming together nicely, and all four of us started getting excited about the adventure we were about to take. Picking up stakes and moving to a strange place where we didn't know a soul made us feel like early pioneers headed out west to homestead. The thought was both exciting and frightening. I was kind of used to running off to some strange place, but in those days I didn't have a family to care about.

That night, we drove to the city and checked into a hotel. After dinner, we drove to the train station where I bought a one-way ticket to Shelby, Montana. From there I would take a Greyhound to Butte,

Montana. That's where we would all meet up, in the likely event I had to make a break for it. We purchased the ticket in my new name, Timothy C. Dunn.

I found the name in the obituary section of the local newspaper. Next, I went to the Office of Vital Statistics and paid to have a copy of Mr. Dunn's birth certificate. Then, I went to the DMV and applied for a new state I.D. card. Just like that, I was a new man. I would be leaving my old life as Charles Dudrey behind me, and starting fresh – new family and all. Even though I wasn't really a new man, the new identity gave me a sense of freedom, and I loved it.

I was really looking forward to moving to Washington. I had spent a summer there with my Dudrey grandparents as a kid, and had returned a few years later, when at age seventeen, I was on the run from the County Home. Hoquiam was a two or three-hour drive from Morton, and I was excited about going back to the area. I was glad the little silver boot had landed on a town in Washington. Of course, I had no idea that there was a bigger plan behind all of this, one over which I had no control.

That night, it was hard to sleep. That was only partly due to the drama of the situation. There was also fear that something might go awry with our plans, something that might keep us from making the trip west. The reality of the situation was, I was going to be in a courthouse with deputies everywhere, which meant that there was a very real possibility that in spite of all our planning, something might go wrong, and I would be sent to prison.

Early the next morning, we finished breakfast and went over the plan one more time. Finally, it was time to drive to the courthouse. I had been to that building many times, as a bond agent. But this was the first time I was going to be there on my own behalf.

When we got to the courtroom, my attorney was waiting. Charley had defended me more than once over the years, and we had a good relationship. The rule I went by was, never lie to your lawyer unless you had no other choice. So, as usual, Charley knew everything about my case. I'm pretty sure he believed that I was innocent of the charge. In other cases, I had told him up front that I was guilty, when, in fact, I was. I always believed that your lawyer will fight harder, if he or she believes you.

Two years earlier, Charley had defended me in a case in which I could easily have been sent back to prison. I remember that day well. I thought I was going to do serious time, so on the morning before court,

I told Charley that I didn't have the money to pay my attorney fees. I did have a new computer, I explained, that had never been taken out of the box. I asked him if he would accept the computer as full payment. He said he would.

At the end of the day, I got six months in jail, instead of prison. It could have been a lot worse. The charge was perjury, and knowing that judges don't like being lied to, I was happy with the deal Charley got me. In the process, I had been fair to him regarding my attorney fees, and he appreciated that.

Charley, however, was not having the same kind of good fortune with my new case. As the proceeding moved along that morning, it became increasingly clear that things were not going to go my way. Right before lunch, Charley and I sat down and talked. He explained to Diana and me that the District Attorney wouldn't make a deal for less than five years. Worse yet, he made it clear that five years was probably the least amount of time I would get.

It really bugged me that the prosecutor wanted me to go to prison for five years for something he most likely knew I hadn't done. He knew he was holding all of the cards because he knew he had a good chance of getting a conviction, whether I was guilty or not. From a strategic perspective, the prosecutor had an ace up his sleeve. The charge I was facing was aggravated forgery, and I had been convicted of forgery in the credit card scam I had done a few years back with Dad and Susan. That fact alone was probably enough for everyone to assume that I was guilty this time, as well.

Charley was always a straight shooter with me. He looked me in the eye and gave me the bottom line. "Either take five years in a plea deal," he said, "or possibly face much more time."

Five years is a lot of time. If you've never been in a situation like that, it's hard to comprehend the stress. You know you didn't commit the crime, but you have to assume that the prosecution has enough to make you look guilty. You can roll the dice and go to trial, and maybe win. But if you lose, and they throw the book at you, you might get ten or fifteen years in prison for something you didn't do.

On the other hand, you can take the deal and spend just five years in prison. That might seem like the better deal, but think of it this way. That's 365 days, lived one long, boring day at a time, times five long, hopeless years of being locked up in a cell. The anguish of a choice like that is mind numbing, and even more so, if you are innocent.

There's one aspect of plea deals that is rarely discussed, and it is perhaps the most frightening. When you make a plea deal, it always includes you standing before a judge and declaring that you are guilty of a specific crime. You make a deal beforehand with the prosecution. Both sides agree to how much time you will serve for the crime, then you stand in front of the judge and say, "Guilty, Your Honor."

The judge then asks you if anyone promised you anything or threatened you with anything in exchange for the guilty plea. You have to say in response to both questions, "No, Your Honor." Otherwise the judge can't accept your guilty plea.

You have to say you were not promised anything or threatened with anything, even though it is a bold-faced lie and everyone knows it. You were just promised a deal for less time in exchange for not forcing the government to go through the time and expense of a trial. And you were just threatened with having to do more time, if you didn't make the deal. In other words, the legal system requires you to lie and say there were no promises or threats, if you want to make a deal. They call this, "Getting your 'orals' right."

But here's the scary part. After you have said in open court that you were not promised anything or threatened with anything as part of the plea you are entering, the judge is not legally bound to the terms of the deal you made with the prosecutor. The judge can say that he or she understands that the prosecution has recommended a sentence of five years and then sentence you to that term; or the judge can say that he or she is rejecting the prosecution's recommendation for a five-year sentence and instead sentence you to the maximum, which might be five or ten years for every single fraudulent check you allegedly wrote.

The minute between the judge accepting your guilty plea and the judge announcing your sentence is the most dangerous, vulnerable minute in a defendant's life, and especially so if the defendant is actually innocent. Judges are not parties to plea agreements and can accept or reject the deal you thought you made. Once you have entered a guilty plea, however, you are entirely at their mercy and can't take back what you said.

People don't like to hear this, but prosecutors send innocent people to jail all the time. Defendants would rather take a one-year or two-year or five-year sentence than face the possibility of a stiffer sentence, if they go to trial and lose.

I apologize for that little tangent. Let me just say this: Sitting there, in the hallway of the courthouse with Charley and Diana, my mind was fully made up. I was not going to roll the dice in a trial or make a plea deal. My family and I were taking off.

"Charley," I said. "Go tell the prosecutor that I'll give them my answer after the lunch hour. Oh, and by the way, I won't actually be there, so it has been nice knowing you. I'm out of here."

Charley and I shook hands. He wished us the best. Then Diana and I walked calmly to the elevator. Once the elevator door closed, I quickly changed outfits and put on a hat and some sunglasses. We got off the elevator, left the building, and walked to where the car was parked. We hopped in and drove directly to the hotel.

I knew that as soon I didn't appear for court, a warrant would be issued for my arrest. That meant there was no time to waste. That evening, I told Diana and the kids that I would see them in three days and boarded the Amtrak train for Shelby, Montana.

The train ride took about twenty hours and I think I slept the whole way. I was completely drained. Once again, I was on the run. This, however, was different from all those other times. This time, I had no intention of ever going back. I planned on spending the rest of my life under a false identity while the law searched in vain for some guy named Charles Dudrey.

Chapter 38

The Ancient of Days Steps In

S tanding in the front yard of our new home in Hoquiam, I could see Grays Harbor. The smell of the sea breeze flooded my senses, and I absolutely loved it. I had made a clean getaway, and felt like a new man.

Sure, I knew that there would be a warrant out for my arrest, but "Chuck" was long gone. As far as I was concerned, I was now Tim Dunn. I got a Washington driver's license and started getting used to my new name. I had buried my old life somewhere deep in the back of my mind, and had no intention of ever resurrecting it. I had a clean slate now, and no one was the wiser. Only Diana and the kids knew the truth.

We spent the next few weeks making the new place our home, cleaning the house and fixing up the yard. The owners stopped by to introduce themselves and have me sign a formal rental agreement. I liked signing my new name, although every time I did I felt a little twinge of guilt. I was sort of surprised by that. So what if it wasn't my real name? I had identification sufficient to prove that I was Timothy Dunn, and that's all that mattered. Besides, Minnesota's unethical attempt to convict me of something I hadn't done had forced me to do this.

I recall one afternoon, when Diana called me Chuck instead of Tim. I had asked her to please go along with me on the name change. I'd told her it was important. Later, I asked her why she still wanted to call me by my old name. She answered simply, "You will always be Chuck to me."

Well, I thought, Charles was Timothy C. Dunn's middle name, so it would be easy enough to explain if someone heard her call me "Chuck." So I was Chuck at home and Tim everywhere else.

It was summer in the Pacific Northwest. The weather was great and everything was green and lush. Of course I had no idea what was coming, weather wise. We spent lots of time at the beach those first few months, picking up sand dollars and other seashells. I told Diana and the kids about how I used to do the same thing, when I was a kid, and hung out with my dad's mom and dad at that very same beach.

If you've never spent a summer in the Pacific Northwest around Grays Harbor and the Olympic Peninsula, you have missed something. The weather is beautiful most of the time, but it still rains enough to keep things mostly green. We had a great time that first summer, getting to know our newly-adopted state.

In spite of all the good times, I continued to wrestle with the fear of being arrested and being hauled off to prison. I knew that it was an unlikely event, but I didn't want anything to ruin the new life we had put together. Still, I was always looking around expecting something to happen. I kept telling myself not to be scared, to buck it up and be tough, but to be honest I was haunted.

Diana found a job, the kids started school in the fall, and I found a job repairing washers and dryers at an appliance shop. I was paid cash, so there were no taxes to pay, and no way for anyone to trace the money back to me. One afternoon, while I was walking home, I saw a man in an alley near our house. It didn't take me long to size him up. I knew the type. That night I went home with a bag of pot to smoke. I was sure some good smoke would make everything easier for me. I could think well and work faster if I had some weed in me. I had been that way for years. Diana knew I smoked the stuff, but had never said much about it. I got the feeling she didn't approve, and certainly she never smoked any herself, but as far as I was concerned that was her choice, not mine.

The way I saw it, my conversational skills improved, and I was more fun to be around than I had been in weeks. What could be wrong with that? I decided right then and there that I would always smoke pot. It slowed me down just a little, and took the edge off. Yes, I was sure pot was good for me.

I recalled back when I was in the treatment program when I was in prison. All of the guys in the group were yelling and screaming at me. They didn't like it when I told them, matter-of-factly, "I'll always smoke weed." The cons tried to talk me out it, but what did they know?

Time passed quickly our first few months in Hoquiam, and before we knew it, it was October. Before long, I would be celebrating my thirty-ninth birthday. Sometime in October, there was a major change in the weather. The rains came. That may be the greatest understatement I've ever made. I was in no way prepared for the amount of rain that started falling from the sky. It rained and rained and then rained some more. It didn't stop day or night. It wasn't always a downpour. Sometimes, it was just steady rain, but it rarely, if ever, let up.

I had never seen so much rain in my life; rain and lots of wind. We were, after all, living very near the ocean and at our backs was a vast mountain range, which stopped the clouds from flying on by. The clouds came in off the ocean, full of moisture, then immediately dumped most of it on us. It was a shock to the senses.

Oh well. Out to the garage I went and smoked some weed. Yes, grass was the drug for me. It even helped me cope with the rain. Plus, the way I saw it at the time, the dope helped with the evil thoughts I was battling. I was really struggling with a desire to go back to Minnesota and take care of some of the people who had done me wrong. I fought hard to drive the thoughts from my mind, but they persisted.

Some days, I was consumed with regret for not killing Barbara that night at the top of the stairs. Memories of things I had never told Diana about started coming back full force. It was as if all of that stuff from so many years ago had just happened. I remembered Barbara's urine-soaked goulash, and the two-by-two beating. I recalled how she beat me and my brothers and sisters with extension cords and with her fists, even little Frances. I remember how she locked my baby sister in a dark closet for hours at a time and made her eat a whole jaw of peanut butter with a handful of salt mixed in.

The more I thought about it, the more details I remembered, which led to an even more powerful desire to see that woman dead. I wanted justice. I wanted to make sure she didn't get away with all of the cruel things she had done. My soul was all but consumed by hatred and bitterness.

The dark thoughts would come to me, seemingly out of nowhere. I wasn't trying to think them. Somehow they just showed up in my mind, uninvited, and started consuming me from the inside. Sure, there were others I hated and wished were dead, but none of them held a candle to the evil woman who had made the lives of me and my brothers and sisters a living hell.

For some inexplicable reason, I always gave my dad a pass on all that stuff. He had obviously let it happen, and in fact, had dished out more than his share of over the top beatings, including sending me to the Mayo clinic with brain damage. And he had almost certainly had our mother killed. But still, I gave him a pass and focused my hatred on Barbara.

I desperately wanted the marijuana to calm those feelings and dampen my rage, but nothing seemed to help with that. The truth is, there was a lot of ugly stuff festering inside me, and I had no idea what to do about it. People spend decades seeing shrinks about issues smaller than mine, and yet continue to struggle.

One day, I saw an ad in the paper for a male Cocker Spaniel puppy. Bringing home a cute little puppy seemed like a good idea, so I went to check him out. The first time I tried to pet the little guy, he bit me. I ignored the nip, deciding he would be okay once he got used to his new home. He had probably been hit or abused by someone and just needed a little nurturing. So, I bought the dog and took him home. We named him Spike. That seemed like a fitting name for a little dog that would dare bite a guy my size.

I sat in front of the TV holding Spike every chance I got, just loving on the little fellow. At the time, the U.S. was at war in the Middle East and my eyes were glued to the television most of the day. The pictures that flashed across my screen were all too real. Bombs with cameras mounted on them were blowing up buildings, tanks were speeding through the desert. It was all unfolding right there on our living room television set.

I wondered if I was possibly looking at the beginning of the end of the world. It was, after all, going to take place in the Middle East. That's what my grandparents had told me as a kid. I remembered them saying something about all the armies of the world coming together to attack Israel. So I sat back, smoked some pot, and watched TV news, often for hours at a time.

Late one afternoon, I decided that my new dog needed a bath. He was stinking. So I grabbed the dog shampoo, and with the dog under my arm, headed upstairs to run some water in the bathtub. I had no idea that what was about to happen was going to change my life forever.

As the tub was filling with water, I started petting the dog and loving him up. I was trying to prepare him mentally for getting in the water. But my plan wasn't working. The poor little guy was trembling with fear. The moment I put him in the water, he turned and nipped me on the hand. My reflex was to slap him, just to teach him a lesson, and then continue bathing him. But the furry little varmint snapped at me, and bit me again.

I reacted more strongly than the first time. I smacked him harder than I intended. I hurt the little guy and he began to shake with fear. At that moment, my puppy looked up at me with the most hopeless look on his face. When I saw the pitiful look in his eyes, it broke my heart. I realize, of course, that a puppy's temporarily hurt feelings were probably not that big of a deal. He probably wouldn't remember the incident thirty minutes later. But the effect it had on me and my raw, tattered emotions was powerful.

Tears started welling up in my eyes. I quickly rinsed him off and dried him with a towel, crying like a baby the entire time and feeling guilty for what I had done to my innocent little dog.

After I'd dried him off, I picked him up and walked down the stairs and out the door. It was a stormy night, but not too cold. I walked aimlessly through the darkness for several blocks, holding the puppy tightly in my arms. The wind and rain were blowing in my face, so I cuddled the puppy close to keep him warm. A steady stream of tears continued to roll down my cheeks and mixed with the raindrops.

Charles Dudrey, certified tough guy and career criminal, was sobbing and crying like a baby. I felt like I was breaking apart inside, all over a stupid little dog that shouldn't have nipped me in the first place.

When through the darkness, I saw out in front of me the weathered boards of the pier, I realized that I had walked quite some distance and was now standing by the river. I stood there for a minute, looking out over the water, then suddenly started sobbing out loud. I wept uncontrollably. The emotion began to pour out of me in what seemed like a torrent. My chest heaved in and out with each breath.

Something was going on inside me and it was much deeper than the thing with the dog. I could feel it in the very core of my being. The pressure that was welling up was so powerful that I couldn't catch my breath. Suddenly, words started bursting forth.

"God, I need you. Oh please, God, help me." It was my own voice, but it sounded desperate, as if my life was at stake.

I was silent for a moment, then began to weep and sob even harder than before. All of a sudden, every bad thing I had done in my entire life started gushing forth from my memory. All the people I had hurt, the crimes I had committed, the lies, the deception, the immorality. Everything I was ever guilty of, things I hadn't thought about in years, all flashed before my mind's eye, as my soul pleaded with God for help.

The guilt and anguish was so great that my guts hurt. As my memory dredged up a lifetime of sins, I began to feel a great emptiness deep inside me, and sense that I was lost, totally lost. It was from that place that I called out to my Maker from the depth of my soul.

"In Jesus name, God, help me, please. I am so scared. Please forgive me, oh God, for what I have done. Please, I am so sorry."

I stood there weeping, pouring everything out, then all of a sudden a calmness came over me. It was like it was consuming me. The anxiousness and emotional turmoil left me, and I felt a clearness of mind.

I began to notice where I was standing and what was going on around me. The wind had stopped blowing, and the night air around me had become still. The rain had stopped. I was standing there, breathing in the fresh clean night air, when an overwhelming peace began to flow into me. I could feel it entering my body, filling me up. At that moment I realized that I was free.

I had never felt or sensed anything remotely like that. I could feel the presence of God, right there with me. My mind was at ease. I felt clean. I felt free. I knew that I had been forgiven by the one Person who can fully and completely forgive and wipe clean a human heart.

The tears came again, but this time the tears that rolled down my cheeks were tears of gratitude and thankfulness. I was smiling from ear to ear and thanking God. I was smiling so big, that it almost made my face hurt. I had never felt so complete, and so at ease.

I noticed that I didn't feel high anymore. The effect of the weed I had smoked earlier was completely gone. I started praising God, something I had never done before. No one preached to me that night. I hadn't followed any formula or script I knew. In fact, I had no idea what I was doing. All I can say is I encountered the Son of God on a rainy, nighttime walk through the streets of Hoquiam, Washington. I felt his forgiveness and mercy sweep over me and wipe away every rotten thing I had ever done.

When I turned and started back toward home, I was a new man. I knew it. And I knew that nothing would ever be the same.

Still, I had a lot to learn. God had indeed wiped my slate clean. He had forgiven a lifetime of sin. But that didn't mean that man's law was done with me. That didn't mean I was done with being locked up. But whatever lay ahead of me, from that night forward, I knew that I would no longer face it alone.

Chapter 39

Me, a Church Guy

W hen I awoke the next day, I was still filled with the same great joy I had found the night before, down at the pier. I was the most upbeat and excited I had ever been. I walked around all day thanking God and praising Him for the forgiveness I had been granted. It was all so real, and so unlike anything I had ever experienced.

It was hard to wrap my head around the change that had come over me. I had never been a religious person. Far from it, actually. But here I was, walking around the house, talking about Jesus and the goodness of God like some Bible thumper.

Diana took it all in stride. She accepted and even encouraged my new found spirituality. She had been raised Roman Catholic, so believing in God and Jesus was something she took for granted, even if her belief had no real impact on her life. The kids, on the other hand, were kind of overwhelmed, especially Stacy. And who could blame them? They had no frame of reference for what they were seeing, and I wasn't exactly wise in the way I approached them about it.

I had found the most amazing thing in the world, and I wanted everyone else to have what I had. I thought they should trust and believe in God, just like I did. They should realize that they were sinners and have their sins forgiven, just like I had. And immediately. I must have been overbearing to say the least.

God had likely spent years getting me to the place where I was willing to accept the reality that without Him I was lost, but I expected William and Stacy to see the truth right then, right on the spot.

I withdrew from them, at least a bit, and began searching the television guide for Christian programming. I came upon a listing for CBN, the Christian Broadcasting Network. Once I found that channel, I sat and watched it for hours on end, soaking up everything they said about living the Christian life. I sat in front of the television, singing along and praising Jesus. I found myself singing some of the old hymns I had heard at my grandparents' church, when I was a kid. I was surprised by how many of the lines came back to me, even if just in bits and pieces.

Sometimes it was hard to sing, because I had tears in my eyes and was completely choked up. It was the strangest thing. I was weeping and feeling totally peaceful at the same time. One of the preachers on TV talked about, "Peace that surpasses all understanding." That was it. That's what I was feeling.

I couldn't escape the feeling that I needed to go to church and be around other people who loved Jesus. I had no idea which one to pick, but I knew I had to find one and go. I talked to Diana about it and she agreed that if I believed I should go to church, then I should. The next day happened to be Sunday, so I picked one and went.

I sat there feeling good about being in church, and yet feeling uncomfortable at the same time. We sang three or four songs and then the preacher went forward and started talking. I had been listening to the guys on TV, so this was the first time I heard a preacher in person. I had no basis for judging whether he did a good job, but it was okay. When the service was over, I met a few people, shook a few hands, and then headed out the door.

I was on my way to the car, still thanking God for saving me and forgiving me of my sins, when suddenly I found myself thinking about my family. Diana and the kids had left everything they had ever known, just so we could all be together. Even though I was wanted by the law when we left Minnesota, three months earlier, they believed me when I told them that we would all start a new life together in Washington, and it would all work out. And so far it had. We had a comfortable home, and life was going well.

But something was bothering me. Diana was a special, beautiful woman, and I loved her. In fact, I was more impressed with her with each passing day. Her two youngsters were amazing, too, and I thought of them as my own. I realized that I was fortunate to have three such wonderful people in my life, and I did not want to hurt them or drive them away. But I wanted them to know Jesus, and they didn't.

Something strange and new happened after church that day. On my way home, I heard God say something to me. I know that sounds strange, in and of itself. And if I told you how God spoke to me, you probably wouldn't believe it, so I won't elaborate. But the message I heard was simple and clear. I was not to go back to that church again. I had no idea why, but I never did.

Chapter 40

Going All In

After that day, I continued watching Christian television as much as I could. All this religious stuff might sound a little nuts, maybe more than a little, but I was just living in the moment, loving God and appreciating what He had done for me. There is a story in the Bible that might better explain why I was behaving the way I was.

There was this woman of the streets, someone the religious people considered unclean. She somehow found her way into a room where Jesus was having supper with some religious leaders. She sat down at his feet and began washing them with her tears and drying them with her hair. The religious people in the room were incensed, and began chiding Him for letting this unclean woman, someone who had been a prostitute, touch his feet.

Jesus looked down at the woman and gently told her that her sins were forgiven.

As you might imagine, that really upset the "holier than thou" people at the dinner. They protested, saying, "Only God can forgive sins."

Then, Jesus explained to them something that, I think, explains what was going on with me. He reminded his hosts that when He had walked in off the dusty street, none of them had washed his feet, or had even offered him water, as was the custom of the day, so he could do it himself. But this woman, He explained, had not ceased to wash his feet with her tears and dry them with her hair.

Then He summed it all up for them with this simple, but profound declaration, "To whom much is forgiven, the same loves much."

That was it. That was why the woman had so loving caressed Jesus' feet, washing them with her tears and drying them with her hair. She had been forgiven of so much that she could not help but love the One who had forgiven such a great load of sin.

That's how it was for me. My sins were so many, and they were so awful; I had hurt so many people, and broken so many of God's laws, that I was completely overwhelmed when He forgave me. I was acting the way I was, because I was overwhelmed with love for the One who had stooped down and touched such an unclean man, and made him clean.

As for religious or moral people, who think they are good people already and don't need much forgiveness, well, they're really missing out. And I suspect they might not have a really honest picture of their own hearts. The Bible says, "The heart of man is deceitful and desperately wicked above all things, who can know it?" I think that statement is for everyone, not just people like me whose rottenness was painfully obvious.

So, I kept praising and thanking God and watching Christian television as much as I could. I could tell, though, that others in the house were starting to get upset with me for being so "religious." I didn't want to make them uncomfortable, so I went to the bedroom and closed the door. I wasn't embarrassed. I just didn't want to upset the rest of my family.

That evening, it occurred to me that I needed to talk to someone about what was going on in my life, maybe a pastor or a minister. It was almost nine at night when the impulse hit me, but I wanted to call someone right away and at least leave a message for them to call me back. I started thumbing through the phone book, looking for the church section. I ran my fingers down the page, stopped, and dialed one of the numbers I saw there.

To my surprise, a man answered the telephone. I didn't really know what to say. Recalling the events of the past few days and the shows I'd been watching on television, I just blurted out, "Are you a Spirit-filled church?"

His answer was, "Well, what do you mean by Spirit filled? If you're asking, do we trust in the Spirit of God? Then yes, we are a "Spirit filled church."

I was so excited to speak with someone who understood what I was talking about. The man explained that he was the pastor of the church. He sounded kind.

He asked me my name. I lied, and told him I was Tim Dunn. I felt a twinge of guilt. He invited me to join him and some of the others from the church at their next meeting, which was on Wednesday evening. I told him I would be there.

I had no sooner hung up the phone, when suddenly, out of nowhere, I started hearing voices in my head. These were not like the voices I had grown accustomed to hearing when I'd struggled over things that had happened in my past. This was different. These were not my own thoughts. They were coming from outside of me.

I tried to think about something else, but that didn't work. The voices were still there. I theorized that maybe I was having a battle in my own mind, arguing back and forth in some kind of internal struggle. But what I was hearing, sounded like lots of voices, and they were real. They were saying things like, "Call the cops now, and tell them you're wanted by the law in Minnesota. You're a liar; you're not a Christian. Look at all the things you've done. You stabbed that guy in the chest for attacking you. Remember that? He almost died. Remember when you burned down that garage? Call the Pastor and tell him about that. See if he wants you at his church, then."

The voices were ridiculing me. They were screaming and yelling. They were laughing at me, and making fun of me. It was frightening, and I wondered if maybe I was going crazy. It felt like I was fully awake, and yet having a nightmare. My head started pounding.

Suddenly, like a frightened child, I cried out, "Jesus, help me!"

I didn't think. I just cried out.

The moment I spoke those words, the voices retreated. I could sense that they were still there, but they were moving away from me. It was like they were fleeing, like a mist that is being blown out to sea by a strong wind.

I felt at ease. I had peace again.

I could sense that the voices were not completely gone. They had retreated some distance, and then stopped, as if waiting for something.

I had never been in a spiritual battle before. I had no idea what had just happened. All I knew was that powerful voices had been screaming at me, mocking me, accusing me, ridiculing me, but just when they were about to overwhelm me, I called on my God and they fled when I said His name. That was not an experience I would soon forget.

Wednesday night finally arrived. I had really been looking forward to the meeting. I walked in with several other people, who had also just arrived. The pastor came over and greeted me and began introducing me to the others. I took a seat in the third row from the front and settled in for the class.

The group was in the middle of a Bible study on the Book of Ephesians. The pastor talked about spiritual battles. He explained the difference between the spirit life and the life of the flesh, or the soul. He explained that these two often battle one another, and that the struggle takes place in our minds.

I thought that maybe this was what had happened to me two nights earlier, when I'd heard the voices. It had seemed like a spiritual battle, all right. But, I was pretty sure that the voices I'd heard were not my own mind talking.

From that night on, I started going to all of the meetings at the church, and soaking up as much as I could. I always wanted more.

Back at home, however, relationships were being stretched, especially with Stacy. She was nearly eighteen, and was not fond of the idea of living with a hyper-religious father figure in her life. She was not sure she liked this new me, all that much. She preferred the old, non-religious version.

But that was not my only problem. I was becoming increasingly aware of the fact that I was in a living arrangement that was not pleasing to God. Living with a woman to whom I was not married was not exactly biblical. But what could I do? This amazing woman, a woman I deeply loved, had left everything she knew and loaded up her kids and traveled across the country with me. I couldn't just walk away from her. What would she think of the God I had found, if my meeting Him broke up our family?

I had talked to them about Jesus, and had explained who He was. The problem was, I had shared my faith from a position of judgment, telling them about the wrath of God, and about the hellfire and brimstone they faced if they didn't get saved. I hadn't balanced that with the love of Jesus, and the peace and forgiveness that God gives.

I realize now that I had been sharing my faith from the place I was in, when I got saved, a place of fear. I was scared, and had every reason to be. When I encountered the Lord down by the pier that night, I was overwhelmed by the sheer volume and ugliness of my sins, and that's what caused me to call out to God in desperation.

It's true that sin offends God and there is such a place as hell and judgment, but that's only part of the message. The Christian message is called the "gospel" for a reason. The word gospel means "good news."

I had indeed experienced that good news the night God washed away my sins. But I hadn't yet learned how to share the truth of it.

None of that, however, changed the fact that Diana and I were not married and were living together. I felt strongly that this was not okay with God. So, I sat down with Diana and told her that I loved her, but that I had to move out of our house. I told her how much it would hurt to leave the warmest and most loving place I had ever lived, but I had to go.

Right or wrong, there was no way I could feel good about doing that. There was no way it was fair to her. She had completely uprooted her life to be with me. She and her children had run away to Hoquiam with me, based merely on the toss of a Monopoly game piece.

It is probably fair to say that, even though my life with God was good at the time, the rest of my life was a total mess.

The easy answer to our dilemma was to just get married, but there was a problem with that, too. Diana had made it abundantly clear that she wasn't willing to marry me as Tim Dunn. I'd asked her, but she'd said, "No." She told me that she would only marry me as Charles Dudrey, not under some fake name. The woman had her principles! She would rather let me move out than marry me under a false name.

What could I do? If I used my real name on a public document, it would be just a matter of time before the law would catch up with me, and I would end up back in prison. Given that reality, we found ourselves at an impasse, so I moved out.

At one point I told God that I hadn't signed up for this, that it was just too much. I was saved and wanted to serve Him, but at the same time I was a fugitive living under a false name and on the run from the law. I was like a man sitting straddled across a picket fence. Life was hurting.

I was calling myself a Christian, but deceiving people about my true identity. I tried telling myself that I wasn't the same person as before, so it just made sense that I have a new name. But something inside me kept telling me that I had not taken care of business.

Life can change quickly. Mine was changing on several fronts, all at once. I was one hundred percent certain that I had experienced the presence of Almighty God, the one the Bible refers to as "The Ancient of Days." What had happened was not some figment of my imagination or something I had just made up. I hadn't gone off the deep end. I had met Jesus, and it was as simple as that.

Still, something had to give. My faith had to reach into these other areas of my life and make them healthy, too. But that was not going to be an easy matter.

Chapter 41

The Vision

I continued to attend church. I loved it and wanted to absorb as much as I could.

One day, one of the couples invited me and some other folks over to their house for dinner after the Sunday service. I felt a little uncomfortable about going. I barely knew these people, and that was the first time I had been invited to anyone's home since I was saved.

Once I got there, though, everyone made me feel right at home. Their house was very cozy and well kept. The walls were covered with lovely family pictures, all nicely framed. I got the impression that they were collectors of picture frames, because each one was unique and beautiful.

While the ladies worked in the kitchen preparing the meal, the men sat in the living room and visited. The design of the house was open enough for the women to join in, so everyone was engaged in the same conversation. It was a warm and friendly atmosphere and whatever it was they were cooking smelled really good.

Out of nowhere, I was overcome with a strange drowsiness. Two or three times, I caught my head falling forward, as I started to doze off. Like most people, I get sleepy if I eat too much, but I don't tend to doze off while I'm waiting for lunch.

I can't explain what happened next without using a word that will make some people nervous, so I'll just say what happened. I had a vision. It wasn't like a normal dream. I was very aware of everything I saw, and more importantly, when it was over, I remembered it all.

I was standing at the bottom of a ladder that led up to the hayloft of a large barn. Standing next to the ladder was a man I recognized as one of the elders from the church I was attending. He looked at me, and without saying anything, motioned for me climb up. I took hold of the ladder and climbed the rungs to the top and stepped off. I stood there on the floor of the loft for a moment, then I heard a voice that I knew was God. He told me to turn and look to the right. For some reason, I turned and looked to the left instead.

What I saw there was troubling. There was a clothesline that stretched from one end of the loft to the other. Hanging from the line was a full set of clothes. A man's shirt was fastened by two clothespins, and pinned to the bottom of the shirt was a pair of pants. The shirt and pants were moving in the wind. Then the wind picked up, and the clothes started whipping back and forth violently. The scene looked like a man caught in a severe thunderstorm and being blown about.

The sky overhead was pitch black. The wind was extremely cold and I began to shiver. Above my head I could see heavy, dark clouds moving quickly across the heavens. Bolts of lightning flashed in every direction, lighting up the sky from one horizon to the other, and the thunder was almost deafening. I stood there watching, trembling with fear.

Then, I turned and looked to the right, the direction I was told to look in the first place. Before my eyes I saw rolling hill after rolling hill of fields of golden wheat and corn and barley, all glimmering in the autumn sun. The grain was swaying back and forth as a soothing and gentle breeze blew across the fields. The sun was warm and I felt the breeze blow gently on my face. The sky above was decorated in stunning pastel colors of soft orange, red, and violet. The clouds were moving swiftly through the heaven, like on the other side of the loft, but they were large, fluffy white, beautiful clouds, unlike anything I had ever seen before.

For a moment, I attempted to open my eyes and snap out of it, but they were so heavy that they closed again and the vision moved to another scene. This time I appeared to be standing outside one of the "cheese caves" that are carved into the cliffs back in Minnesota. In my vision, the large, oak double doors that cover the mouth of the largest cave had been refinished. They were stained and polished, looking as beautiful and brilliant as the day they were made, years earlier. All of the other doors to either side of the large double doors looked old, wet, and weathered, almost like they were falling apart.

I was told to open the nice-looking, well-kept door. Stepping forward, I unlatched the bolt and pulled the door open. Peering inside I saw that the cave behind the door was extremely deep, and dark and cold. The breeze that came from the inside the cave was chilling. As the cold breeze coming from inside the cave blew over me, I started to shiver.

Then it was over. I felt my head drop forward for a moment. The forward motion startled me, and I was immediately wide-awake. I thought I had fallen asleep and apologized to my host for my rudeness. He told me that I hadn't fallen asleep. I thought that was odd. He said he had been sitting in the chair right next to me, and would have noticed if I had fallen asleep. That's when it occurred to be that I must have seen some kind of vision.

I had never experienced anything like that before. I tried to understand what it meant, what God was perhaps saying to me, but I had no idea. I decided that I should talk to someone who might be able to make sense of what had happened, so I called my pastor.

In the brief time I had known him, I had become fond of the man, and had grown to respect him. I could see the love of Jesus in his eyes and a genuine sense of peace emanating from him. True, he still didn't know my real name, and that troubled me, but that was an issue for another day.

I made an appointment to see the pastor. We met in his office and I gave him a general description of the reason I wanted to see him. The pastor said it sounded to him like I had received something from the Lord, and asked me to share with him the details of what I had seen. I began at the beginning and told him everything about the two sides of the hayloft and the caves with different kinds of doors. When I was finished, he sat there for a moment without saying anything. Then he began.

He said that the vision in the barn was simple. The clothes on the clothesline, blowing in the storm, was me, and showed what my life would be like if I turned from God's will and chose to walk in disobedience. Life would be full of hard times. The rolling fields of grain blowing in the autumn sunshine, on the other hand, would be my part of the harvest of souls for the Kingdom of God, if I walked in obedience.

Talk about mind-boggling! I was completely overwhelmed by the thought that God had a real plan for my life, that He could somehow use someone like me to save others. What a powerful thought. I was called to be a child of God and to do His will.

But what about my other problems? What about my legal mess? Would that ever be over or would it always be there, haunting me and holding me back?

When we were done talking about the vision, the pastor and I prayed. I said, "Please God, use me to do whatever it is you want me to do with my life." And I meant it.

I had come to the place where that was the thing I wanted most in all the world. I wanted for my life, the life I had wasted doing selfish, evil things, to now be used for good, for whatever God wanted to do with it.

But once again it occurred to me that as clean as I was before God, thanks to the mercy He had shown me, I was not at all clean before the law and the powers that be. To be honest, I couldn't escape the thought that that part of my life was just too big and too risky for me to fix.

Chapter 42

Coming Clean

Wintertime in our part of Washington was not like any season I had ever known. Like I said before, it rained, and then continued raining, leaving one with the impression that it might never stop. I thought it must be easy to be a weatherman in our county, at least in the wintertime. All you had to do was predict rain. Talking about the weather forecast, someone said, "If you can't see the hills, it's raining. If you can see the hills, it's going to rain." That was about right.

You might think I'm exaggerating, but I'm not. They don't measure the rain in inches up here; they measure it in feet. Eight feet, ten feet, or twelve feet per year. All are possible.

One Sunday night, I was sitting in church when to my complete surprise Diana came in and sat down beside me. I was so happy to see her. She was looking good and her smile was as warm as always. She leaned over and said she had something to share with me. She said that she now understood what it was that I had been trying all along to explain to her.

"Chuck," she said, "when you first got saved it all seemed crazy to me, so completely foreign to anything I had known. I was raised Catholic and went to church, but it was never serious, like what you were into. To me, it seemed like you were suddenly speaking a different language, a foreign language that I didn't understand.

"Then when you moved out because of God, it hurt me deeply. I didn't understand how you could love me and move out." I could tell she was hurt, that I had hurt her.

She went on to explain that she and William had been going to church faithfully for months now, and that both of them had been saved and baptized. She almost glowed when she told me that. That was such wonderful news. I could hardly contain my excitement. I knew right then and there that God had been working in both of our lives, even when we were separated.

In all of the months we had been apart, we had continued to meet from time to time and maybe have a piece of pie and chat. But after I learned that she had come to know the Lord for herself, we began spending a lot more time together.

I had missed Diana the whole time, but I still believed that even though she had given her heart to the Lord, it was still important that we do the right thing before God. So we continued to live apart.

Looking back, I am still surprised that Diana stuck with me. Our backgrounds were almost polar opposites. Diana had never been in trouble with the law. She never even had a speeding ticket. No one in her family had ever been arrested or gone to jail. On birthdays and holidays, they always gathered as a family, and celebrated in a loving, caring atmosphere. The kind of family life she had known growing up was completely foreign to me. None of the families I knew lived like that, or were close like her family was. That's why it was so hard for me to leave her and the kids and the home we had created together.

With her becoming a believer and the two of us spending more time together, there were some serious challenges, or should I say, temptations. We had lived together like a married couple for some time, and now we were two unmarried people with the same physical attractions. Some days, we were able to overcome the temptations, and then there were days when we failed and had to do some serious repenting.

I found myself caught up in that battle I had heard several preachers talk about, the one between the flesh and the spirit. It was a struggle between my will versus God's will. I felt like one of the apostles, when Jesus said to them, "The spirit is indeed willing, but the flesh is weak." I very much wanted to live like a follower of Jesus should, but I was having such a difficult time doing so. Denying my desires was not an easy thing.

The thing is, I knew that God still loved me, even when I blew it. I knew He wasn't disowning me as a child, and tossing me aside because of my weakness. But still, my conscience was sensitive, and I knew when I was displeasing Him.

One afternoon I received a phone call from one of my friends at church telling me that some young men had come into his gun store, wanting to buy a gun. They'd told him that one of their friends had a mother, who had a boyfriend, who was an ex-bounty hunter. They said they wanted a gun for protection.

I recognized right away that the "friend" they were talking about was Stacy, who had moved out of her mother's home some months earlier. And of course, the bounty hunter was me.

Obviously, there was some serious friction between Stacy and me. In those days, when I talked to people about God, I didn't give much thought to where they were in their own lives. That was especially true when it came to Stacy. I had all but forgotten that when I was sixteen, I too had run away.

I decided that I ought to find my daughter and try to make things right. I wanted to apologize for the way I had acted toward her.

That particular afternoon, however, I had other priorities. I was more concerned about those kids trying to buy a gun to use on me. Rather than praying about the problem, or trusting God to take care of it, or seeking wise counsel before acting, I did what most ex-cons do when confronted with a challenge, I rashly and impulsively leaped into action and handled it the way I had in the past.

I did a little research and then drove over to the house where the guys were staying. Wasting no time, I crashed through the front door, looking for the guy with the gun. One of the guys who was staying at the house stood up to face me, throwing a few choice words my way. I busted him upside the head. He tried to call the police, so I grabbed the telephone and yanked it out of the wall. Then I turned around, having accomplished nothing for my troubles, and left.

The next day I staked out the house, watching for the guy who wanted to buy the gun. I sat in my car for about two hours before I saw the boy I was waiting for come walking down the street. I timed his steps, so when he got close to my car I could jump out and confront him. The new me, the Christian me, had gone into hiding. At that moment, I was the old me, stalking my prey and ready to pounce. I might as well have been there to beat up some punk that Jimmy the car salesman wanted to teach a lesson.

"So you want to shoot me," I demanded. Just to make sure he knew who I was, and that I was not to be messed with, I punched the guy a few times. You know, to kind of educate him a bit. "I'm the guy you want to shoot, you little punk."

Then I turned around and got in my car and drove away. I was confident that I had changed this guy's mind about taking me on.

Later that day, it sunk in what I had done, and a battle started raging in my head. I drove out to the ocean and sat there in my car, watching the waves break, feeling guilty about losing my temper and using my fists to fight my battles. On the one hand, I was feeling bad about punching the kid. On the other hand, I was doing my best to justify my actions, telling myself that the guy had only got what he had coming. How dare he even consider using a gun on me!

Eventually, I broke down weeping. I began to repent, asking God to forgive me for what I had done to those two guys. I had fallen back in to the "old me's" survival mode, never letting anyone threaten me. I knew I had sinned, and the feeling was ugly. I hated it. I had given away the freedom God had given me; I'd submitted again to my pride and my temper. I stayed there at the beach until I'd made my heart right with God.

When I got back to town, the police were already looking for me. I stopped by Diana's work and told her what I'd done. She was not one bit pleased. In fact, she gave me a good scolding. When she was finished, she suggested that I go somewhere and get some rest and see her again when she got off work. We agreed on a time and place.

That night, we talked for hours. We talked about everything that had happened, and how we had come to the place we were in. Then we talked about where we wanted to be. I asked her again if she would marry me, and her answer was the same as the other times, "I will marry you when you have your real name back."

After a lot of talking and praying, we decided that evening that it was time that we put all our trust in the Lord, time to come clean about everything. We decided that the first thing I needed to do was talk to the pastor and tell him my story. Diana said she would go with me, so I made an appointment.

I didn't know how our pastor would respond when he heard about my past, so I began by telling him that what I was about to share was in confidence. "If that's what you want, Chuck, that's the way it will be," he replied.

"Pastor, my name isn't really Tim Dunn."

"Well, what is your name?"

"It's Chuck Dudrey."

"Well then, I'll call you Chuck."

241

I was somewhat surprised by his calm, matter-of-fact response. The news that I had been living under a fake name didn't seem to faze him. Of course, he hadn't yet heard what was behind the name change.

The pastor asked me if there was anything else I wanted to share with him. He was kind of a laid-back fellow, but he knew there was more to the story than just a name change. So we began. We told him our entire story, including the fact that I was on the run from the law, and how it was that we had come to live in Washington. We talked for more than two hours.

When we got in the car to head home, I told Diana that it felt good to be clean. The lie I'd been living had been affecting me a lot more than I'd realized. I decided, then and there, that from that day on, being open and honest with our pastor would be a way of life.

Before our meeting wound up, I asked my pastor if I could address the congregation that Sunday night, and ask for their forgiveness for my deception. I loved those people. I didn't want to lie to them anymore. They had been open and caring with Diana and me, and I needed to come clean. I was finally ready to do that.

When Sunday night rolled around and the time came for me to come up front, the pastor gracefully set the stage. He explained that I had something important that I needed to share with them. With that, I walked up front and explained that I was on the run from the law and why I had changed my name. I told them the story from start to finish, and assured them that I was committed to doing whatever it took to clear up my legal situation.

I'd be lying, if I said I wasn't nervous about talking to those folks, and coming clean, but I have to tell you, they were so very gracious about it all. People who have truly come to terms with their own sin, and have been forgiven of every bad thing they had ever done or said or thought, are people not quick to condemn others for their faults, or to conclude that someone else's sins are worse than theirs. I guess that's why they say the ground is level at the foot of the cross. We all come there on the same terms.

After the service, every person in the church came up to me and thanked me and shook my hand. Diana and I had never before felt more loved and accepted than we did that night.

The time had come to face the fallout that was sure to follow my coming clean.

Chapter 43

What Is Your Real Name?

Y ou probably know that familiar saying, "No matter where you go, there you are." Well, my bad ways had followed me to Washington. To be more accurate, I had brought them with me.

Yes, God had forgiven me and saved me, but I still had some pretty bad habits from the past, and they liked to pop to the surface from time to time. You know, things like kicking in the front door of a house, and punching out some guy I didn't even know. That's not exactly Christian behavior.

As might be expected, the guys I'd smacked around filed a complaint against me. Thanks to my own behavior, there was a warrant out for my arrest in my new home town, the place where I had hoped to start over with a clean slate.

I wasn't sure how to respond. I realized that I was the one who had made the mess, but knowing that didn't mean I knew how to fix it.

Over the past few months, I had taken my family on an emotional roller coaster ride, one not entirely of their choosing. It was time to settle down, think things through, and then do the right thing. We decided to take a trip as a family, and gather our thoughts. Wasting no time, Diana, William, and I hopped in the car and took off for Northern California. I don't know if leaving town at the moment was the right thing to do, but I kind of assumed that we could think a little clearer, if we weren't listening every moment for arresting officers to come knocking at the door. In other words, I was running, but this time not permanently. I tried to think of that as progress.

When you first become a Christian, you don't immediately become a mature believer. On the inside, you become a new person with a clean slate before God. That is possible because of the sacrifice Jesus made on the cross to pay for all of your sins. But the old ways don't always disappear in one day. You make mistakes, you stumble and fall, then you get back up, brush yourself off, and start again.

The amazing thing about that process is, even when you do something wrong that you know displeases your God, your Heavenly Father, you know that He is displeased, and you feel guilty about what you did, but at the same time you know that He still loves you. It's like we continue to love our own children, even when they have done something wrong.

Once you've given your life to God, and are one of his kids, He might chasten you when you need it, but the mistake you made or the sin you committed does not separate you from His love. Even when He sends tough things into your life to guide you in the right direction, it's always aimed at redemption and restoration, not judgment. The judgment I deserved all went on Jesus' shoulders at the cross, and He gave me a clean slate instead.

In my case, the Lord was directing me in a way that would force me to come clean, not just with Him, but also with the law. However, just because God was the one bringing the agents of change into my life didn't mean the process was going to be easy.

It wasn't for me. I had gone from being wanted by the law in one state to being wanted in two states. Clearly, I had not learned how to stay out of trouble. There was no way to know it at the time, but I was going to get into even more of it down the road.

Diana and William and I decided that I should leave the matter up to the Lord and trust Him, no matter what happened. I found a Bible verse that helped me move forward. It said, "The battle belongs to the Lord." I decided that my legal battles, which were most definitely larger than I could handle, should be left in God's hands.

Even after accepting that this was the right direction, I still needed a few days to wrap my mind and heart around the very serious ramifications of that decision. The possibility of spending ten or fifteen years in prison back in Minnesota was not an easy pill to swallow. But either I was going to trust God or I wasn't.

The first thing we decided was that Diana and I would get married, with my real name on the marriage license. That was a huge step. Filing a legal document with my real name on it opened the door to so many things I had worked so hard to avoid.

We decided that the wedding should take place in a few days. In the meantime, I would lay low to avoid getting arrested before the wedding. We owned a small piece of property about a mile outside of Hoquiam, and it had everything I would need. I was sure the police would never look for me there, so that bought us a little time.

After agreeing on a plan for going forward, we returned to Washington. I spent the next few days in that little hideaway, praying and seeking God regarding my legal mess. Interestingly, I wasn't having any of those intense spiritual battles I'd experienced a few weeks earlier. I had made my mind up to trust the Lord, and with that decision came a peace that seemed to overpower the fears and anxiety, which earlier had been overwhelming me.

I was at peace because I had come to a very simple conclusion. I had trusted God to save my soul from hell, and to forgive me for everything I had ever done in my life. That included some pretty ugly stuff. Some of what I had done people knew about, but there were secret things too, rotten things that no one knew about, stuff the law would never punish me for, because I had gotten away with them. Jesus had cleansed me of those things too.

So, if I could trust God with my eternal soul, I decided that I could, and would, trust Him in this comparatively small matter of prison time. After all, He is God and there is nothing too hard for Him.

With that decision behind me, the real battle, the one that takes place on the inside, was settled.

I should say something about Diana's heart. This sweet woman, who had never had a run-in with the law herself, was prepared to marry me, even though she knew that the law was looking for me, would now catch up with me, and very possibly send me to prison. It's hard to fathom that level of love and trust. She has always amazed me.

Finally, our wedding day arrived. Everyone we had met since moving to Washington showed up to witness Diana and me exchanging our marriage vows. My dad even flew out for the wedding. He was there, with a suit on, busily taking pictures for us.

I didn't know it until just before the wedding, but Diana actually knew my dad. Her ex-husband Jay had been involved in Scouting before his snowplow accident. Diana had met my dad through some Scouting events. Of course, she had no idea what Dad was really like, she just knew his face and name.

Our daughter Stacy also came to support us, and to be in the wedding. That meant a lot. Diana and I were both excited to have her there with us. From the very beginning, Stacy had been more freaked out about my new faith than Diana and Will. With all three of us having become committed Christians, she felt left out of things, even though they were things she wanted nothing to do with anyway. She loved us, just the same, and there was no way she would have missed our wedding.

Finally, everything was in order and ready to commence. My heart was pounding like crazy when the music started. I walked to the front of the church and stood in the same spot, where a few weeks earlier, I'd stood to ask the congregation's forgiveness. This time, though, I was waiting for my beautiful bride to walk down the aisle and become my wife. Our son William stood next to me. Our good friend Ed, a man we had met since moving to Washington, was my best man.

Everyone stood for the wedding march. Diana, walking down the aisle in a gorgeous wedding gown, looked so beautiful. As she made her way toward me, I whispered a prayer of thanks to God for giving her to me. My heart was so full that I thought it might burst. The pastor started the ceremony and led us in our vows. Fifteen minutes later, he pronounced us man and wife. It had taken us a while to get to there, but we were finally a married couple.

On that happy day, I was a long way from Church Street, far removed from the life of fear and abuse I had known as a child. That was all in the distant past. I now had a real family of my own. Even having my dad at the wedding was not enough to bring back the pain of my childhood. It was a day of celebration with nothing to mar it.

I moved back in with Diana and William, and life started again where we had left off, only we were all believers. As for my legal issues, well, I really hadn't given them much thought. But as you might expect, that was about to change.

I was out in the front yard, a few days later, and had just finishing mowing the lawn when a police car pulled up and a uniformed policeman got out. I had seen this particular officer several times before. He lived just up the hill from us. That day, though, it was all business.

He was courteous enough when he spoke, but he made it clear that he needed to talk to me, because, he explained, there was some question as to my true identity.

He said he had a warrant for my arrest, and that the charge was assault. My heart sank, but I took a deep breath and accepted that it was time. I'd known the day would come; I'd just hoped it wouldn't come so soon. As the officer opened the back door and politely directed me to get into the backseat of his squad car, I began to pray.

I asked the Lord to watch over and protect my family. I said, "Lord, you are God and you can do anything. Please help me through this trouble, and help me to rely on your strength. Please open my eyes, so I can see this situation as you see it."

Down at the station I was led to a holding cell. The door closed behind me and the lock slid loudly into place. The sound echoed against the concrete walls of the jail. I had heard that awful sound far too many times. I felt fear trying to break through and take hold of me, so I prayed some more. I prayed out loud and asked the Lord to guide me through the next few days. "Father God," I said, "whatever it is you want of me, I will do. I submit my life to your will."

In a few minutes, the officer returned. He asked me several questions, then said he needed to know my real name. I told him the truth. He asked for my birthday, and after writing the date down in his little pad, he left. While he was gone, I prayed some more. I knew that there were authorities in Minnesota who were not at all happy with me for not returning to court the day we skipped town, and I prayed for them.

All of a sudden, this amazing peace and calm swept over me. I heard the Spirit of the Lord say to me, "As I set Peter free, I will set you free, also." Peter is an apostle in the Bible. He was in prison and locked in chains and God miraculously released him from his shackles and opened the prison door for him.

I was amazed. I had heard the still small voice of the Lord! My God had spoken to me. He had assured me that it was going to be okay and that I would be released. I can never get over what a special thing that is. God doesn't talk to me all the time, but when He does, it's a powerful thing, something to treasure.

I had no sooner heard the Holy Spirit speak to me, when the officer returned to the holding cell. This is what he said, "Minnesota called us back and said they don't want you anymore. They told us to set you free."

He explained that I would still have to face the local assault charges, but that I would be out of jail within the hour. Then he said something else, and he had a puzzled look on his face when he said it. He told me, speaking of the call from the authorities in Minnesota, "I have been in law enforcement for twenty years, and I have never seen anything like this happen before."

Well, neither had I. But I knew whom to thank. While I waited to be released, I praised God some more. The Minnesota situation could have gone very, very differently. I could have been extradited and stood trial there and tossed in the penitentiary for ten or fifteen years. Instead, I was free. God had worked a great miracle on my behalf. He had opened the prison door and set me free, just like the Holy Spirit had said.

I wish I could say that that was my last time behind bars, or even my next to the last time, but alas, that was not to be. I still had lessons to learn.

As you might expect, I couldn't wait to share with Diana and William, and the people from church, what the Lord had done for us. No one could think of a good explanation for why the authorities in Minnesota had let their check fraud case slide, but they had. That entire debacle was over and done with, and for a little while I could just settle in and be happy with my family.

As for the local assault charges, the county settled that case with some probation and a requirement that I pay for the repairs related to the phone being ripped out of the wall. I deserved worse, but I gladly accepted the mercy I was handed.

Chapter 44

Bumpa

I began to notice that our daughter Stacy seemed a bit lost in life. She was a very smart girl, and when it came to helping others, she had a heart of gold. But she clearly lacked direction. It occurred to me that a stint in the military might afford her an opportunity to remedy that.

It just so happened that I knew a man who worked as a Navy recruiter out of an office located in the local shopping mall. One day, I drove over to see him. I told him I knew of a really sharp young woman who would probably join the Navy, if he would pay her a visit. He did precisely that, and with little or no hesitation, Stacy enlisted.

A few months later, when she'd finished her basic training, we flew to Florida to watch her graduate. We went a day early, because the Space Shuttle was scheduled to launch from Cape Kennedy the day before the graduation, and we wanted to see it. To our disappointment, the launch was scrubbed, due to weather conditions. The next day, however, while Stacy's graduation was proceeding at the parade grounds, the shuttle launched. We had a spectacular view of the launch from our seats in the bleachers.

Our daughter served her country well, and afterward came back to Grays Harbor to live. I think the Navy did Stacy some good. If nothing else, that's where she met the man she would marry in a private ceremony back in Virginia. By the time Stacy and her husband Brian arrived in Washington, they already had our first grandchild, a baby boy named Connor.

Our house was easily large enough for the three of them to live with us, so we invited them to move in until they could get on their feet. They both wanted to go to college, so staying with us for a while made good sense. They could live cheaper, plus have two willing and able live-in babysitters.

It didn't take long for me to fall in love with that little boy. Connor was a joy to have around, and I took advantage of every opportunity I got to pick him up and hold him. I especially loved the look on his face when I went into the nursery to get him when he woke up from a nap. He would look up at me and smile, hold out his arms for me to pick him up, then snuggle in close, with his little head resting on my shoulder. My heart still melts when I remember those moments. The joy I felt was worth the world ten times over.

When my daughter Jacqueline was small, I went to prison for three years, missing the opportunity to be a daddy and to hold her and love on her. One of the greatest regrets and losses in my life was not being around to watch that little girl grow up. Spending time with baby Connor gave me a little bit of that back.

It became a family routine for everyone to leave for work or school in the morning, and let Grandpa take care of the baby. When I was the only one there, I changed him, fed him, and took care of all the baby stuff. I loved walking around with him and showing him things. I would let him rub the leaves on our herb plants, then smell the fragrance. I was always looking for something new or different to show him. I tried to make every moment we spent together a learning experience.

The first quarter of college was just wrapping up when Stacy and Brian told us they wanted to go to Mexico for a week. They asked if I would mind watching the baby while they were away. I readily accepted.

The first few days went as smoothly as could be expected. Connor was starting to crawl and discover things on his own. He was pulling himself up and standing next to the coffee table. It was exciting to see how bright he was and how quickly he was learning. I enjoyed getting down on the floor with him and playing at his level. My wife sweetly reminded me, more than once, that she knew a thing or two about raising a child, and that Connor was her grandson too. So, we shared. Diana and I spent many an enjoyable evening in the living room, playing with our grandson.

One day, while I was holding Connor and playing with him, he looked up at me and called me "Bumpa." Where that came from, I had no idea, but throughout the day he kept saying it. After that, I was no longer Chuck Dudrey. I was Bumpa.

There is something magical about your grandchild knowing who you are, and holding up those little arms for you to take them and hold them, but when little Connor called me "Bumpa," it was as if I was instantly someone important.

Another day, except for Connor and me, the house was empty. Stacy and Brian were still on vacation, and Diana was working. Connor was crying, so I changed his diaper, thinking that might quiet him. But even with a dry diaper, he kept crying. I held him and patted his back, thinking maybe he needed to burp. That didn't seem to be the problem, so I started walking around the house talking to him, trying to comfort him. That didn't help either. He just cried all the more.

"Oh, little guy, you're okay. Bumpa's here," I whispered in his ear. "It will be alright, it's okay to cry."

I sat down in the recliner, pushed the leg rest out, and leaned back with the baby lying on my lap. Connor was looking into my eyes as if he was trying to touch my soul. Before I knew it, I felt a tear roll down my cheek, followed by another. If you would have walked in right then, you might have thought it rather strange, a grandpa and a little baby boy sitting in a recliner, both crying.

I just sat there, holding him on my lap, rubbing his tummy and letting him cry. A few moments passed, and then the crying gave way to sleep. There was something wonderful and powerful, perhaps even profound, in that little boy drifting off to sleep lying in my lap. It was as if little Connor was saying, in his own way, "I trust you. I am at peace resting here with you."

Jesus said that if we would enter the kingdom of heaven we must become as a little child. Verses like that are not always easy to understand with your mind. Sometimes you need a picture. God used little Connor to help me understand what it means to totally trust Him, to lie back and peacefully rest in His presence.

Without saying a word, that little boy taught me a lesson that I would never forget.

Chapter 45

Smoking dope

O ne evening, at the church's youth group meeting, our son William met a girl named Christy. She must have made quite an impression, because when he came home that night he announced to us that he had met the girl he was going to marry. Diana and I just smiled. He was young and happy, so we let him dream.

That Saturday, I happened to be driving by the church and noticed a pickup parked out front. The church was closed, but I knew that people who were in need sometimes dropped by to see if the food donation pantry was open. I worked with that program, so I had a key.

I parked next to the pickup, got out, and asked the folks if there was anything I could do to help. It turned out that they were new in town. They had traveled across the country to Grays Harbor with a story not all that different from ours. I had a heart for people who needed help, so I invited the family to our house the following day for Easter dinner. They accepted. I was sure Diana wouldn't mind. She was a people lover, too.

The next afternoon, right on time, our guests pulled up out front. William could hardly contain his excitement when he saw them get out of the car.

"That's her," he whispered rather loudly. "That's the girl I was telling you about, the one I'm going to marry."

And he was right. William and Christy were married and soon surprised us all with a set of twins. Diana and I got to be grandparents again, and Christy's parents and her brothers became our lifelong friends.

Around that time, my little brother Kenny was killed in a motor-cycle accident. Dad called to give me the news. After I hung up the phone, I just sat in my chair in the living room and wept. My brother had never come to grips with the abuse he'd suffered as a little boy on Church Street. He was never able to get past it. And now he was gone.

Then, out of nowhere, I heard from my ex-wife Helen. She wanted to talk to me about our daughter. Jacqueline was sixteen, and Helen wanted to know if she could come to Washington and live with Diana and me. We said yes.

A few days later, I went to the bus station and picked up my daughter, whom I had not seen since she was a toddler. It became clear, soon enough, that Jacqueline had a serious independent streak. That may have been the reason why her mother wanted her to visit her dad. She didn't want to go to high school. In fact, she wanted nothing to do with school. I was fortunately able to talk her into getting her GED.

Jacqueline went to church with us every Sunday, and to youth group meetings. During the day, she helped me with the property manage-ment business I was running. That allowed us to spend a good deal of time together. However, one day, about a year after she'd arrived, Jacqueline called her mother and pleaded with her to let her move back to Minnesota. Her mother acquiesced, so we put her on a Greyhound and sent her back to live with Helen. That was not the end of our rela-tionship. We still talk on the phone pretty much every week, but have never been as close as I would have liked.

One thing I learned from that experience with my precious daughter is that you can't put your grown child back in the cradle and make up for all the time that was lost, or messed up. You just do the best you can, love them, and pray a lot.

There's no need to elaborate, but something happened at the church that made me decide to stop going altogether. That's not an uncommon mistake. Many Christians have made it. But it is a costly one on several fronts.

I decided that I didn't need church, that I could just serve God on my own. I could read my Bible and pray at home just as well as at church.

I did my best to rationalize that philosophy, but I can tell you with certainty that the Bible teaches otherwise, and that Christians need to be in a local church, connected with other believers. I would learn that lesson personally.

People are the living stones or bricks that make up God's house. The enemy, the devil, is a thief who likes to steal bricks. A brick that is mortared into place between other bricks is hard to steal. A brick that is just lying off by itself, well, that's a different story.

Also, when you are trying to be a Christian off by yourself, there is no one to rub against you, like iron sharpens iron, and keep you sharp. Your spiritual senses become dull. The thing is, you don't even know it's happening. Here's why I'm telling you this:

If you recall, I used to be a pretty dedicated pot smoker. But when I accepted Christ, I stopped smoking the stuff. That evening, when I met the Lord on the waterfront, He took away the high I was on. It left instantly, and I didn't have any desire for pot after that. Frankly, I was happy to leave that piece of my life behind.

But then, later on, maybe five years after I was saved, I started buying a bag of weed from time to time. I would kick back, smoke some pot, and get stoned. It's hard to explain my erratic behavior. I would stop by a friend's house and tell him about Jesus, decline his offer to get high with him, only to go back a few days later and get stoned with the same guy. I was slowly slipping back into the lifestyle from which God had delivered me.

Many times, I would buy a bag and get stoned in the car on the way home, then later start feeling guilty about it and throw the bag out of the car window. The next morning, I would drive back to where I'd thrown the bag out the window the night before and search the side of the road for my pot. I was a mess.

I had been set free from things that had once held me captive, but had willingly crawled back into the chains and fastened them around me. I had made myself a prisoner of something from which God had released me.

Eventually, I became a fully committed pot smoker. I started growing the stuff in my garage and in the attic. Sometimes, when I had a few plants ready to harvest, I would get paranoid. I was so sure the cops were watching me that I would pull up all my plants and throw them away.

I was under so much condemnation, and so overwhelmed with guilt, that I stopped praying altogether. That's where I was at the time; no going to church, no fellowship with other believers, and then no praying.

After a year of smoking pot every day, I came to the conclusion that I actually needed it. I didn't just like marijuana, I needed it. I was sure I could think better, be a better conversationalist, and work faster than when I wasn't using.

I could even show you a verse in the Bible where it says that God made the herbs for man. I was working overtime trying to justify what I was doing. I didn't need the devil to deceive me; I was doing a pretty good job all on my own.

The one thing that made me question whether smoking pot was okay was the fact that it was illegal. I couldn't find a way around that. Then, one evening, I heard a newscaster talk about this thing called "medical marijuana." That was the answer I'd been looking for.

After hearing that, I made it my mission in life to find a doctor who would give me a prescription. It took weeks, but eventually I found one and got a prescription for pot "to help with my back pain."

My problem was solved. I could grow and smoke pot in Washington legally. No more worrying about the cops catching me. I could be back in favor with God and smoke all the pot I wanted. All I had really proven was the truth behind the old saying: People believe what they want to believe.

Chapter 46

The Hotel and Café

Do you recall the vision of the shirt and pants being whipped about by powerful winds? That was a picture of me, if I chose to walk in my own way instead of the path of the Lord's choosing.

Diana and I had always talked about having a little hotel, or a bed-and-breakfast. That was our dream retirement plan. We could cook for people and serve them, which was something we both liked to do anyway, only we would get paid to do it. We decided that if we found a place like that, we would pack up and move wherever we had to.

William had married Christy, and they had their own family, starting with a set of twins. So, it was just the two of us in that big house all by ourselves. Maybe it was that old desire to hit the road. Maybe it was just empty nest syndrome. But whatever it was, we were looking to make a move.

We started watching the real estate ads and eventually found a hotel for sale in Central Oregon. We made the six-hour drive so we could check the place out in person. We loved what we saw. The hotel was picture perfect. It was cozy, neat and clean, and ready for us to take over on day one.

So we made an offer to buy it. Buying this hotel represented a major change in life, but I never really gave much thought as to whether this was something the Lord wanted us to do. We wanted to do it; that's all that mattered. So we commenced the work of making our dream come true.

Reading this, you might be thinking, "Hey Chuck, it's your life; you're free to do whatever you want." I get that. I really do, but it's only sort of true. God didn't steal my free will when I became a Christian. I was free to make my own choices. But I did give Him my life, and I did agree that He would be the Lord, my Lord. I willingly decided to trust Him to lead me and guide me, so I could best do His will. That commitment was not without meaning.

When a Christian decides to go off and do his own thing and ignore the will of God for his or her life, he steps outside the divine protection and the assurance that God will direct his steps. One of the difficulties of being in that place is the fact that we are only human and can't see around corners, or anticipate every eventuality, like God can.

The closing on the property in Oregon did not go smoothly. That should have at least made us stop and consider the possibility that this was not a door God was opening for us. Every time I was about to close the deal, something would come up and it would fall through and set us back to square one. This went on for nearly three months. I had to go back and forth with the bank the entire time and work with two different appraisers to make the deal work.

I had made some tough deals in my life, but that hotel, well, it was easily the hardest. Nonetheless, thanks more to my persistence than anything else, the pieces eventually came together and we closed the deal.

We talked with William and Christy, and they agreed to move into our place, so we didn't have to worry about renting out the house, or selling it before moving.

With the deal closed and our house in Hoquiam no longer a worry, all we had to do was pack our bags, load our stuff into a truck, and drive six hours from Hoquiam to our new property in Mitchell, Oregon. We loaded up the rigs and formed a caravan, of sorts. My buddy Bob drove the moving van, Diana drove her car, and I drove my pickup truck with all of my pot plants in the back. Couldn't forget those! And off we went.

The little hotel we purchased was located on the main street of a small town. The population of Mitchell was 168 people, and the total number of county residents was under twelve hundred. We chose the place because the town is located on a tourist highway. In the summertime, people from all over the world came to the area to visit, and see the Painted Hills and the rugged terrain of the high plains desert. Also, I was sure a tiny town like Mitchell would be a perfect place to set up a growing room for my "medical marijuana."

The hotel itself was an historic building. It looked like the hotels you see in movies about the Old West. Much of the original decor still existed. Diana and I moved into the owners' quarters on the first floor. The building had a basement that ran the entire length of the building, some eighty feet. The facility had been completely remodeled and was already operating, so it was more or less a turnkey business.

We were sure this was a good move for us, and that we would be retiring and living happily ever after in Mitchell, Oregon.

Everything started just as we had planned. Within a few weeks, the hotel was full every night. Of course, being busy meant there were lots of rooms to clean and lots of laundry to do. Man, did we ever have laundry! It felt like the washer and dryer never stopped running. But we weren't complaining. To a retail business, being busy sure beats the alternative.

Plus, we were having a good time. We thoroughly enjoyed sitting on the front porch, visiting with our guests every evening and the first thing every morning. I would get out my guitar and play and sing some of the old songs I knew, like "Crazy," by Patsy Cline, and "Bad, Bad Leroy Brown," by Jim Croce. I would start picking and singing, and sometimes the guests would gather around to listen or they would join in and sing with me. I was having fun and everything looked promising.

The winter came and went. Business was slower in the winter season, but we rented a few rooms to some hunters and hikers and made ends meet. We never got bored. And thanks to my little medical marijuana project in the basement, I had all the dope I wanted to smoke.

By this time, I had become a full-blown proponent of medical pot. I joined many of the online groups where I could get tips on how to grow better marijuana and find out which plants would best help with my back pain.

We didn't completely forget about God. Diana still read her Bible a lot. We even started attending church services on Sundays. For some reason, though, I never felt at home like I did at the church back in Washington. I missed the fellowship we had there, and all of the friends we had made over the years.

I had never lived in a town as small as Mitchell, and I was caught completely off guard by all the gossip. Gossip in Mitchell was a way of life. Everyone talked about everyone else. It was somewhat of a culture shock. You'd find it hard to imagine all of the things people in that town were saying about one another. There was nothing too small or too personal to escape their attention.

I started going to the Thursday morning men's group at the church, but to my surprise they gossiped there, too. I refused to engage in the sport, but that didn't stop anyone else.

One time, I mentioned to someone in town that I didn't like people gossiping about me. He responded by saying that at least when they were talking about me, they weren't talking about someone else. It kind of reminded me of a saying I had heard, "God made the country, men made the cities, and the devil made the small towns." If gossip is a sin, and it sure enough is, then the devil was having a field day in our little town.

Next to our hotel was a small café. The owner approached me one morning and asked if I wanted to buy his place. He told me he was fed up with the people in the town and wanted to sell and move on. I explained to him that I didn't have much capital on hand to make the purchase, but that didn't stop him from bringing the subject up every time he got the chance. I tried to encourage him to stay, but he made it quite clear that he wanted out, and the sooner the better.

One day, I asked him how much he needed for the business. The price was okay, but when he told me that we could walk into the place, a fully operational café with all the inventory, for just $2,000 down, he had my attention. I spoke with Diana about the offer, and she agreed that we should move forward. Just like that, we had a hotel and a food service operation for our guests. I was feeling pretty proud of myself. Diana and I now possessed two of the nicest properties in the entire county.

We went right to work putting our stamp on the place. We cleaned and scrubbed the café from top to bottom, and gave it a fresh coat of white paint. With the new curtains Diana made for the windows, our little café was a show piece. We hired three or four employees to help us run the place, and opened for business.

One Thursday morning, at the men's breakfast at the church, the topic of conversation turned to a certain man who was causing a great deal of trouble for the people in town. The guys described how this fellow was scaring the neighbors, and even shooting guns over the heads of their horses to frighten them. I didn't know who the man was, but he sounded like some piece of work. Supposedly, he was also doing things like cutting fences and damming up the water in the spring. In cattle country, that's serious business.

Almost all the group did that entire morning was gossip about that one man. The group's leader not only did nothing to discourage the gossip, but was right in the thick of it. In all the years I had attended church, I had never heard such talk from a pastor. I was very disappointed. I didn't say anything about it at the time. I just made up my mind not to participate. I didn't know the guy, but I was pretty sure he couldn't be as bad as they were saying.

Things continued to go well for us at both the café and the hotel. The cafe was busy all day long. The cash flow was sweet, and we were able to make all of our financial commitments on time. One afternoon, while I was sitting on a bench in front of the café, I saw a man standing on the sidewalk across the street, looking my way. I gave him a nod, and he, in turn, did the same. Then he turned and walked away.

The town was alive with people that day, but I noticed that a lot of them drove through town without stopping. While I was standing there, watching them drive by, I got an idea. I fetched my guitar, and started playing and singing songs out on the sidewalk in front of the café. Before long, people started gathering around to listen. I invited them to come inside, and some of them did. I knew that I was on to something. After a few days, I started playing and singing inside the café on a regular basis. It was great fun. I even started getting tips.

One day a reporter from *The Oregonian* newspaper out of Portland came to town. He was writing a travel piece about Mitchell. Here are a couple of excerpts from the piece the reporter, a man named Foster Church, wrote:

> I had made reservations at the Oregon Hotel, a commodious two-story structure with an inviting veranda. The owners, Chuck and Diane Dudrey, play Patsy Cline CDs on the veranda, and it seems to capture the atmosphere of the place and town. The hotel, to be honest, is the kind of hostelry that could be a dump with cockroaches watching every move, or it could be a jewel. The Oregon Hotel is definitely in the latter category. The rooms are airy and spacious and furnished with handsome quilts and antique radios...

> That night, I ordered takeout hamburger steak from a local cafe and ate it on the hotel veranda, listening to Chuck Dudrey play the guitar and salute passers-by. After living in Mitchell six weeks, Dudrey offers two observations: The stars in the clear night sky take on

depth and dimension invisible in the cities, and the town's haunting silence guarantees a good night's sleep.

One day, I noticed that the man I had seen earlier standing on the corner watching me was back again. Apparently, he was trying to get my attention. I invited him to come on over and have a cup of coffee and some pie on me. He accepted, and within a week he was there every day. He was pleasant to the customers, and sometimes he even put on an apron and cleared tables. He seemed to be having a good time, just hanging around.

One day, one of my regular customers asked if he could speak with me outside, so I went with him to hear what he had on his mind. He told me that he and the other ranchers would not be coming back to the café, as long as Robert was there. I asked him why, and with a con-fused look on his face, he replied, "You don't know?" I assured him that I didn't; then he told me that the man who was bussing tables for us was the "crazy man" they had been talking about at the men's meeting. He told me that this guy was big trouble.

I brushed him off. I told him that as long as Robert behaved himself at the café, he was welcome to stay. Well, that didn't go over well with the ranchers, but I stood my ground. They could say what they wanted, but I wasn't going to tell this guy that he wasn't welcome anymore, based solely on other peoples' beef with him. Why should I? Robert had been no trouble to me.

Over the next few weeks, it became increasingly clear that the people in the community didn't approve of my position regarding Robert. I explained that the man hadn't been any problem for me, but their response was always, "You wait and see."

My wife and I eventually gave Robert a room in the hotel, so he would have a place to sleep when he was in town. Diana even bought him some blue jeans and a couple of shirts.

One afternoon, I was headed to the café after taking a nap at the hotel, when I saw Robert out front. He was embroiled in a heated argu-ment with some guy. I asked Robert what the trouble was, but he didn't respond. I told him that he needed to take the yelling elsewhere. Robert made it clear that he didn't appreciate me saying that, but he did leave.

A few days later, we were hard at it, gearing up for the busiest day of the year at the café. It was the town's yearly festival. We had hired lots of extra staff, and had set up a grilling station outside on the lawn, hoping to capture some extra business from those folks who simply wanted a burger and a cool drink, as opposed to a full sit-down meal. We had everything all set up and ready to go, when out of nowhere, Diana and I both came down with the flu.

Keeping things going while we were both sick was a nightmare. In the afternoon, we would go to the hotel to sleep and try to break the fever, then we would get up and go back to the café to work the dinner rush, all the while being careful not to spread germs.

One particular afternoon, I took some cold medicine, so I could work. But all that did was put me to sleep. After I had slept for a little while, I dragged myself out of bed and got dressed. I encouraged Diana to stay in bed and rest, while I took care of closing the café.

When I walked outside, I saw Robert. He was standing on the sidewalk between the hotel and the café, arguing with one of the young girls who worked for us. He had a firm grip on her hand and when she would try to pull away, he wouldn't let go. I told him to knock it off and release the girl. I told him that his behavior was not acceptable.

He responded by directing his yelling at me. He was so loud that I was sure everyone in the hotel could hear him, and it was already past ten. I tried to talk him down. I told him to go home and we would talk in the morning, but there was no talking to the guy.

I continued walking toward the café. I had things to do. But, Robert walked along beside me, still yelling and hollering. He was clearly losing it. I kept asking him to quiet down and thought I'd convinced him to leave.

As he walked toward his truck, I asked him what I might possibly be able to do to help him. He climbed up onto the bed of his truck, still yelling and screaming. It wasn't just the loudness. Some of the words he was using were not fit for polite company. He even threw in a few insults about my mother, if you know what I mean.

While I watched, Robert knelt down in the bed of his pickup and starting pouring gasoline into a coffee can. I had no idea what he was up to. Suddenly, he turned and jumped off the back of his truck and attempted to douse me with the can of gasoline. What could I do? I was carrying a nightstick at the time, something I often did. I swung it, and hit him in the arm that was holding the can of gas. The coffee can fell to the ground and gas splattered all over the pavement. I must have swung pretty hard, because the impact broke the man's arm.

Robert got back on his feet and took off running, holding his broken arm with his good one. The man was obviously in a dangerous state of mind, so I gave chase, hoping to nail him again. Fortunately for Robert, and perhaps for me, he was faster than I was, and got away. I went on to the café and finished up my work, then went back to bed, still sick with the flu.

But that would not be the end of my encounter with Robert. In fact, far from it. The man would turn out to be a real thorn in my side for quite some time.

Chapter 47

The Longest Days

I t felt like I had just gone to bed that night, when suddenly it was morning again. I was still as sick as a dog, and the events of the night before were still fresh in my mind. I really hadn't wanted to hit Robert, and I definitely didn't mean to break his arm, but I wasn't about to let some lunatic throw gasoline on me. I'd seen that move before. First the gas, then the Zippo lighter, a combination that never makes for a happy ending.

I was having trouble wrapping my head around the whole situation. All I'd done was offer the guy a helping hand. I was nice to him, when the whole town despised him. And what did I get for my troubles?

Still feeling weak, I crawled out of bed, got dressed, and walked outside. As I headed toward the café, several of the local citizens approached me. They were all excited. Every one of them wanted to shake my hand and make the point that it was about time someone dealt with Robert. "Good job!" several of them said. "Sorry we missed it."

One thing about a gossiping town, is news travels fast, true or false. That morning, townspeople came from everywhere to thank me for dealing with the town tormentor. Some of them even gave me their phone numbers, so we could stay in touch. They told me how glad they were that I had moved to town.

I shook everybody's hand, but inside I wasn't feeling all that good about what had happened. I'd liked the guy. I was sorry that he'd pushed things to the point where I had to decide between hitting him or possibly being set on fire.

"We told you there would be trouble, once he started hanging around," they said. I wished they'd been wrong about that, but it didn't look like it.

At any rate, today was the big day and the town was really starting to come alive. Everyone was preparing for the afternoon parade, which was scheduled to start at one o'clock. The tables outside the cafe were all set up, and we were looking forward to the thing most businesses want, a high cash flow day. As I walked back toward the hotel, I was greeted by two sheriff's deputies. They wanted to talk to me about the event of the night before. I invited them into the hotel so we could sit down and talk.

One of the deputies had a smile on his face. He began the conversation with, "Job well done."

He explained that, nonetheless, for purposes of their report, they still needed to hear my side of the story. I told them that Robert had been acting crazy, yelling and screaming. I explained that he was holding one of our waitresses by the arm, and wouldn't let go in spite of her protestations. I told them that I had attempted to quiet Robert down, but he'd jumped off of the bed of his truck with a can of gas in his hand, trying to douse me with it. I assured them that's the only reason I'd hit him, and that I hadn't intended to break his arm.

With that, one of the deputies told me that they would like to see what was I was doing down in the basement. He told me that Robert had reported to them that I was growing marijuana down there. I told them that I didn't have to show them anything, without a warrant, but because I wasn't breaking the law, they were welcome to take a look.

With that, I led them downstairs and showed them my medical marijuana plants and my legal permit to grow them. They seemed satisfied that my operation was on the up and up.

We went back upstairs and they were just ready to leave, when one of them stopped to tell me that they had talked to the waitress involved, and that she was willing to testify that she had seen the whole thing and that I'd had the "patience of Job," when dealing with Robert. Then he said that he wondered how I could have taken all of the threats and insults, for as long as I had, without reacting. As they got in their car to leave, the lead deputy told me that he doubted that there would be any charges filed.

A short time after they left, I walked outside and there stood Robert, yelling and screaming again. He was telling everyone in town that I was growing pot for the cops, and that the cops had paid me to beat him up. The street was full of people in town for the parade, and Robert's yelling and screaming was turning them away from our business. He stood on the corner, twenty feet from our café, and carried on. Well, he got the result he was after. He succeeded in driving most of the customers away from our business.

Robert's antics went on for hours. On what should have been the busiest day of the year, our café was almost empty. I couldn't help but think of another time and place, and how I would have handled the problem then. It was a struggle to not give the guy a good "old school" beating.

I pleaded with the sheriff's department to do something, but they declined. Finally, about noon, the deputy and his wife, who happened to be the festival director, tricked Robert into following them into the feed store. I don't know what they said to the guy, though I suspect that their chat might have included a threat of bodily harm, but when Robert came out of the feed store, he left town for the day. Business at the café picked up for the rest of the afternoon, so the day was not a total loss.

The next day, with the festival behind us, the town was quiet again. The café, however, was unusually busy. In fact, it was the busiest it had ever been. All everyone wanted to talk about was the night someone finally dealt with Robert. Locals I had never met were anxious to tell me their stories about Robert, and complain that the law never did anything to stop him. It was fascinating to learn of all the torment this one man had inflicted on so many people.

Conversations about Robert went on for weeks. Finally, I had heard enough. I was sick of hearing the man's name, and hoped I would never see him again. But alas, that was not to be. One day, I received a letter from the county grand jury, ordering me to appear in the matter of the "State of Oregon versus Charles Dudrey." I couldn't believe it.

I actually knew the county attorney from planning meetings I'd attended. He seemed to be a nice enough guy, so I fully expected that I would not be charged with anything. I thought the deputies who'd interviewed me the morning after the incident would have made it clear to the district attorney that there was no case to bring. Nonetheless, when the grand jury summons you to appear, you appear.

When the time for me to testify arrived, the official running the affair read me my rights and swore me in. Then he asked me a series of questions about the night in question. I told the members of the jury, a group of everyday folks, the entire story from start to finish. They seemed satisfied with my answer, so that afternoon I was back at work.

For months after that, the Robert saga continued. The guy never let up. He set up camp on the sidewalk across the street from our hotel. That was a bit discomforting. The guy who had tried to douse me with gasoline was camped a hundred feet from where my wife and I slept every night. When I would get up in the middle of the night to look out our bedroom window, there he would be, standing across the street, staring in our direction. As soon as he would see the bedroom light go on, he would move back into the shadows.

Eventually, Robert upped his game a notch. He brandished a firearm at me. I called the sheriff's office and reported what he'd done, and told them that I felt threatened. They replied that there was nothing that they could do about it. I told them that the man was stalking us, and therefore, I wanted a protective order from the court. They informed me that there was no anti-stalking law in Oregon, which was true at the time.

I had to come to grips with the reality that Robert had been doing stuff like this to the rest of the community for years. The law hadn't protected anyone else, so they weren't likely to help us either.

Then one day, the cops showed up and placed me under arrest and charged me with assault. I couldn't believe it. I'd had enough. I was sorry that I hadn't taken care of Robert the way I'd taken care of such problems in the past. I wasn't thinking about God at the moment, or the verse that says, "Vengeance is mine, I will repay," says the Lord. I wanted to put the hurt on the guy myself.

The only reason that I hadn't was because of how Diana might have responded. Still today, I'm sure Robert has no idea just how much pain my wife protected him from.

I think part of what had me so riled up was the county's ill-advised decision to indict me in the first place. Hitting Robert was clearly an act of self defense. There was even a witness to that effect. As far as I was concerned, some elected district attorney with political ambitions had decided to come down hard on me for reasons that probably had little to do with the incident itself.

As soon as they booked me, I went before a judge, posted bail, and was released pending trial. But, I'd had enough of their nonsense. Early in June, I told Diana that we were moving. We were putting "hell town" behind us. That was okay with her. We liked our business and had enjoyed running it, but the affair with Robert had taken all the fun out of our lives. And I was definitely taking the threat of jail seriously. As I've said before, being innocent is no guarantee that you won't be locked up. I was forty-nine at the time, and did not want to spend another day of my life in a cell.

We decided to leave Mitchell on the Fourth of July. There would be no fanfare; we would just drive away and not look back.

The night we made the decision to leave, I awoke from my sleep with a troubling thought on my mind. It was recalling the vision I had seen years earlier, the one with the dark clouds overhead and the shirt and pants hanging on the clothesline, being whipped back and forth and blown about by the strong winds.

That was me, alright. It was me living a miserable, unhappy life outside the will of God. I had chosen the left side of the hay loft, not the right. And the way I saw it, it was up to me to get myself out of the mess I'd made.

Chapter 48

Our Missouri Hide Out

W e drove away from Central Oregon with everything we owned in a pickup truck and a twelve foot U-Haul trailer. We were headed for Missouri by way of Montesano, Washington. We wanted to see William and Christy and the grandkids before disappearing, and we were fairly certain that the first place Oregon officials would look for me, if I didn't show up for trial, was Washington.

As planned, we left Mitchell on Independence Day. We were liberating ourselves from that awful place. We'd sold everything we could, then left the rest behind. Fortunately, we'd been able to sell the hotel on a contract. That gave us some hope of recouping at least part of our investment. The café went back to the seller, who was holding the contract. But, even the knowledge that we were taking a bath on the business end didn't deter us from walking away from what I had come to see as the biggest mistake I'd made since becoming a Christian.

It wasn't just the town or the people in Mitchell that bothered me. It was more my disobedience in moving there. God had played no part in the decision, and now I was reaping what I had sown.

I was a conflicted mess. When I fired up the engine and started out of town that day, I felt sick and liberated, both at the same time.

As for the Robert affair, if I would have agreed to plead guilty, the county attorney would have settled the case with me serving a thirty-day jail sentence. I just couldn't agree to that. It was the principle of the thing. I had done nothing wrong. There was no basis for their case against me. None. So they could just keep their stupid county, and "hell town," too, as far as I was concerned.

Down the road, I would come to realize that I would have been better off just taking the thirty days. But, there is no way you could have persuaded me of that at the time.

After a brief stay in Montesano, Diana and I headed east and eventually ended up in a small town called Ink, Missouri. The town had two houses. That's it; nothing else. I don't know how it even got to be called a town. We rented a house from a man I'd hoped to be working for, at least part time. But as it turned out, that was an empty promise and we would soon be as poor as church mice.

That winter, I sold our pickup truck to make the rent payments and buy a computer. That's was about the time I accepted the truth that I had walked away from God's will for my life. That's where I also acknowledged the reality that my poor wife was suffering the consequences of my disobedience. You can't make Jesus Christ the Lord of your life and then live as if He isn't.

There's a verse in the Bible that says that the steps of a good man are ordered by the Lord. Well, my steps were obviously not being ordered by the Lord. One day I would pray and repent and ask for God's forgiveness and the next day I would plan and do things my way all over again. I was living a life the Bible describes as that of a "double-minded man." I was trying to go two different directions at the same time.

My wife, on the other hand, was reading her Bible every day and spending time in prayer. If anything, she was probably doing more of that than ever before. I must confess that it bothered me. I got to the place where I didn't want to see her with her Bible in her hand. I would walk right past her, and pretend that I didn't see what she was doing. Oh sure, I would occasionally pray some anemic prayer, just so I could tell myself that I still prayed, but then I would turn right around and continue going my own way.

Then one day, Diana asked me to sit down. She said she needed to talk to me about something. I recalled, as I took a seat, something my pastor had said to me years earlier. He said, "Chuck, you're like a large ship in the ocean. When you get going in one direction, it takes a long time to get you turned around." He continued, "Large ships have a small rudder that controls their direction. That rudder can set the ship on a new course. Chuck, your wife is your rudder. When she has something to say, you need to be still and listen."

Diana sat across from me, and looked at me the way only she can. Then she started talking. By the time she was finished I knew I had plenty to think about. She ended with, "You're my husband and my spiritual covering, but you have holes in your armor. You need to get your life back on track."

There was nothing I could say. This amazing, faithful woman, the woman God had given me, was right, and I knew it. Other people might get away with wandering around in the darkness, never knowing that they are missing the will of God for their life, but a sincere Jesus follower cannot. God sees around corners and knows the future. We don't even know, with any certainty, what's going to happen just one minute later, even when we think otherwise.

I had ignored God and left Washington on a whim. I had left a good church and lots of friends. I had launched out into the deep and left my compass behind. Now I was lost.

What I'm going to say now might sound kind of odd, but the Bible says that men cast lots, or in common vernacular, roll dice, but "the outcome is of the Lord." That passage is not talking about playing craps or gambling, per se, but it just might apply to something like blindfolding a child and having them toss a monopoly game piece onto a map of the United States. It is quite possible that even before I knew Him, God directed us to the place we needed to be. Looking back, I'm sure that is what happened. Hoquiam, Washington was our home. It was where God had placed us. But, we had nonchalantly abandoned it and cut off all of the roots we had put down there. So, of course, we were hurting.

After a few months of hiding out in Missouri, we were pretty hard up. With no work, and also no truck, we were forced to live each day from hand to mouth. Then suddenly our ship came in, so to speak. A couple of years earlier, we had made an investment. We had no idea it was going to happen, but that investment paid off right when we needed it. We received a check in the mail for twenty-five thousand dollars and sixty-eight cents. As you can imagine, that money was a real life-saver.

We needed a car and a place to live. So, we immediately started looking at houses for sale. One day we drove out to the country to look at a place, and as soon as we saw it, we knew that it was the one we should buy. We agreed with the realtor that we would meet up with him right after lunch.

While we were sitting in the parking lot, ready to go in, Diana looked me in the eye and told me that I was to offer a really low price. I was almost embarrassed at the price she said to offer.

Nonetheless, I did as she suggested. To my surprise, the sellers accepted without making a counter offer, and we closed the deal right on the spot. Literally. We got keys that same day.

Just like that, we were homeowners again. Part of the offer we made was we that we would give the sellers one year's worth of payments, at closing, in a separate check. They liked that idea, and for us, the thought of not having to make any house payments for a year was pretty sweet. We could work on our new home, and relax for a while.

Our little house on five-acres was located about thirteen miles outside of town. Interestingly enough, the name of the county we lived in was Oregon. Once we got settled in, I felt better than I had in some time.

The day we moved in, a boy from down the road stopped by and invited us to visit his church on Sunday. He looked a little surprised when I told him we would see him there. After I made that promise, I wished I'd have kept my mouth shut. I had just committed to going to a church that I knew nothing about, and to meeting a bunch of new people. But we did as I'd promised, and went.

Oak Hill Missionary Baptist Church was a small country church with about 60 members. When we walked in the front door, the pastor introduced himself and gave us a warm welcome. The church was very different from the kind we'd attended, back in Washington. We were used to lively churches, where people clapped their hands and said, "Praise the Lord." The message was good, though. It was solid Bible preaching. So, in spite of our cultural differences, I liked the pastor right from the start. Even though I was in a pretty sinful state of mind at the time, I could still recognize that the Spirit of God was with this man.

I remember thinking on the way home that day that perhaps things were looking up again. I was back in church and getting back on track.

Springtime in the South is very different from the Northwest. People put in their gardens early in April, and by May they are already eating fresh beans. Our five acres gave us plenty of room for a garden. Following our neighbors' lead, we planted ours, and before long we had fresh radishes to eat.

As we got acquainted with the people at the church, we came to see that they were as good an example of Christianity as you could ask for. People who love God are in many ways the same no matter where you go. If they aren't caught up in some starchy religiosity, warmth and generosity just flows from them. People from our little church were always stopping by the house and giving us fresh produce and fresh eggs.

As soon as we started back to church, Diana and I started reading the Bible and praying more. Still, even though I kept it to myself, I was continuing to smoke pot regularly. I had some left over from my old growing room in Oregon. Plus, I'd already planted a new crop by the side of our house, just to keep my supply up.

To make sure there was some cash coming in, I found a job working in a telephone call center. After work, I would come home and tend our garden and work on the house. One of the reasons we got such a steal on our house was that it needed a lot of work. I had to put on a new roof, plus we decided to rebuild the back porch area and turn it into a larger bathroom. But I liked doing that kind of work. It felt good to build something again.

Diana found a job, too. She started working for a social services organization. With two incomes, we were doing better than we had for the past couple of years.

Then one evening, I decided that it was time to quit smoking pot for good. The prayer and Bible study was beginning to do what it's supposed to do.

I was pretty much married to the stuff, so, as you might imagine, that was a major decision, one I was sure Diana would be pleased to hear about. That night, I took my pipe apart and threw the pieces in every direction. Then I called my wife and told her what I'd done. Diana was elated. While she was still on the phone with me, I poured fuel on my stash and set it all on fire. By the grace of God, I was finally free from the stuff.

People who smoke pot all of the time will tell you that it doesn't have a hold on them, but it does. It's just more subtle than other drugs. I had smoked weed all day long almost every day for three decades, except for some of the time when I was in jail. It took me a long time to realize that pot had become a religion to me, but it had. For years I had carried a pipe and tin of pot in my pocket at all times. I would fill the tin with pot every morning, even before I had a cup of coffee.

I had been living in denial about it, but my use of marijuana was a large part of the spiritual battle that had been waging in my spirit for so long. Jesus said a man cannot serve two masters because he will love the one and despise the other. I had allowed this drug to rule over me, and in so doing had let my heart be led away from my God.

When a man searches the internet for the best seeds for growing the best pot, when he joins clubs and forums to learn how to get the best highs, when he joins efforts to make the use of marijuana legal, he just might have a pot problem. All I can say is, the day I finally let it go, I felt freer than I had in many years.

After that day, sitting at the kitchen table every morning and reading our Bibles together and praying, became a way of life for Diana and me. I came to the place where I could hardly wait to study. There is a verse in the Book of Romans that says, "Faith comes by hearing and hearing by the Word of God." That really proved true for us. The more we read our Bibles, the more our faith grew and the more we trusted God.

Diana and I began praying for the people in Oregon who had caused us so much trouble, especially Robert and the district attorney. We asked the Lord to make my Oregon legal issues go away, so we wouldn't have to be concerned about them any longer. We prayed for the sheriff, and everyone else involved in the matter. We even asked that they would forget me.

Well, that was not going to happen. God had a different plan. He heard our prayers and the cry of our hearts, but He answered in his own way, as He is prone to do.

Eventually, we joined the church we were attending, and became official members. It felt really good to be back in fellowship with other believers again. There were about seven hundred people in the community we lived in and fifty or sixty of them were members of our little church. I remember telling Pastor Edward one day that the Lord had given us the finest people in the county to be our friends.

Every local church has its own uniqueness, or what some people call "spiritual DNA." Oak Hill's DNA was the awe inspiring love the people there had for one another. They were really something special to behold, and just what Diana and I needed.

In the Ozarks, at least back then, a lot of people heated their homes with wood. Every fall, all of the men got together to cut firewood for those who needed it. And if, for some reason, someone was hurt or off work, there would be a food drive on Sunday night, we would collect food for them, and then deliver it their house. I'm talking serious amounts of food. Coolers of frozen meat, dozens of eggs, boxes of fruits and vegetables, dairy products. This was just a way of life in this little country church. The people were always looking for an opportunity to serve and help someone.

One afternoon, I was looking out the front window and saw two police cars drive past the house. That was the first time I had seen a police car on our road. I continued to watch as they went down the road and then turned around and came back. My heart began beating faster, when they drove into our driveway. I went outside just as they came around the corner of the house. As soon as they saw me, they asked if my name was Charles Dudrey. I told them it was.

I asked the officers if they would like to step inside the house so we could talk. Before we sat down, they informed me that there was an outstanding warrant for my arrest in Oregon.

As I mentioned earlier, Diana and I had been praying that it would all be over. I calmly asked the officers if I could change clothes and have a moment to pray with my wife. They said that would be alright. Diana and I spent a few moments praying together. I hugged and kissed her, and then the deputies hauled me off to jail.

I was surprised by Diana's attitude when I left. She assured me that she was not afraid. She told me that her faith was strong. She said the Lord was going to make it all work out. Those are easy words to say when there not two cops standing outside your door with handcuffs, waiting to take your husband away and put him in a cell. But when my wife needed her faith the most, it was there. I could tell, because I saw no fear in her eyes that day.

Chapter 49

The Oregon Trail

Getting hauled off to jail was not exactly what I had in mind when I prayed and asked God to take care of my "Oregon problem." But, by now, I had enough experience with God to know that He answers prayers in his own way, and in his own time, and He makes no mistakes.

We can ask God to deliver us, and He will hear our prayer, but often we have no idea what that deliverance is going to look like when it arrives. That's why faith in God means trusting Him regardless of circumstances.

That night I went to sleep in another jail cell. Over the years, I had slept in plenty of cells, but this time was different. This time I went to sleep with my Bible beside my bed. The jailer had been gracious enough to let me keep it.

When you enter a cellblock for the first time, the other inmates immediately size you up. They want to know your story, starting with why you're there.

In my case, they already knew who I was before I even got there. I was the fugitive from Oregon who had been caught hiding out in their little community, and arrested on numerous assault charges. The story had been all over the local news.

I settled into my bunk, got as comfortable as a guy can get on a steel platform and a thin mattress, and tried to get some sleep. I lay there thinking that I had been arrested and jailed far too many times, and that every time was supposed to be the last.

Later in the evening, I called home and talked with Diana. That night marked the first time I had been in jail, overnight, in all the years we had known each other. I was concerned about how my being jailed might affect her, but my worry was misplaced. It was Diana who encouraged me that night. She was totally good with what was happening and said she knew that God was working on our behalf.

I also took some comfort in knowing that our friends at church would look after Diana while I was away. Pastor Edward would see to that. He was the kind of friend you could count on.

As for me, my real troubles would come further down the road, in Wheeler County, Oregon. Judging by the way my arrest warrant read, the District Attorney was more than a little unhappy with me for running off. He had added some additional charges. Instead of one assault charge, the charges were assault in the first degree, second degree, and third degree. On top of that, he had added a theft charge. I had no idea what that was about. There was also a charge for delivery of a controlled substance. That one, too, was a mystery to me.

Ambitious or overly aggressive district attorneys do that sort of thing. The more charges they bring, the more potential jail time the defendant faces. The scarier the downside, the easier it is to get the defendant to accept a guilty plea with a promise of a lesser sentence. It's a rigged system and it amounts to legal intimidation, but it's common practice with prosecutors.

But I was neither worried nor intimidated. I was confident that God knew what he was doing. Times like these test the genuineness of one's faith. You can't really trust God and worry at the same time. The two behaviors are polar opposites. In my case, I had chosen to trust God, which meant that the final disposition of things was out of my hands.

As I waited for my court hearing, I thought about fighting extradition back to Oregon. If they wanted me that bad they would have to get a signed warrant from the Governor of Missouri. However, instead of seeing how clever I could be, I began to pray and ask the Lord what He had in mind. I asked Him to use me for His purposes, no matter what.

Every day, I spent hours in my cellblock reading my Bible. One afternoon a young man asked me what I was reading, so I shared with him something the Apostle Paul talks about in the Book of Romans. It's one of the greatest principles in the entire book. Paul said, "All things work together for the good for those who love God..." At the moment, that promise meant everything to me.

Then I told the young man, "Son, let me tell you something. God has me here in this jail for a reason, and that reason could very well be you. Do you want to meet Jesus? Do you want to be forgiven of every ugly thing you have ever done or thought about in your life? Do you want to be free from the guilt and the hurts and pain in your life? Do you want Jesus to save you?"

He replied, "Yes, I do."

Then, just as I was about to pray with him, another man spoke up. "Wait! Please. I want to get saved too. I want to be free!"

And so I prayed for them both, right then and there. Those two inmates accepted Jesus as their Savior that afternoon. They became free men, even though they were locked up. The three of us had ourselves a little church service, right there in the county jail. We thanked God and praised Him for saving our souls.

Pastor Ed came to visit me at the jail on several occasions. One morning, while I was waiting to go into a courtroom for a hearing, I had a sit-down in the hallway with Diana, our pastor, and another brother from the church. While we were talking, a man from my cellblock came up to us and asked me to pray for him before he went to court. The four of us stood and prayed for him that God would intervene in his situation.

That's one of the amazing things about putting God in charge of your life. No matter where you are, or whether things look good or bad, if you trust Him and act from a position of faith, He makes a way for you to touch the lives of others. There's even a story in the Bible of one of the apostles, while he was locked up, leading his jailer to faith in Jesus. God just does stuff like that.

I had spent most of the past few years walking in disobedience to God, but now that I was back on track, He was opening doors for me to give hope and faith to others. I had been living on the dark and stormy side of the "hayloft," but was now looking out at fields of ripe grain, ready for the harvest.

Shortly after we prayed for my jail-mate, the clerk called my case. A decision had been made, and I was headed back to Oregon. All that was left was for the Oregon authorities to send someone to get me.

One day, while Diana and I were sitting in the visiting room talking, a young man from my cellblock sat close by, talking with someone who had come to visit him. He looked to be about twenty. After our visitors left, the two of us sat waiting for the jailer to come get us and take us back to our cells. We had a few moments alone, so I turned to him and asked, "Son, do you know who Jesus Christ is? Have you ever prayed and asked Him to forgive you of the sin in your life, and to save your soul?"

He was silent for a moment, but in a matter of a few seconds, I saw tears in his eyes. Then he told me that he hadn't.

I said, "Sir, you have never met me before and will likely never see me again after today, but listen now. This is the time to ask Jesus to save you. Are you ready? Don't pray because I asked you to. Pray because you want Jesus to save you from the sins in your life. Do you want Jesus to come into your life?"

"Yes," he said, with tears rolling down his cheeks. We prayed together, and that young man was saved right there on the spot. He wept openly, and I saw God begin doing something wonderful in his life.

Walking back to my cellblock that day, I realized that God's timing is never off. Three souls had been saved in that Missouri jail. God had used me, a flawed man, to share with three young men the message of salvation, which can only be found in His Son, Jesus. I would gladly spend three weeks in jail to lead three people to Jesus and see their souls saved and their eternal destinies rewritten.

Some people don't believe in jailhouse conversions. They say they don't stick. But I have known lots of men and women who were not open to finding God until they had reached the end of their own rope. Besides, God is not fooled by anyone, not ever. He knows our hearts. If we call on Him from a sincere heart, He hears and answers. Just ask the thief on the cross, if you ever meet him. He was being crucified and was near death when he called on Jesus, and the Lord told that man, a condemned criminal, "This day you will be with me in Paradise."

Lots of men and women have given their hearts and lives to the Lord and been saved while sitting or kneeling alone in their jail or prison cells. What God asks of us, no matter who we are, is that we come to him in faith. We must confess with our lips and believe in our hearts that Jesus Christ is the Son of God, that He died for our sins, and that God raised Him from the dead. It's that simple. Anyone can do that. Any time. Any place. The path is the same for a convict as it is for a businessman/woman, a construction worker, or a stay-at-home mom.

Three days after my hearing, the sheriff arrived from Oregon to take me back to stand trial for failure to appear in court, and several other matters. One thing I learned back in my bail bonding days is that judges get pretty upset when someone fails to show up in court as ordered.

So off we went, with me shackled and handcuffed, riding in the backseat of a rental car headed for Oklahoma City. From there we would catch a flight back to Oregon.

But God wasn't finished working on my behalf. It just so happened, that the sheriff hadn't come alone. One of the judges from Wheeler County came with him. The three of us had a very interesting conversation on our way to the airport. We talked about Jesus.

Chapter 50

Vengeance is Mine

During the flight back to Oregon, I asked the sheriff if he would set up a meeting between the county attorney and me. He assured me that he would. I didn't have that bad of a relationship with the officials in Wheeler County. I had cooperated with them throughout the entire process, up to sitting in jail for some baseless charge.

There were two things hurting my case and making it harder to make this all go away. One was my criminal record from twenty-five years earlier, and the other was my failure to appear in court.

When we got the courthouse, I sat waiting for the district attorney to come and talk to me. He knew that Robert was the county troublemaker. Everyone knew that. He also knew that Robert was about to douse me with gasoline when I hit him, so mine was clearly a case of self-defense.

When the District Attorney arrived, we shook hands and made some small talk. Then he explained that I had ticked off the judge by leaving the state, and because of that he had no choice but to add charges to my case. After our brief chat, I was booked into the county jail. There was nothing for me to do but sit and wait for my next court appearance.

I sat there for two months, praying the entire time that this mess would soon be over. I was coming to the conclusion that things were not looking good. With all the charges I was facing, I could serve a total of one hundred and thirty months in jail, if I was found guilty of everything. That's more than ten years.

As usual, the court appointed an attorney for me. I drew the same guy that I had fired three years earlier. He looked like Opey Taylor from the Andy Griffith Show. He even dressed like him. There was nothing about the guy that instilled confidence in me. The more he talked to me, the more obvious it was that he didn't like me and didn't want to represent me.

Court appointed attorneys generally get paid the same to defend you, whether they file one piece of paper and settle the case, or go through a full-blown trial. With a set up like that, if the attorney doesn't like you, you shouldn't expect much. They go through the motions and give you the minimum defense, then forget about you. The only times that is not true is when you have enough money to hire the best, or if someone is defending you in a high profile case and wants to win to enhance his reputation.

I had several issues to address with my attorney and needed to ask him a few more questions, but he told me that he didn't have time to talk further. I decided, then and there, that I was going to have to hire a real attorney, if I was going to have any chance of winning. Before our meeting ended that afternoon, the guy told me that he had fifteen more clients to see that afternoon, and wanted to get home. With that guy in my corner, I might as well have had no attorney at all.

So I called Diana that night and described the situation. She agreed that we needed to hire a real attorney. The problem was, we didn't have five thousand dollars needed for a retainer. That evening I lay awake praying and thinking. Before I went to sleep, I decided that in the morning I would call Pastor Edward back in Missouri. Fortunately he was there when I called, and after a brief chat, told me politely that he would see what he could do.

A short time later, Diana flew from Missouri out to Washington. From there, she called to tell me that she and William were driving to Oregon to see me and talk about my case. She also informed me that before she left Missouri, a man from our church had given her a $5,000 check to cover my attorney fees. "Take this, and go to Oregon and bring your husband home," he'd said. We thanked God for that man's generosity.

Leave it to our son William. He had grown to be quite the young man and was not at all shy about getting things done. He called the jail ahead of time and talked to the superintendent, who then arranged for us to meet in the lawyer's visiting room for as long as we needed.

It was so good to see Diana and William again, and I thoroughly enjoyed our visit, but I didn't see any evidence that things were changing on the legal front. From where I sat, judging by pure logic and my past experiences in court, it was all but certain that I was going to go to prison. My wife reminded me to trust God and not my own logic, but I was struggling.

I had surrendered my life to Christ and my life was no longer my own. But sometimes, when circumstances are rough and things seem hopeless, rather than trusting the Lord, the natural tendency is to rely on your own strength and judgment. My faith must have been weak that day, because when our visit ended, I sent all of my personal belongings home with Diana, just in case.

One morning, about a month later, I was sitting in a holding cell waiting for the sheriff's deputy to come and get me, so we could make the sixty-mile drive to court. I happened to be looking out the cell window, when to my surprise, I saw Robert. He was being placed in another cell. I hadn't seen the guy for three years, and it seemed odd that he would be in jail at the same time I was, especially considering the fact that I was being held for allegedly assaulting him.

Instantly, almost like it was a reflex, I felt myself starting to hate him, but then I caught myself. I remembered that morning, sitting at our kitchen table at our home back in Missouri, when I had forgiven him. I had no right to take that back. In fact, that would have been a dangerous thing for me to have done.

One of the things Christians often forget, when they pray the Lord's Prayer, is the condition it places on forgiveness. In that prayer, Jesus taught us to ask God to forgive us of our trespasses or sins, "as" we forgive those who sin against us. "As" is a tiny word, but it carries a powerful punch, and a scary one, if we have not forgiven those who have sinned against us. If God forgives us to the same extent that we have forgiven others, and we haven't forgiven others...

With that in mind, I started praying for Robert. I asked God to heal his heart. I asked God that Robert would come to know Him. Then I asked God to make sure that my actions would bring honor to the name of the Lord.

When it was time to go, you can imagine my surprise when the deputy put Robert in the back seat of the patrol car, right next to me. The two of us were going to ride to the courthouse together. The deputy told Robert that he had better behave himself. I thought I saw a faint smile on his face when he said that.

There I was, seated next to the guy who had cost me so much, someone I had once powerfully hated. I was sure God wanted me to love him, but I was definitely going to have to work at it.

All the way to the courthouse I prayed for Robert. I refused to let the hate come back. But all the while I kept thinking that this car ride was probably no accident; it had been planned. Someone meant for Robert and me to ride side by side for the sixty-mile trip to court. Back at the sheriff's office, the deputies were probably laughing about the whole thing, wondering if Robert would run his mouth, and if I would try to knock his head off.

When we reached our destination, they led us to a holding cell in the middle of the sheriff's department. It was odd that they would stick Robert and me together in a cell. They were really pushing it. Nonetheless, I continued to pray and ask God to reveal to me what He was doing. We sat there for a while, and then Robert signaled that he wanted to tell me something. He was whispering and trying to get my attention, but being careful not to let anyone see him talking to me.

His behavior reminded me of the way he'd acted three years earlier, back in "hell town." Robert was the sneakiest man I had ever met, so my guard was up. After he got my attention, he whispered to me that if I would tell the judge that the sheriff's department had paid me to beat him up, he wouldn't testify against me in court. He said, "Tell the judge that you were growing dope and the sheriff's department was in on it with you." I was surprised that even a man as odd as Robert would suggest such a thing. I wondered if he was perhaps even more delirious than when I had known him before.

Robert kept at me, trying to persuade me to lie for him. I kept thinking, how dare this man ask me to do something for him. For a moment, I felt sorry for him again. I remembered how I had once liked the guy, and how Diana and I had tried to help him.

Then Robert told me that the cops had paid someone else to beat him up, too, someone besides me. He showed me his bottom lip where, according to him, the guy the cops allegedly sent to beat him up, had bitten it off. His lip looked pretty ugly. When I acknowledged that his lip did indeed look bad, he started begging me to help him get out of his troubles. The scene felt almost surreal.

Finally, the bailiff came and took us both up to court. He motioned us to sit side by side on one of the benches and wait for the judge. Robert's turn came first. Based on the list of charges the clerk read, the man had continued harassing people just like he was doing back when we lived in Mitchell. Plus, there was a charge for trespassing.

When it was my turn to stand in front of the judge, I pled "not guilty" to all charges. Apparently, I had been driven all that way, just to be arraigned, because as soon as I had entered my plea, the judge ordered me back to jail to await trial.

As we were being led back down to the holding cell, I mentioned to the deputy that I wanted to speak to the sheriff before I went back to jail. I told him that it was important and that I wasn't trying to waste anyone's time. He said he would pass my message on.

Sure enough, the sheriff agreed to meet with me. I was brief and to the point. I told him about the lies regarding his department that Robert wanted me to tell the court. I assured the sheriff that as crazy as it all sounded, I wasn't making any of this up. He said he believed me. He said the only way I could possibly have known these things was if Robert had told them to me. Before I left, I said to the sheriff, "How convenient that Robert and I should be here together today."

He smiled and said, "Isn't it though."

All the way back to the jail, Robert continued whispering. I wanted him to shut up, but I starting to suspect that Robert's antics were perhaps part of God's plan. The Bible says, "Vengeance is mine; I will repay," says the Lord. That means we are not to seek vengeance against people who have harmed us, even when they deserve it. God claims that right for Himself. And according to the Bible, his instrument for bringing judgment on the bad guys, is usually civil government. So it was possible that God was going to give Robert what he deserved for all of the harm he had done, and He was going to use the government to do it.

About a week later, my attorney showed up at the jail to talk to me. I could tell by the look on his face that he had some news for me.

He explained that the county attorney had made me an offer. If I would enter a plea of guilty to the charges, he would agree that I would only have to serve six months in jail. They would credit the time I had already served, so I would be out in about a month. There was one additional stipulation. After I was sentenced, I would be required to testify before the grand jury in a case the county was bringing against Robert.

Robert was going to be charged with witness tampering, and I was going to be the witness.

Chapter 51

A Promise that Had to Be Kept

After completing the final month of my sentence, I was released from the county jail. I said goodbye to Oregon and took a Greyhound back to Missouri. Diana met me at the station, and I have to tell you, when we pulled into our driveway, it felt really good to be home. I had been on quite a journey. I'd spent six months in jail for things I hadn't done, and I'd pled guilty to crimes I hadn't committed. But, on a more positive note, instead of facing years in prison, I was released a free man.

As it turned out, the district attorney and the sheriff were so eager to get Robert (for trying to get me to testify that they were working with me in a drug enterprise and had paid me to hurt him), that they let me off the hook so they could get him. The way things turned out, our "coincidentally" riding sixty miles to court together, and our being placed in the same holding cell, were the key to my release.

You might be wondering why I chose to plead guilty to crimes I hadn't committed and would have preferred to fight. Well, there are times when you stand on principle and fight to the death, so to speak, and there are times when you just walk through the door that has opened for you. I already had enough bad stuff on my criminal record that the new charges didn't matter much. Getting home and back to my family seemed more important than risking spending years in prison, if I went to trial and lost.

Sometimes you just say your best prayers, ask God for guidance, and then make the decision that is best for your family, unless, of course, you hear the Lord tell you otherwise. My wife had been through enough already and I had the opportunity to end all that, so I prayerfully took the deal.

As part of my plea agreement with the State of Oregon I had to be on probation for three years, plus pay a lot of money to the county for court costs and fines. In many cases like mine, probation is a waste of everyone's time. But they tack it on anyway, because it allows the district attorney to say he got a longer sentence in the plea agreement than he actually did.

So, when I got back to Missouri, I was assigned a probation officer there. The officer I drew was a likeable man. After reading my case file, he wondered out loud why I had been charged with a crime in the first place. I had asked myself that question many times over and never came up with an answer. Maybe I had gotten away with so many crimes in my life, before coming to know Jesus, that the Lord let me serve at least some time for all the times I hadn't been caught.

Our first Sunday back at church, all our friends were delighted to learn that I was a free man. We thanked God together for finally getting all that legal stuff behind us – once and for all.

When the folks at church heard my story, especially the part about Robert and me riding to court together, everyone agreed that God had intervened on my behalf.

God can take evil and use it for good. I am confident that is exactly what He did for me in Oregon. And let's not forget that while I was in jail in Missouri, waiting to be extradited, three people came to know Jesus. Plus, I had the opportunity to pray for several more. That alone made the whole affair worthwhile, many times over.

God makes no mistakes. He is in charge and if we will submit to his will, He will use people and situations to accomplish His purposes in our lives. My life is proof of that.

Diana and I got serious about finishing the remodeling on our house and praying about our future. Eventually, we came to the conclusion that the Lord was directing us back to Washington. That was our real home, and we were really missing our son's family and the grandchildren, and longed to be closer to them.

Diana flew back to Washington for William's birthday party in December. When she returned from her trip, all she could talk about was being a part of our grandchildren's lives. I think that kind of did it for us. Once we'd settled it in our minds that we were moving back, we began to feel better and better about it.

To get the ball rolling, I put a "For Sale" sign out front and placed an ad in the local newspapers. To our delight, we started getting calls right away. People came and looked at the house, and a few seemed like they really wanted to buy it, but we didn't get any offers.

In April, Diana was offered a job working for the company she had worked for when we'd lived in Washington. We decided that she should take the job and I would stay in Missouri and sell the house.

Eventually, I gave up on selling the house myself and enlisted the aid of a real estate broker, a lady who went to our church. She placed ads in the newspaper and on several websites, but still there were no offers.

Eventually, it occurred to me that God might have a different plan than mine, so I stopped being anxious about selling the place and just peacefully continued making improvements. The house would sell when it was time. As you will soon see, God did have a plan and it would unfold at the perfect time.

One evening I got a telephone call from a friend from church. His elderly father was in failing health and had been in the hospital off and on for the past few months. I decided to go see him. Enos Hand was a lovely man with a kind and gentle spirit. Diana and I knew Enos from church, and had grown to love him and his family very much.

Pretty much anyone who knew Enos would have described him as a godly man. He spoke with a gentle voice. He was honest clear to the core. He loved God, and he always had a kind word to say. The world could use a lot more men like him.

During one of our visits, Enos told me that back in the 1940s his father's family had grown sweet potatoes on the very spot where our house sat. Back before his health started failing, Enos and I spent many a morning sitting in our kitchen, visiting, drinking coffee, and eating Diana's homemade desserts. I confess that I truly loved that dear man.

The doctors determined that Enos didn't have much time to live, so they sent him home. Once he got settled, I started visiting him every day. He would take my hand and ask me, with his soft, failing voice, to please pray for him. More than once, Enos said to me, "Brother Chuck, please pray for my family, that they would all come to know Jesus." And so I did.

Holding the hand of a man who is about to die can be an emotionally numbing experience. I had nothing in my memory with which to compare that feeling. I loved Enos, and it was very difficult to watch him slipping away.

On Father's day, Enos Hand drew his last breath and went to be with the Lord. It was kind of strange how I felt at that moment. I was sad, but at the same time I was filled with joy, knowing that my dear friend was now sitting at the feet of Jesus, his first love.

The Bible says, "Death, where is your sting?" That is the great hope of everyone who knows Jesus. Death only releases them to be with Him.

Eight days after Enos's funeral, I went shopping for a pickup truck to pull our trailer, packed with all our stuff back, back to Washington. I had planned to drive to West Plains and look for one there, but when I stopped at the stop sign where I was supposed to turn right, the Holy Spirit spoke to me and told me to turn left instead. It's easy to be foolish about such things, and think you're hearing from God when you're not, but that day I knew the Holy Spirit was leading me.

So I whispered, "Okay, Lord, I will turn left. Let's see what You have in mind." As I was driving along, I saw a pickup for sale in a yard alongside the highway. My first thought was; this must be the one God wants me to buy. I asked the Lord, "Is this the one?" I got no response, so I continued driving.

A few miles later, I came to the intersection of another highway and was just about to pull into the right lane when the Holy Spirit said to me, "Turn left." So I turned left again, which put me on the highway headed toward Arkansas. I passed three more car dealers, but heard nothing from the Lord. I drove to the town of Mammoth Springs and then turned into the first auto dealership I came to, which happened to be closed.

I had the dogs with me that day, so I got out to stretch my legs and let the dogs run around a bit. Glancing around, I saw a nice-looking, pewter-colored, quad pickup truck. I liked it the moment I saw it. As I was walking toward it, the Lord said to me, "This is your new truck." I placed my hand on the hood said, "Thank you Lord." I had never had the Lord direct me to buy a truck before, but oh well. I drove away confident that the truck would be there when I came back the next day, when the lot would be open.

On the way home that morning, I had to drive right by Enos Hand's house. Like I had done so many times before, back when Enos was alive, I pulled into the driveway. From the car, I could see one of Enos's sons and his niece sitting on the front porch enjoying the morning sun. Enos's nine-year old granddaughter was with them.

I got out and we all cheerfully greeted one another. I went over and sat down on the step next to the granddaughter, little Ashley. With no warm up conversation, I earnestly asked her, "Ashley, is today the day you're going to ask Jesus into your life?"

She instantly put her arm around me and gave me a tight hug. "Yes it is, Brother Chuck. I want Jesus to save my soul." Her young heart was full of faith and ready for the invite.

So, on that fine July morning on the front steps of Enos's house, I prayed with his nine-year-old granddaughter, and she gave her heart to Jesus. I had no more than said "amen," when she jumped to her feet and ran into the house, yelling, "I got saved, I got saved, I accepted Jesus into my heart."

Everyone in the house came running out to see what all the commotion was about. Little Ashley kept saying over and over again that she had found Jesus and that she was saved.

As you may recall, this was Enos Hand's final prayer before he drew his last breath, that all of his family would come to know Jesus. Little Ashley was the last one.

God was faithful and answered that dear old man's best prayer. With my work there completed, I said "so long" to everyone and got into my car and started on the short, two-mile drive home. I had gotten less that a hundred yards down the road, when the Lord spoke to me. He said, "Now you can move. Your mission here is complete."

I had no more arrived back at the house than the phone started ringing. It was my real estate broker telling me that our house had sold just ten minutes ago. The buyers had offered the full asking price, and wanted to move in on August first.

The Lord had kept me around until I'd completed the one thing He had left for me to do in Missouri. Once I had led Enos's granddaughter to the Lord and that dear old man's last prayer was answered, I was free to go.

The way things worked out, the people who bought our house signed their offer at almost the exact same time that little Ashley prayed her prayer and gave her heart to the Lord.

Chapter 52

The Little Ones

G od is a restorer of things the enemy has stolen. In my case, as with so many others, the enemy had stolen a lot. He had stolen my childhood. He had stolen my character and my integrity. He had taken years of my life, leading me to spend them robbing and plundering the lives of others and then sitting in some jail or prison cell paying the price for what I'd done. Altogether, I spent more than seven years of my life locked up.

Sometimes we lose things and don't realize they're missing. That was certainly the case with me. I had lost the ability to love unselfishly. For a long time, my heart was calloused. Whether it was the childhood abuse that led me to shut down my emotions, or the years I'd spent taking advantage of others, for a long time I was unable to truly love.

God, however, kept his promise to give back more than the enemy took from me. He took away my emotional poverty and made me rich in the things that matter most.

There is a verse in the Bible that says that the Lord sets the solitary into families. That is such a powerful concept. It foretells an end to the loneliness that so many of us struggle with while we're growing up, and often on into adulthood. For me, a man who had known nothing but dysfunction and heartbreak, it meant being surrounded by a family of loving, caring people, and the freedom to love them back.

God brought me to a place in life where I could pour myself into the lives of at least a few little ones, and make sure that they enjoyed lives of happiness and safety, far removed from the abuse, constant fear, and bitterness that had been my life growing up on Church Street.

I determined that the cycle of abuse that had been perpetuated by Barbara and my dad, and his dad before him, would end with me. The beautiful, awesome children that the Lord had placed in my life in my "old age" would know love. Even if it wore me out.

I wasn't sure I could take another night of flashlight tag. I was still recovering from all the wrestling on the living room floor the night before. It was, after all, as I gently reminded my three grandchildren, already two hours past my regular bedtime.

I had tried two hours earlier to get the three-year-old and the two seven-year-olds to go outside and play. But "No," they insisted. "It's not dark enough yet."

I sighed, smiled weakly, and rolled my eyes, resigning myself to my fate.

When it was finally dark enough, I put my shoes back on and headed outside to try to keep up with the little ones. They seemed to find great delight in hiding from me in the dark.

"Bumpa, it's your turn. You're it! Count to a hundred, then come find us."

I took my sweet time counting. I needed to catch my breath.

"Bumpa, we're waiting. Come and find us."

I was sure they could see me coming, because every time I would get close, they would run and hide somewhere else.

"I see you," I called after them.

"No you didn't, Bumpa," they said, giggling.

"Lying is a sin," I shouted back, laughing as I spoke.

Only an hour earlier, on the living room floor, I had pleaded with them, to no avail, to "not jump on Bumpa's belly." Taking my plea "not to," as a request to climb aboard, all three of them had climbed on top of me and started wrestling.

"Tickle me, Bumpa, tickle me some more"

"No, it's my turn," one of them said.

I was already worn out. I had spent the afternoon playing with William's three children. But, I told myself, they would go home soon enough and I could rest then. That is one of the well known joys of grand parenting; you play with them, and then you send them home. Tonight, we would have fun while we could.

When I was seven, the same age as the twins, I had almost been killed by an adult. My life was never the same after that. But now, in a way, God has given me a chance to be seven again, and go outside and play hide-and-go-seek with the other "kids."

Some might find it a little unusual for a man my size and my age to be down on the floor wrestling and playing with three little kids, or building them a fort out in the woods. But who cares? I was loving them and they were giving me part of my life back. They were making me rich. Just knowing them was making me a wealthy man by all meaningful measures.

I am thankful that I have a family that understands me and cares enough to let me show the heart of a Bumpa to these little ones. It is only by the grace of God that I get to spend time playing with three precious grandchildren and I'm not sitting in some prison cell, playing solitaire, or trying to figure out how to run a game on some other inmate to get another pack of cigarettes. Seriously. That could very well be my life today.

I will never forget something a minister said to me at church one night, more than twenty years ago. I was standing in the front of the church praying, when he walked over to me. I had never met the man and he knew nothing about me. But he laid his hand on me and began to pray over me. "Son," he said. "Hear what the Spirit of the Lord has to say. God wants to restore unto you what the moth and the cankerworm has destroyed. He wants to heal you from all the pain and hurts in your life caused by the hand of your father."

I stood there with tears streaming down my face as he continued. "God wants you to know that He has plans for your life, and that He will give you a beautiful wife and a family to love, and to love you."

I began weeping that night and thanking God for the things He was willing to restore back into my life. Looking back, I can say with confidence that those words have more than come true.

"Bumpa, I want Tootie Fruities for breakfast."

"Bumpa, I want Coco Crunch and cinnamon toast."

"Bumpa will you help me get dressed?"

"I'll be there in a moment. You guys, don't spill your milk, and hey, no fighting."

When I spend time with my grandchildren I am constantly reminded of where I've come from and the place God holds in my life today. I know that if it weren't for his love, and mercy and grace, none of the things I enjoy today would have ever come to pass.

"Why is Bumpa crying, Grandma?"

I knew why. Sometimes I am just so grateful that my God saw fit to drag me out of the pit in which He found me and give me such a wonderful life. This old criminal has turned into a soft hearted man who loves to love.

Tenderly, I continued to dress my sweet little granddaughter and tie her tiny little shoes for her, completely ignoring her question about the tears.

"I love you, Bumpa," she said.

Something about that scene triggered in me a memory of one morning when Barbara was dressing my little sister Frances. Frances was three at the time, and she must have squirmed or moved in some way that Barbara didn't like. Barbara jerked Frances's hair violently and snarled, "Stand still you little ____." Then she slapped her in the face. "Now hold your foot still, you _____, so I can put your ____shoe on you."

Barbara twisted Frances's arm and dug her dirty fingernails into her skin and turned her forcibly around, jerking her like she was a ragdoll.

"What are you crying for? Knock it off!" she hissed

That's the way Barbara had treated an innocent little girl, a child whose mother had been murdered only a year-and-a-half earlier.

When those memories came flooding back I had to excuse myself from the room. The memories are old now, but they still break my heart.

Chapter 53

Diana's Turn

Today, Chuck and I make our home in the beautiful Pacific Northwest near the foothills of the Olympic Mountains. And yes, it rains all winter still. We live near the ocean, surrounded by fresh air and evergreen trees. We continue to be involved in the lives of our grown children and our grandchildren.

We attend a great church in Aberdeen and continue enjoying the love and fellowship that can best be found by building relationships with people in a local church setting.

Our lives are full. We don't have a lot of material things, but we are happy. Chuck is in charge of the men's groups in the church and stays busy helping other men avoid the mistakes he made early in life. He spends time on the streets every week, praying for people's needs and sharing the gospel with them. If you went looking for Chuck, you might find him in some dirty back alley in the roughest part of town, kneeling down by some lost and hurting homeless person, telling him or her about Jesus. That's what he does. That's who Chuck is.

I have grown accustomed to my cell phone ringing and the call being Chuck telling me that he wants to bring some down-and-out person home for a few days. I trust his judgment, and always say yes. At least he always checks with me first. I'm thankful for that. Loving people is what Chuck is about, so we do all we can.

The Bible says that we freely received and, therefore, we are to freely give. Chuck and I have been forgiven of so much, and have been shown so much love and mercy, that we cannot help but share our faith.

Besides, it's so rewarding. Every time someone accepts Jesus and gets saved, we feel that our lives have been worthwhile.

It's not uncommon for us to share the gospel with someone, and when they hear about Jesus they want to give their heart to him and get saved, but they don't know how to do that. There are a lot of people in this country who have never prayed and don't know how to talk to God. There's no formula to follow, but the Bible says, "If you declare with your mouth, 'Jesus is Lord,' and believe in your heart that God raised him from the dead, you will be saved. For it is with your heart that you believe and are justified, and it is with your mouth that you profess your faith and are saved." Romans 10:9-10 (NIV)

We often lead new believers in a simple prayer that goes something like this:

> *"Heavenly Father, thank you for loving me so much that you sent your Son, Jesus, to die in my place. I believe in my heart that Jesus Christ is the Son of God, that He died on the cross for my sins, and that He was raised from the dead. I ask you, Jesus, to forgive me of all my sins, all my mistakes, and to come into my life and be my Savior, my Lord, my Boss, and my Friend and my King. And by your grace and by your power I will serve you for the rest of my life. In Jesus name, I pray. Amen."*

Then we hug them and tell them, often through tear-filled eyes, "If you prayed that prayer by faith, you are now in the family of God! You are a Christian. It's that simple. If you died today, you would go to heaven because Jesus Christ just wiped away all of your sins."

Of course, we make sure to tell them to get involved with a local church where they can get baptized and get good Bible teaching, so their faith will grow. Chuck and I made the mistake of not staying connected to a local church for a few years and consequently suffered through some tough times that were probably not necessary.

Some of the people Chuck talks to on the streets are a lot like he was, before he met the Lord. I don't think I would be able to relate to some of them today, if I had not met and fallen in love with Chuck and seen God work in his life.

When I first met my husband and learned of his criminal background, it was all a little shocking to my senses. I had never known people from the world Chuck had lived in. Like I told him back then, my family and relatives were all law-abiding people. None of us had ever been in trouble with the law, let alone been sent to jail or prison.

Chuck, on the other hand, had been on the run from the law since he was a young teenager. He had done a lot of bad things. Still, I could tell that deep down inside Chuck wanted to be a good man. In spite of all of the abuse he had suffered, he was still capable of treating people well.

The way he treated Stacy, William, and me was...it was as if we were the most important people he had ever known. Chuck could not have been a better dad to my two kids, if they had been his own.

By the time Chuck got arrested coming home from William's birthday party, that long ago night, I already felt that I knew him well enough to trust him. But still, it was pretty weird to be calling a bail bondsman about getting my boyfriend out of jail. That was my first experience with the world Chuck was from, and I felt very much out of place.

I hope people know that I would never have agreed to take my two kids and move to some far away place with a man who was on the run from the law, if I hadn't feel strongly that Chuck was a good man, and that in time we would have a good life together as a family. And I was not alone in that. Stacy and William both felt the same way about Chuck, and that was before he met Jesus.

Plus, I believed Chuck when he said he hadn't written those bad checks. I suspect the police eventually figured that out on their own, because down the road they dropped the charges. Either that, or God just told them to forget about it. I'm just as thankful either way.

After we moved to Washington and got settled in and comfortable, Chuck came home one night from walking in the rain with our puppy, and was so different that our whole world got turned upside down. It was as if he had gone out for a walk with the dog and come home a different Chuck. I had no frame of reference for what I was seeing. Being raised Catholic, I'd had a religious upbringing, but Chuck was taking things to a whole different level. It seemed so strange to me, but I thought I would just wait and see where this was all going.

Then, when Chuck told me he had to move out because it wasn't okay with God that we live together, without being married, I was deeply hurt. I had given up everything I knew to be with this man, and now he was leaving me and moving out because he'd met God. That was a hard pill to swallow. But I hoped, and held on.

We continued to meet for coffee and talk, and Chuck continued to tell me that he loved me and believed we were meant to be together, but that for the time being, we could not live together.

I thought about just going ahead and marrying him under his adopted name, Tim Dunn, but something in me was just not willing to have a sham wedding. It would be the real thing, under his real name, or we would not get married. It was that simple. I think God was in that decision, because, even though it led us down a tough road, it ended up with all of those legal issues being gone for good. It was a great relief when there was no more hiding, or wondering when the police were going to show up and arrest my husband.

As hard as that time was for us, William and I continued going to church, and eventually God began dealing with both of us and William and I both got saved and baptized. That's when I began to understand what all the fuss had been about. Knowing Jesus for myself, changed the way I saw everything in life. I began to understand why Chuck had acted the way he had. He had not become religious; he had met Jesus. And now I had, too.

A lot of people might not realize this, but it was a big step for Chuck to step out into the light and marry me under his real name. Going public with his real identity opened some doors that he had worked so hard to keep closed. But it was the right thing to do. We both knew that. It took a few years and some hard times to get all of that legal stuff behind us, but it was a path that the Lord led us along, day by day, sometimes in spite of our stubbornness.

You might think that when you come to Jesus and get saved, and all of your sins are forgiven, that all of your problems will just go away. You might even hope that there will be no more consequences for all of the bad things in your past, but that's not usually the way it works. It takes time, and God has to help you work through things to change the way you think. He promises to be there through it all, but your walk with God requires faith all the way through, just like it did in the very beginning. I saw that working out in my husband.

Even after Chuck became a believer, every once in a while I would see him lose his temper, or become seriously angry. I had no idea where the outbursts were coming from. It was not like him. I didn't realize that, even though Chuck had told me early on about his criminal background and all of the bad things he had done, he had told me nothing about the things that had been done to him. I knew nothing about the abuse.

It was when he started working on this book that I learned about the hell that he and his little brothers and sisters lived through on Church Street. It broke my heart to learn of the suffering those poor little kids endured. Some of it was so shocking I almost didn't want to know it. Some of what happened was so bad that it is not even in this book.

My husband is truly a miracle. He is a trophy of God's grace. Our whole family is. Chuck could have been killed a hundred times. He could have spent his entire life in prison. He could be a man consumed by bitterness, hate, and rage. Instead he is a sweet, loving man who loves nothing more than telling others what God has done for him, and what He can do for them – and then bringing them home to stay with us for a few days, if they need that.

My husband and I love God, and we deeply appreciate the goodness He has shown us.

Our daughter Stacy lives back east, and has three kids of her own. She has her PhD, and teaches at a University.

William and Christy and their three kids live near us and attend our same church. William was the youth pastor for a while, and is now the associate pastor. Ironically, he also worked for several years in a prison, and is well-trained in law enforcement issues.

Chuck, after all of his unpleasant experiences with the police, now routinely works with law enforcement and even has several friends on the force.

Chuck's grandparents, the Mausolf's, came to Washington to visit us a few years before they passed away. Chuck got the chance to share some special times with them and talk at a level they had not been able to when he was a rebellious kid. His grandma, Ora Mausolf shared how she had come to the Lord at one of those southern tent revivals back when she was young.

When they first arrived here in Hoquiam, Chuck gave Ora a big hug. Her first comment was how much better he looked without facial hair. Chuck had grown a beard and Ora didn't like the way he looked, or the feel of facial hair rubbing against her face when he hugged her. That night, Chuck shaved off his beard just to show his grandma how much she meant to him.

Chuck's dad passed away a few years back. Chuck went back to see him a couple of months before he died, and hoped to end things on a warmer note. Chuck reached out and things were cordial between them, but when he returned home, Chuck seemed disappointed. There had been rumors that his dad had come to the Lord, and God alone is the final judge of such things, but Chuck said he didn't see any sign of it. He told me that when he asked his dad about how he was doing spiritually, his dad replied, strangely, I thought, "I promised God a long time ago that I would never eat pork, and I have kept that promise."

Chuck's dad had a knife collection, and while he was back there visiting, Chuck told his dad that he would like to have one of the knives to remember him by. His dad told him to pick one out, and he would let him have it for ten bucks. There's something telling about that. A different man might have said, "I'm not going to be around much longer, and I love you, son. So, take as many as you want. I've enjoyed them, now you can." But sadly, not Chuck's dad.

Barbara, the last we heard, was living in a nursing home in Minnesota. Chuck has forgiven her for all the things she did to him when he was little. He refused to let all of that old bitterness and hatred fester inside of him and eat him up, so he let it go. Occasionally we still pray for her, that she will come to know the Lord and find forgiveness before it's too late. God can forgive anyone, if they will humbly bow their knee, and ask Him, out of a repentant heart of faith.

In preparation for this book, Chuck got in touch with some of his siblings that he hadn't spoken to in quite some time. To our great delight, we learned that Susanne and Frances are both Christians now. The enemy did his best to destroy them when they were young and vulnerable, but the grace of God prevailed and they now belong to Him. For that I say, "Thank you, Jesus!"

Author's Note

When I first met Charles Dudrey, or Chuck, as he prefers to be called, I had no idea that he had such a story to tell. He was a pleasant, affable fellow, who cooked the barbecue and baked the cookies for the church dinners and picnics at Harbor City Church. Just meeting Chuck, one would never guess the kind of life the man had lived.

Chuck and I quickly discovered that we both liked Merle Haggard songs. One of us would break out singing one of Merle's tunes, and then surprise one other with how many of the words we both remembered. The difference was, Chuck could easily reach all of the low notes that Merle was famous for, and I couldn't come close.

After hearing bits and pieces of Chuck's story, his pastor, Doug Cotton, encouraged him to write a book. Chuck attempted to do that, but found that as compelling as his story was, he just wasn't a writer. He gave me a copy of what he had written and I read it, as did my wife. I told my wife, "Chuck is not a writer, but his story needs to be told." Cindy agreed.

I approached Chuck about maybe writing his story for him, and he humbly and graciously agreed. What you have before you is the product of my interviews with Chuck, in person, and by text, email, and phone conversations over the several months I worked on this manuscript. I was also able to interview one his dad's sisters, and Chuck's sister Susanne.

When I started writing, I will tell you that there were times that I had to lean away from my keyboard to avoid the possibility of tears shorting-out my laptop. There were other times when I became angry and wished I could go back in time and rescue those five little kids. At times, I found myself wanting to personally put the hurt on some of the characters in this book.

Chuck's story may be extreme, but there are countless kids in this world who have lived through the same kind of abuse. Some to a lesser degree, but some even worse. Most kids are warped for the rest of their lives by experiencing the kind of things the Dudrey kids lived through. Chuck almost was, but he found the one answer that can turn any life around. He met Jesus and God fixed him. God turned Chuck into another man. He healed his soul.

I hope you enjoyed this story. I hope you were touched as much by reading it as I was by writing it. Chuck assures me that it's all true, at least as far as he can remember.

Chuck told me that he wanted his story told, not so people would feel sorry for him or to exalt the bad things he had done in his life, but rather so that others could see what God, through his Son, has done for him. And in seeing that, might let Him do the same thing for them.

There's one more thing I want to add. When Chuck went for a walk with his puppy on that rainy night in Hoquiam, and met the Lord down by the pier, he called out for help and forgiveness in the name of Jesus. He knew to do that because his grandparents had taken him to church as a kid, and had talked to him about the Lord many years earlier. The seed they had sown was further watered by the Bible-believing foreman whom Chuck met in the prison furniture shop. That man fearlessly shared his faith, even when mocked by other inmates.

Those seeds might have been buried deep in Chuck's heart and mind. He might have forgotten them altogether; but still contained in them was the power that is always inherent in the Word of God, the power to change a man or woman from head to toe and make them alive again. What burst forth from Chuck's lips that stormy night was the result of years of work the Holy Spirit had been doing in his heart. It might not have visible. Chuck might not have been aware of what God was up to, but when his day of salvation came, he called on the name of the only one who can truly save a man's soul, the Lord Jesus Christ, the Son of the living God.

Hell on Church Street is available on the retail market through most major booksellers. The book is also distributed free of charge to jails and prisons across the United States by "Free Anywhere Prison Outreach, Inc." If you would be interested in helping fund the distribution of this book or other books the nonprofit distributes to those behind bars, you may contact them at www.freeanywhereprisonoutreach.org.

<u>*Books by Bill Sizemore*</u>

Escape from Jonestown (published under the pen name, Billy Rivers)

The Fractured Church

Hell on Church Street

The Valley of the Rajneesh (coming soon)

The Valley of Trust (coming soon)

CPSIA information can be obtained
at www.ICGtesting.com
Printed in the USA
FFOW03n1720100418
46221937-47552FF